W9-CLX-160

For Reference

Not to be taken from this room

Modern Collectible Dolls

VOLUME VI

IDENTIFICATION & VALUE GUIDE

PATSY MOYER

COLLECTOR BOOKS
A Division of Schroeder Publishing Co., Inc.

Front cover:
Top left: 20" composition Ideal "Shirley Temple" marked "Cop. Ideal//N. & T. Co." on head, NRA tag on dress, wig in original set, hazel sleep eyes, real lashes, painted lower lashes, feathered brows, open mouth, six upper teeth, five-piece composition child body, original blue organdy pleated party dress with pink ribbon trim, combination underwear, socks, center strap shoes, Shirley Temple button and marked original box, unplayed-with condition, circa 1934, $1,700.00. Courtesy McMasters Doll Auctions.

Top right: 10" vinyl Robert Tonner Doll Co. "Ann Estelle," a Mary Engelbreit character, #ME0112, "Dancing Into My Heart," blonde wig, blue eyes, closed mouth, gold rimmed glasses, rigid vinyl body, black and white dress with black pompon trim, white hat, tights, shoes, red flower corsage on wrist, 2001 line, retail $89.99. Courtesy Robert Tonner Doll Co.

Bottom left: 8" hard plastic Vogue Cabbage Rose Ginny from the Botanical Babies Collection, blue sleep eyes, closed mouth, rose felt petal dress with green top and felt rose trim in blonde synthetic hair, 2001 line, retail $39.95. Courtesy Vogue Doll Co.

Bottom right: 15½" vinyl Alexander Doll Co. doll in Ocean Drive Outfit #31380, a turquoise and white patterned silk dress featuring a keyhole halter neck that crosses at the front and wraps to the nape in the back, white straw picture hat, shoulder bag, white sunglasses and sandals, and gold hoop earrings finish the look. Three pastel shopping bags included. Costume only, retail $44.95, 2001 line. Courtesy Alexander Doll Co.

Back cover:
15½" vinyl Ashton-Drake Gene and Trent; Gene wears a pink silk "Love in Bloom" sheath with embroidered flowers on train, long white gloves, and matching shoes. Limited edition of 5,000, 2001 line, $120.00. Trent wears a black tux in "Formal Introduction," 2001 line, $110.00 retail. Courtesy Ashton-Drake Galleries.

Cover design: Beth Summers
Book design: Sherry Kraus
Book layout: Melissa J. Reed

COLLECTOR BOOKS
P.O. Box 3009
Paducah, Kentucky 42002-3009
www.collectorbooks.com

Copyright © 2002 Patsy Moyer

The current values in this book should be used only as a guide. They are not intended to set prices, which vary from one section of the country to another. Auction prices as well as dealer prices vary greatly and are affected by condition as well as demand. Neither the author nor the publisher assumes responsibility for any losses that might be incurred as a result of consulting this guide.

Searching for a publisher?

We are always looking for people knowledgeable within their fields. If you feel that there is a real need for a book on your collectible subject and have a large comprehensive collection, contact Collector Books.

Contents

Dedication..........................4
Credits..............................4
Introduction 5

Great American Dolls of the Twentieth Century

Advertising Dolls 8

Alexander Doll Co. 11

American Character 30

Arranbee Dolls.........................36

Artist Dolls...........................42

Barbie Dolls...........................57

Betsy McCall Dolls 72

Black Dolls 82

Cameo Dolls 88

Celebrity Dolls........................89

Chalkware Dolls 97

Cloth Dolls 100

Comic Dolls...........................106

Composition Dolls 107

Deluxe Reading Dolls 115

Disney Dolls 117

Effanbee Dolls 119

Ethnic Dolls 129

Fashion Dolls.........................141

Girl Scout Dolls 166

Hard Plastic Dolls 171

Hitty Dolls 174

Horsman Dolls.........................176

Mary Hoyer Dolls 178

Ideal Dolls 182

Kenner Dolls 185

Klumpe Dolls..........................186

Lenci Dolls...........................187

Monica Dolls 190

Nancy Ann Storybook Dolls 192

Nurse Dolls 196

Old Cottage Toys......................198

Raggedy Ann & Andy Dolls 207

Scarlett O'Hara Dolls 209

Shirley Temple Dolls 214

Terri Lee Dolls 218

Robert Tonner Doll Company 222

Vogue Dolls 235

Collectors' Network...................248

Bibliography..........................252

Index.................................254

Dedication

To Trudy, Jim, Jack, and Margaret,
the world's best brothers and sisters.

Credits

Debra Adorni
Chelle Albonico
Alexander Doll Company
June Allgeier
Barbara Andresen
Ashton-Drake Galleries
Gay Baron
Sandy Johnson Barts
Charlotte Beeney
Dorothy Bohlin
Vivian Bourcher
Judy Brown
Flo Burnside
Kathleen Campbell
Stephanie Cauley
Judie Conroy
DeAnn Cote
DeDee Crowe
Jane Darin
Sally DeSmet
Judi Domm
Jacques Dorier
Merilee Ellsworth
Bruce Endersbe
Marlene Engeler
Elizabeth Fielding
Yvonne Flipse

Cornelia Ford
Betty Jane Fronefield
Donna Fronefield
Julie Ghavam
Pat Graff
Bonnie Gvokas
Adrienne Hagey
Amanda Hash
Carolyn Haynes
Marilyn Henke
Janet Hill
Claudi Huber
Barbara Hull
Judith Johnson
Sharon Kolibaba
Lebba Kropp
Anita Ladensack
Nancy Lazenby
Denise Lemmon
Diane Little
Rita Mauze
Karen McCarthy
Shari McMasters
McMasters Doll Auctions
Pidd Miller
Peggy Millhouse
Art Mock

Tom Morris
Pat Moulton
Michele Newby
W. Harry Perzyk
Celeste Pestlin
Rose Pitzer
Stephanie Prince
Joan Radke
Marilyn Ramsey
Pat Rather
Merlyn & Tina Richards
Jill Sanders
Myra Sherrod
Joan Sickler
Harlene Soucy
Grace Steuri
Betty Strong
Ellen Sturgess
Linda Lee Sutton
Stephanie Thompson
Robert Tonner Doll Company
Sandra Tripp
Atelier Bets van Boxel
Carol Van Verst-Rugg
Vogue Doll Company
Louise Williams
Goldie Wilson

Introduction

With the changing times bringing us stricter security and a new wave of patriotism, doll collecting remains a treasured hobby for collectors. They can find new enjoyment in this endeavor where they can forget the pressures of the outside world. The Internet continues to influence collectors worldwide with a constantly changing level of participation. This technological tool has leveled the playing field, tossed aside old considerations, and brought a whole new outlook to today's collectors. It has made objects that were unavailable to many in their lifetime actually obtainable and has brought with it also a horde of novice collectors and sellers who have little knowledge of what they have or are seeking. While the influx of new collectors brings new items to the marketplace, it also skews the market as unsophisticated collectors may pay astronomical prices for some things that previously had modest values.

To help seasoned collectors keep up with all of that and to help new collectors more realistically look at collecting, this book brings you examples of what is available or has been recently sold. Doll collecting ranks in the top ten of collectibles, with Barbie finishing the millennium as the most popular doll today. As with any collectible, as an experienced or novice collector you want to get the most for your money. In all cases, knowledge is power.

You need that knowledge to get the most for your money. Unless you have won the lottery or made your million in software or the stock market, you probably have a limited budget. Those of us who are not independently wealthy need to know that we are spending our money wisely — perhaps so that when the time comes for us to part with our collection, it will have increased in value. Thus your next doll might be considered a portable asset.

The novice collector needs to learn as much about doll collecting and your chosen niche as possible. This means you need to see a large number of dolls so that you can tell the good from the bad. You need to find out as much about your next doll as possible — perhaps to ease your conscience when you want one so badly, it is nice to know that you got a good buy. This book provides some of those answers in that it is a showcase of dolls that collectors have acquired. It can help you when you need to find an example of a certain costume, and it gives examples of how some dolls that were new many years ago may look now.

Perhaps "modern" is a misnomer for dolls over 70 years old but still considered by doll collectors to be modern. One factor influencing this, however, is that some doll companies that made dolls at the turn of the century are still operating and producing dolls. For this book, I am grouping dolls made of composition, cloth, rubber, hard plastic, porcelain, vinyl, and wood as modern as opposed to dolls of bisque, wax, wood, and china that were made before World War I or earlier. There are no easy cut-off dates, and some spill over from one category to the next. This book will give you examples of dolls for you to compare for identification.

Collectors wanting to know more about the dolls they have or wanting to start collecting have several ways to gain knowledge. One way to do this is to research and arm yourself with books, periodicals, and magazines that deal with the subject and also to seek the counsel of other informed collectors. Beginning collectors should begin to list their dolls, with the prices paid, the size, marks, notes about materials, and other pertinent facts, such as originality and condition. Collectors need to be able to identify their dolls, and one way to do this is by noting the material of which they made.

One very basic thing beginning doll collectors need to understand is that experienced doll collectors refer to a doll by whatever material is used for making the doll's head. So a composition doll has a composition head but may have a cloth, composition or wood body. A doll with a vinyl head and a hard plastic body is a vinyl doll. The head commands the order of reference to the doll in relation to materials used to produce it. A doll made entirely of vinyl is referred to as all-vinyl.

It is also helpful when exact measurements are given to describe the height of the doll. The doll's height is important because it immediately confirms the identity of certain dolls, and the height of the doll influences its value. Usually larger dolls are more valuable than smaller dolls, but sometimes smaller dolls or a certain size doll has unique characteristics that make them more sought-after.

When collectors find a doll they wish to identify without any packaging or box, they first need to examine the back of the head, then the torso, the usual places the manufacturers place marks, and then the rest of the body. Some dolls may have only a mold number or no mark at all. Nursing students are often given the task of writing a physical description of their patient, starting at the top of their head, down to the bottoms of their feet. This is also a good method for describing dolls and their attire.

Collectors like to meet and network with other collectors who share their interests. For this reason we have included a Collectors' Network section in the back of this book. There are many special interest groups that focus on one area of doll collecting. These are experienced collectors in a certain area who will network with others. It is considered proper form to send a SASE when contacting others if you wish to receive a reply.

In addition, a national organization, the United Federation of Doll Clubs, has information for doll collectors who are wanting to form or seeking a doll club. The goals of this nonprofit organization focus on education, research, preservation, and enjoyment of dolls. They also sponsor a Junior Membership for young doll collectors. They will put you in contact with one of 16 Regional Directors who can assess your needs and advise you about any doll club in your area accepting members. You may write for more information to UFDC, 10920 North Ambassador Drive, Suite 130, Kansas City, MO 64153, or FAX 816-891-8360, or at www.UFDC.org.

Beginning collectors need to do their homework and gain power (knowledge) about dolls before spending their money. Most collectors have to budget and do not have unlimited funds. It seems prudent to investigate thoroughly all avenues regarding an addition to one's collection before actually making a purchase. What should the buyer consider?

Novice collectors may wonder where they can find dolls to buy. There are many different ways to locate the doll of your dreams, including finding dealers or shops that specialize in locating a particular doll for you. There are numerous focus groups that list special sales and their locations. Collector groups usually post doll shows and sales in their newsletters.

Auctions may also prove to be an aid in finding additions for your collection. Some offer absentee bidding which is most helpful if you do not live near where the auction is being held. Some also offer over-the-phone bidding if you want to be in on the actual bidding. Auction houses usually send out catalogs and are most helpful answering questions over the phone or faxing if you need more information. See Collectors' Network at the back of this book for more information.

One of the latest and greatest shopping malls is the Internet. And this is where it does get scary. Not only is the novice collector unsure of what she actually wants to buy, but also she may be dealing with an unknown person at the other end of her computer. And there is this great place called eBay that has thousands of dolls on auction every day, 24 hours a day, seven days a week, year in and year out — barring electrical disturbances and Internet traffic jams. More and more, eBay is becoming the acceptable spot for collectors to shop and sell. The site also features a query section that will allow you to look at prices realized in closed auctions.

Again, novice collectors need to arm themselves with as much information as they can find as they begin to build their collections. Not only are books, magazines, and videos available for collectors, but also simple observance of dolls at museums, doll shows, and displays provides a wonderful way to learn about dolls. To help the novice collector, we have added simple tips on what to look for in dolls under consideration for addition to a collection.

Just as the three most valuable qualities that make real estate desirable are location, location, and location, a doll collector must consider condition, condition, and condition. This is by far the most important thing to consider when buying a doll. You need to be able to recognize what a desirable condition is and how that relates to the age, originality, and desirability of the doll. Dolls with good color, original clothing, tags, brochures, and boxes will always be desirable.

The trick is to find those dolls that also have rarity, beauty or some other unique quality that makes them appealing to the collector. It could be that only a few dolls were made. It could be that a collector recalls his/her childhood dolls with nostalgia. Or it could be that a doll's production, presentation or identity makes a historical statement. Other factors can also contribute to the desirability and popularity of a doll. Cleanliness, good color, and good condition are always desirable qualities. We have included "What to look for" tips with each category.

Keep in mind that if your collecting is an investment, you need good records. Even though you think you will never forget what you paid for a single doll, after a few years and many dolls later, the memory becomes hazy. A simple, easy way to keep track of the money spent on doll collections is to utilize the Quicken money program on your computer. Using a number and description to keep track of each doll, enter the amount you spent when purchasing it. If you sell the doll or dispose of it, the doll can be checked during the reconciling procedure and thus will not be seen when you wish to see a list of your current inventory. This is a very simple way to utilize something you also may use to keep your checkbook in order.

With time, collectors' interests vary, but playthings seem to remain a consistent, enjoyable hobby. This book does not mean to set prices and should only be used as one of many tools to guide the collector. It is the collector's decision alone about which doll to purchase. It is the responsibility of the collector to choose his own area of collecting and his method of pursuing it. This book is meant to help you enjoy and learn about dolls of our past and present and to share indications with the thoughtful collector on the trends of the future.

Happy collecting!

Advertising Dolls

Manufacturing companies often use dolls as a means of advertising their products, either as a premium or in the form of a trademark of their company. Sometimes dolls were given as a reward for subscriptions to a magazine. This entrepreneurial spirit has given us some delightful examples and can bring a whole new realm of discovery for the collector. Primarily not meant as a collectible but as a means to promote products or services, the advertising doll has been around since the late 1800s and continues to be a viable form of advertising. Advertising dolls now can be made just as a collectible item — look at the Christmas ornaments that advertise Barbie or space adventurers, and the McDonald's premiums in their "Happy Meal" boxes. All these dolls or figurines that promote a product or service are called advertising dolls. Early companies that used dolls to promote their products were Amberg with "Vanta Baby," American Cereal Co. with "Cereta," American Character with the "Campbell Kids," Buster Brown Shoes with "Buster Brown," Ideal with "Cracker Jack Boy" and "ZuZu Kid," Kellogg Company with a variety of characters, and many others.

What to look for:

This is a wonderful field for collectors. Dolls can be made of any material, and those examples mint-in-box or with original advertising will remain the most desirable. Cloth should have bright colors, no tears, little soil, and retain printed identifying marks. On dolls of materials such as composition, hard plastic, and vinyl, look for rosy cheeks, little wear, unsoiled, original tags, labels, boxes or brochures. Retain dates and purchasing information for your purchases when you obtain current products. This information will add to the value of your collectibles.

7½" hard plastic "Dutch Knorr Dolls," advertising dolls for Knorr Soup, a Best Foods product, blue sleep eyes, European look faces with full lips, jointed, will stand alone; the dolls came in pairs, a boy and a girl dressed in costumes representing several countries, circa 1963 – 1964, $15.00/pair. *Courtesy Betty Strong.*

7½" hard plastic "French Knorr Dolls," advertising dolls for Knorr Soup, a Best Foods product, blue sleep eyes, European look faces with full lips, jointed, will stand alone; the dolls came in pairs, a boy and a girl dressed in costumes representing several countries, circa 1963 – 1964, $15.00/pair. *Courtesy Betty Strong.*

7½" hard plastic "Norwegian Knorr Dolls," advertising dolls for Knorr Soup, a Best Foods product, blue sleep eyes, European look faces with full lips, jointed, will stand alone; the dolls came in pairs, a boy and a girl dressed in costumes representing several countries, circa 1963 – 1964, $15.00/pair. *Courtesy Betty Strong.*

7½" hard plastic Ideal "Miss Curity" dolls, unmarked, blonde wigs, sleep eyes (second from left has painted eyes), painted eyelashes, molded and painted shoes/stockings, white nurses' outfits, cap reads "Miss Curity," circa 1953, $85.00 ea. *Courtesy Peggy Millhouse.*

7½" hard plastic "Swiss Knorr Dolls," advertising dolls for Knorr Soup, a Best Foods product, blue sleep eyes, European look faces with full lips, jointed; will stand alone, the dolls came in pairs, a boy and a girl dressed in costumes representing several countries, circa 1963 – 1964, $15.00/pair. *Courtesy Betty Strong.*

23" composition "Miss Curity" advertising doll, (possibly R & B), blue sleep eyes, blond mohair wig, rosy cheeks, all original with original stand, mint-in-box, circa 1940s to 1951, $875.00. *Courtesy Peggy Millhouse.*

Buddy Lee

Buddy Lee is a display doll made for the H.D. Lee Company to promote Lee uniforms and was first offered to dealers circa 1922. The Lee Company's most popular dolls were the Cowboy and Engineer, reflecting their production of denim jeans and overalls. The early 12½" dolls were made in composition and then later 13" dolls in hard plastic circa 1949. This is one doll that really appeals to men, especially men who wore uniforms in their work on the railroad, at gas stations, and in Coca-Cola plants. Buddy Lee was discontinued in 1962. Collectors can look for outfits including Coca-Cola, Phillips 66, Sinclair, MM, Standard, John Deere, TWA, Cowboy, and Engineer in striped and plain denim and also two farmer versions dressed in plaid shirts and jeans.

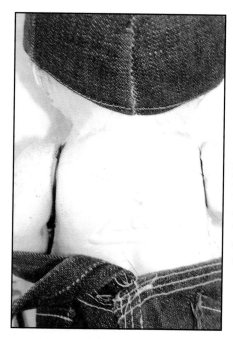

12½" composition "Buddy Lee," trademark doll of H.D. Lee Co. Inc., who made uniforms and work clothes, painted side-glancing eyes, molded painted hair, closed smiling mouth, wearing original overalls and cap, marked on back "Buddy//Lee" (in diamond), circa 1922+, $100.00.
Courtesy Adrienne Hagey.

12" hard plastic Buddy Lee, marked "Buddy Lee" on back, "Union Made//Lee//Sanforized" on pants label, "Phillips//66" on shirt label, molded painted hair, stiff neck, painted eyes to side, single stroke brows, painted upper lashes, closed mouth, hard plastic body jointed at shoulders only, molded painted black boots, original Phillips 66 suit with labeled shirt and pants, black imitation leather belt, circa 1950s, $285.00.
Courtesy McMasters Doll Auctions.

13" hard plastic Buddy Lee, brown painted side-glancing eyes, mouth needs repaint, painted shoes, Lee tag gone off pants, black hat, advertising doll for Lee Rider Jeans, circa 1948+, $325.00.
Courtesy Louise Williams.

Alexander Doll Co.

Alexander Doll Company is alive and thriving, perhaps because a 1995 Chapter 11 bankruptcy led new management to use the Japanese Kaizen flow-type manufacturing. Located in the Harlem section of the New York City borough of Manhattan, the company is owned by TBM Consulting Group. The new management has redesigned the production flow in the turn-of-the-century Studebaker plant to allow groups of workers to oversee the manufacturing process from start to finish on selected items. Instead of each person doing one particular job all day, the group works together to finish dolls within their group, thus increasing productivity and cutting costs.

The financial and production changes seem not to have slowed the interest in Alexander dolls which have increased in popularity under the guidance of the Alexander Doll Collectors Club, a company-sponsored marketing tool that was used successfully by Effanbee during the 1930s and more recently by Vogue with their Ginny club.

Beatrice and Rose Alexander started the Alexander Doll Company around 1912, and were known for their doll costumes. They began using the Madame Alexander trademark in 1928. Beatrice A. Behrman became a legend in the doll world with her long reign as head of the Alexander Doll Company. The company produced cloth, composition, and wood dolls, making the transition to hard plastic after World War II and later into vinyl.

The doll world was shocked these past few years with skyrocketing prices paid for some wonderful collectible Alexander dolls at auction, including $56,000.00 for an 8" hard plastic doll redressed as the Infante of Prague. Alexander's rare and beautiful mint dolls continue to attract young collectors. Alexander dolls continue to increase in value as shown by one-of-a-kind extraordinary, fully documented special dolls as they appear on the market. These gains should continue with the support of avid Alexander fans. And there seems to be no lack of them as premier Madame Alexander Doll Club events are held around the country. For information, write Madame Alexander Doll Club, PO Box 330, Mundelein, IL 60060. Telephone: 847-949-9200; fax 847-949-9201.

One of the Alexander Company's luckiest breaks was obtaining the exclusive license to produce the Dionne Quintuplets dolls after the children's birth in 1934. The Alexander Dionne Quintuplets were introduced in 1935, made in both cloth and composition as babies and toddlers. Some of the rarer groups are the bathtub set and sets with playground accessories like the carousel or Ferris wheel. Other companies tried to fill out their lines with matching sets of five identical dolls even though this brought copyright suits from Madame Alexander. Quintuplet collectors collect not only dolls, but also clothing, photographs, and a large assortment of other related memorabilia.

Quint News is published quarterly by Jimmy and Fay Rodolfos, founders of the nonprofit Dionne Quint Collectors, $10.00 a year, PO Box 2527, Woburn, MA 01888.

What to look for:

Alexander cloth dolls should be clean, all original, and with bright colors. Newer Alexander dolls require mint, all original dolls with brochures, tags, boxes, and accessories to bring top prices.

Composition Alexander dolls may have minute crazing but must have good color, original clothes, labels, tags, and brochures to bring highest prices. Buy dolls with severe cracking, peeling or other damage *only* if they are all original, tagged or mint.

Painted hard plastics are transitional dolls and may be mistaken for composition. Hard plastic dolls should have good color, tagged outfits, and be all-original. The newer the doll, the closer to mint it should be. Alexander dolls were produced in the 1970s and 1980s with few changes, and collectors can find many of these dolls at reasonable prices. The dolls from the 1950s and early 1960s, as well as the limited edition special event dolls, are eagerly sought after.

Composition

Three 7" dolls, "Little Bo Peep," "Alice in Wonderland," and "Czechoslovakia," all marked "Mme//Alexander" on backs, original mohair wigs, painted blue eyes, closed mouths, five-piece jointed composition bodies, molded painted socks and shoes, all original in unplayed-with condition, with original flowered boxes, "Little Bo Peep," circa 1937 – 1941; "Alice in Wonderland," circa 1930s; "Czechoslovakia," circa 1935 – 1937, $350.00. *Courtesy McMasters Doll Auctions.*

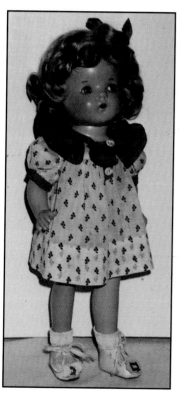

14" "Jeannie Walker," marked "ALEXANDER//Pat. No. 2171291" on body, mohair wig, sleep eyes, closed mouth, jointed composition body, tagged Alexander blue dress with ruffle down front, white socks, black shoes, added straw hat, all original, circa 1941, $675.00. *Private collection.*

13" "Betty," mohair wig, tin sleep eyes, closed mouth, jointed composition body, original tagged "Betty//Madame Alexander//New York" red and white dress with red collar, added red ribbon in hair, white socks and shoes, all original, circa 1935, $400.00. *Private collection.*

16" "McGuffey Ana" marked "Princess Elizabeth//Alexander Doll Co." on head, human hair wig in braids, brown sleep eyes, real lashes, painted lower lashes, single stroke brows, open mouth, four upper teeth, five-piece composition child body, original red plaid dress, white organdy pinafore, underwear combination, socks, and red two-snap shoes, dress tagged "McGuffey Ana//Madame Alexander, N.Y. U.S.A.//Reg. No. 350,781," circa 1937 – 1944, $375.00. *Courtesy McMasters Doll Auctions.*

15" "Sleeping Beauty" (Princess Elizabeth), marked "MME Alexander" on head, blonde human hair wig, sleep eyes, closed mouth, jointed composition body, red velvet gown with gold trim, circa 1939, $475.00. *Private collection.*

19" "McGuffey Ana" marked "Princess Elizabeth//Alexander Doll Co" on head, "McGuffey Ana//Madame Alexander, N.Y. U.S.A.//All Rights Reserved" on dress tag, human hair wig, brown sleep eyes, real lashes, painted lashes, open mouth, four upper teeth, five-piece composition body, red/white dotted Swiss dress, rick-rack trim, red taffeta jacket, straw hat, snap shoes, all original with box, School House wrist tag, circa 1937 – 1943, $1,075.00. *Courtesy McMasters Doll Auctions.*

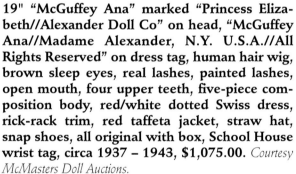

23" "Special Girl," marked "Madame//Alexander//New York U.S.A." on dress tag, original human hair wig, blue sleep eyes, real lashes, painted lower lashes, feathered brows, cloth torso with composition arms and legs, original pale blue taffeta dress with lace and ribbon trim, attached blue panties, original socks and center-snap shoes, circa 1942 – 1946, $750.00.
Courtesy McMasters Doll Auctions.

Hard Plastic and Vinyl

17" hard plastic "Alice in Wonderland," Maggie face, blonde styled wig, blue sleep eyes, real lashes, painted lashes below, eyeshadow, closed mouth, jointed hard plastic body, pink nylon dress with white organdy pinafore trimmed in lace, white stockings, black shoes, circa 1949 – 1950, $650.00. *Courtesy Carol Van Verst-Rugg.*

8" hard plastic "Alexander-kins," bent knee walker, blonde rooted hair, blue sleep eyes, closed mouth, jointed hard plastic body, box says style #500, circa 1956 – 1963, $365.00. *Courtesy McMasters Doll Auctions.*

14" hard plastic "Amy" from "Little Women," marked "Alex." on head, blonde floss hair in loop curls, blue sleep eyes, real lashes, painted lower lashes, single stroke brows, closed mouth, five-piece hard plastic body, flowered dress with white pique bodice and sleeves tagged "Louisa M. Alcott's//'Little Women,'//'Amy,' By Madame Alexander, N.Y. U.S.A.//All Rights Reserved," slip, pantaloons with eyelet trim, black side-snap shoes, circa 1949 – 1952, $550.00.
Courtesy McMasters Doll Auctions.

15" hard plastic "Binnie Walker" in trunk, Saran wig, blue sleep eyes, real lashes, eye shadow, closed mouth, hard plastic body with jointed knees, dressed in black leotard, felt flower appliqués, pink felt skirt, white skates, wooden trunk with white metal covering, wardrobe and accessories, doll and accessories have never been removed from cardboard backing, all clothing tagged "Binnie Walker//©Madame Alexander," circa 1955, $4,600.00. *Courtesy McMasters Doll Auctions.*

16¾" hard plastic "Bride," possibly Madame Alexander, dark blonde wig, sleep eyes, real lashes, painted lashes below, eyeshadow, closed mouth, jointed hard plastic body, white gown with netting over gown, two ruffles at hem, netting is torn, matching veil, lace ruffle at neck, long net sleeves, bouquet tied with ribbon and netting attached to hand, circa 1950s, $150.00. *Courtesy Carol Van Verst-Rugg.*

18" hard plastic Cissy as "Queen Elizabeth II," light brown synthetic wig in original set, blue glassene eyes, pierced ears, jointed hard plastic body at neck, shoulders, hips, elbows, tagged white brocade gown with blue sash and pin, silver tiara, pearl necklace and bracelets, gloves, high heels, nylons, panties, hang tag, circa 1955, $1,100.00. *Courtesy Rita Mauze.*

8" hard plastic "Cowboy," molded painted light brown hair, blue sleep eyes, jointed hard plastic body, original red shirt with gold braid, red boots, white leather pants, printed blue neckerchief, suede cowboy hat, gun and holster, circa 1967 – 1969, $425.00. *From the collection of Vivian Brady Ashley, courtesy Rita Mauze.*

Alexander Doll Co.

14" hard plastic "Groom" (Margaret), auburn mohair wig, blue sleep eyes, closed mouth, jointed hard plastic body, original black tuxedo with top hat, white shirt, black shoes, socks, watch chain, jewel on shirt, mint-in-box, circa 1949 – 1951, $900.00. *Courtesy Rita Mauze.*

18" hard plastic "Lady Churchill" (Margaret), #2020C from Beaux Art Series, light brown synthetic wig in original set, sleep eyes, closed mouth, pierced ears, jointed hard plastic body, pink satin gown with full opera coat of matching material, tiara, earrings, made in 1953 only, $2,000.00. *From the collection of Leigh Sargent, courtesy Rita Mauze.*

17" hard plastic "Maggie Walker," original wig, blue sleep eyes, real lashes, painted lower lashes, feathered brows, closed mouth, five-piece hard plastic body with walking mechanism, tagged blue/white taffeta dress with white collar and cuffs, white taffeta slip/panties, original stockings, black center snap shoes, dress tag reads "Madame Alexander//All Rights Reserved//New York U.S.A.," circa 1949 – 1953, $700.00. *Courtesy McMasters Doll Auctions.*

30" hard plastic "Mimi," synthetic wig in original set, sleep eyes, closed mouth, pierced ears, multi-jointed hard plastic and vinyl body, dressed in #3030 pink formal with matching hat, black velvet slippers, hang tags, mint-in-box, 1961 only, $1,000.00. *Courtesy Rita Mauze.*

8" hard plastic "Prince Charles," #397 (Wendy Ann), blonde wig, blue sleep eyes, painted lashes below, jointed hard plastic body, blue jacket, short pants, matching hat, made in 1957 only, $410.00. *Courtesy McMasters Doll Auctions.*

18" hard plastic "Queen Elizabeth" (Margaret), synthetic wig in original set, sleep eyes, closed mouth, pierced ears, jointed hard plastic body, beige brocade gown with light blue sash, gloves, tiara, bracelet, pin, high-heeled shoes, circa 1953, $1,950.00. *From the collection of Vivian Brady Ashley, courtesy Rita Mauze.*

14" hard plastic "Ringbearer" (Lovey Dove), blonde mohair wig, blue sleep eyes, closed mouth, jointed five-piece hard plastic body, tagged satin shorts and shirt, socks, tie shoes, carrying pink pillow with ring, circa 1951, $600.00. *Courtesy Rita Mauze.*

18" hard plastic "Snow White," Margaret face, black Saran wig, sleep eyes, real lashes, painted lower lashes, closed mouth, hard plastic jointed body, long print gown, gold lamé vest with laces, ribbon in hair, circa 1952, $850.00. *Courtesy Carol Van Verst-Rugg.*

Alexander Doll Co.

18" hard plastic "Sweet Violet" marked "Alexander" on head, "Madame Alexander// All Rights Reserved// New York, U.S.A." on dress tag, synthetic wig, blue sleep eyes, real lashes, painted lower lashes, feathered brows, hard plastic body jointed at shoulders, elbows, wrists, hips, and knees, walking mechanism, original tagged blue cotton dress, flowered bonnet, white gloves, black side-snap shoes, pink Alexander hat box, circa 1954, $1,700.00. *Courtesy McMasters Doll Auctions.*

18" hard plastic "Wendy Bride" (Margaret face), red rooted hair, blue sleep eyes, closed mouth, jointed hard plastic body, white wedding gown, hat with lace and veil, white bouquet of flowers in one hand, carrying pink hat box, mint-in-box, circa 1951, $950.00. *Courtesy Sharon Kolibaba.*

21" vinyl "Jacqueline" marked "Alexander// 19©61" on head, "Jacqueline//by Madame Alexander" on tag on seam of slip, rooted hair, brown sleep eyes, blue eyeshadow, real lashes, closed mouth, pierced ears, hard plastic body jointed at hips and knees, vinyl arms/jointed elbows, adult figure, high-heel feet, original white satin gown, matching cape, taffeta slip/panties, stockings, high heels, bracelet, ring, necklace, purse, earrings, circa 1961, $450.00. *Courtesy McMasters Doll Auctions.*

8" hard plastic "Prince Charles," #397 (Wendy Ann), auburn wig, blue sleep eyes, real lashes, painted lashes below, closed mouth, jointed hard plastic body, blue jacket, short pants, matching hat, white socks, shoes, made in 1957 only, $650.00. *Courtesy Joan Radke.*

Large set of vinyl "Sound of Music;" 17" Maria, 14" Brigitta, 14" Liesl, 14" Louisa, 11" Marta, 11" Friedrich, and 11" Gretl; vinyl heads, five-piece bodies, original colorful outfits, all dolls have original Sound of Music wrist tags, clothing tags have each character name, "From The Sound of Music//©Madame Alexander," except Gretl, whose tag reads "Gretel//©Madame Alexander//New York//U.S.A.," sleep eyes, circa 1965 – 1970, $600.00. *Courtesy McMasters Doll Auctions.*

10" vinyl black "Blue Mist Angel," black hair, brown eyes, hand-painted face, blue gown with a brocade bodice ornamented with pearlescent beaded appliqués cascading over each shoulder, blue satin skirt is overlaid with scallop-edged iridescent white net, and downy white feather wings unfurl behind her, 2001 line, $129.95. *Photo courtesy Alexander Doll Co.*

10" vinyl "Blue Mist Angel," blonde hair, blue eyes, hand-painted face, blue gown with a brocade bodice ornamented with pearlescent beaded appliqués cascading over each shoulder, blue satin skirt is overlaid with scallop-edged iridescent white net, and downy white feather wings unfurl behind her, 2001 line, $129.95. *Photo courtesy Alexander Doll Co.*

10" vinyl "Heavenly Pink Angel," blonde hair, blue eyes, hand-painted face, sparkling sheer pink robe worn over a pink and gold brocade underskirt, both edged with gold binding and rosebud trim, delicate halo of gold and white braid with glittering rhinestones encircles her head, white feather wings, 2001 line, $99.95. *Photo courtesy Alexander Doll Co.*

8" vinyl "Little Love Angel – Pink," blonde upswept curls secured with a single pink rose, blue eyes, hand-painted face, pale pink gown embroidered with slender vines and glistening pale pink sequins, hem of skirt is trimmed with satin, front of the bodice is clustered with flowers, two pink roses attached at the shoulders, pink rose at the waist, delicately embroidered wings, 2001 line, $99.95. *Photo courtesy Alexander Doll Co.*

10" vinyl "Little Love Angel – Lavender," brown hair in ringlets piled on top of her head, brown eyes, pale lavender brocade dress with delicate trailing lace sleeves elasticized and decorated at the elbow with tiny purple rosebuds, the hem of her paneled skirt is trimmed with beaded white garland appliqués, three lavender rosebuds adorn the neckline, feathered wings are spread out behind her, 2001 line, $129.95. *Photo courtesy Alexander Doll Co.*

10" porcelain "Starburst Angel Treetopper," blonde hair, brown eyes, hand-painted face, gown of metallic red organza shimmering with gold iridescence, decorated with gold trim and ribbons, flowing bell sleeves, gold and red metallic stars twinkle on the front of her long gown and the top of her golden halo, underskirt featuring swirling gold flourishes and glittering stars, real feather wings, 2001 line, $99.95. *Photo courtesy Alexander Doll Co.*

8" porcelain "Shining Bright Angel Treetopper," red hair, blue eyes, hand-painted face, fiber optic points of light beneath her sheer pleated silver organza skirt provide a warm, illuminating glow, skirt is trimmed at the hem with gold lamé and the bodice is gold lamé appliquéd with a festive gold star, golden halo encrusted with gilt braid and sparkling rhinestones, wings are of marabou feathers, 2001 line, $139.95. *Photo courtesy Alexander Doll Co.*

8" vinyl "Fall Angel," red hair, brown eyes, hand-painted face, draped from head to toe in the glowing oranges, reds, and golds of Autumn, bodice is russet-red dupioni with short puffed sleeves of orange tulle, layered orange tulle skirt fans out from her waist, surmounted by a gold net overskirt secured with two leaves in gold and brown, headdress of orange tulle anchored by a gold leaf, gold slippers, 2001 line, $79.95. *Photo courtesy Alexander Doll Co.*

Alexander Doll Co.

8" vinyl "Summer Angel," blonde curly hair, blue eyes, hand-painted face, multicolored tulle dress of yellow, green, and pink, lace trim adorns the white bodice, elbows, neck, and hem of the skirt; front of skirt adorned with a long sheer ribbon of pearls and pink and yellow flowers, pink marabou wings, pink slip-on shoes, white flowery halo, 2001 line, $99.95. *Photo courtesy Alexander Doll Co.*

10" vinyl "Winter Angel," brown hair, blue eyes, hand-painted face, luxurious blue ballgown with a voluminous blue tulle skirt embroidered with silver flowers; the hem is edged with fine silver trim, her strapless bodice has attached lace sleeves pinned in place by a sparkling star on each side, blue and silver sash tied into a bow around her waist, star in the center, fluffy white marabou wings, white gloves, 2001 line, $109.95. *Photo courtesy Alexander Doll Co.*

10" vinyl "Spring Angel," blonde upswept hair, brown eyes, hand-painted face, layered pink tulle skirt with picot trim, overskirt gathered in sections by strings of pink, yellow, and purple flowers; pale pink brocade bodice is trimmed at the neckline with yellow and pink flowers, white marabou feather wings unfurl gracefully behind her, hair is crowned with a coronet of ribbon and rosebud appliqués, 2001 line, $109.95. *Photo courtesy Alexander Doll Co.*

10" porcelain "Golden Dream Treetopper," brown hair, brown eyes, hand-painted face, ivory gown embroidered in a burgundy and green floral motif accented with topaz rhinestones; a sheer metallic gold bow at her waist trails down to the hem and a second large bow at the back suggests her angel wings, 2001 line, $99.95. *Photo courtesy Alexander Doll Co.*

10" porcelain "Holiday Trimmings Treetopper," brown hair, green eyes, hand-painted face, a shimmering gold lamé underskirt beneath a fine layer of metallic gold netting hemmed with rick-rack trim, a full taffeta gown of red, gold and green plaid trimmed with bows and gold lame trim; an exquisite halo studded with rhinestones and edged with fine gold trim frames her lovely face, 2001 line, $99.95. *Photo courtesy Alexander Doll Co.*

10" porcelain "Caroler Treetopper," blonde hair, green eyes, hand-painted face, dressed in a red coat with gold trim over a green and gold skirt ornamented with pictures of carolers, white faux fur collar and muff, gold halo, 2001 line, $99.95. *Photo courtesy Alexander Doll Co.*

Alexander Doll Co.

8" vinyl "Best Friend – Blue," ash brown hair, blue eyes, hand-painted face, blue silk dress with square neck, puffed sleeves, a full skirt, hand-stitched smocking on the yoke of the bodice, delicate lace gloves, an organza bag ornamented with flowers and bows, straw hat with flowers embroidered on the underside of the brim and a bow at the crown, ruffled anklets, and white patent leather Mary Janes, 2001 line, $109.95. *Photo courtesy Alexander Doll Co.*

8" vinyl "Best Friend – Pink," blonde hair in a curled bob fastened to one side with a satin bow, blue eyes, hand-painted face, pale pink silk dress with a Peter Pan collar delicately embroidered with dainty flowers, puffed sleeves, full skirt, fine hand-stitched smocking on the yoke of the bodice, ruffled anklets, and deep rose Mary Janes, holds an ornate organza bag, lace gloves, 2001 line, $109.95. *Photo courtesy Alexander Doll Co.*

8" vinyl "Adorable Silk Victorian," blonde curls, blue eyes, hand-painted face, blue and ivory china silk dress with a lace-trimmed ivory overskirt, overskirt is adorned with petite olive green satin bows and a cluster of satin ribbon roses on the bodice, the intricate tucks and folds of her ivory and blue bonnet frames her face and ties beneath her chin with a broad ivory satin ribbon, 2001 line, $94.95. *Photo courtesy Alexander Doll Co.*

8" vinyl "Innocent Silk Victorian," red hair, blue eyes, hand-painted face, intricate silk Victorian style ensemble lavishly accented with rosettes, picot edging, ribbon, and lace, a lace-trimmed bonnet, Mary Janes on her feet, 2001 line, $94.95.
Photo courtesy Alexander Doll Co.

8" vinyl "Victorian Marigold," dark brown hair, blue eyes, hand-painted face, dressed in layers of pale yellow voile and lightweight cotton trimmed with ivory lace, picot edging, and pink and ivory ribbon; the front panel of her dress and her bonnet are embroidered with a tiny pattern, yellow petticoat, and ivory tights and Mary Janes, 2001 line, $79.95. *Photo courtesy Alexander Doll Co.*

8" vinyl "Sophisticated Silk Victorian," red upswept hair, blue eyes, hand-painted face, rose-colored fine silk dress with high neck, lavender over-skirt edged with ivory lace and matching oversleeves; the bodice is centered with an appliqué of a single blossom and three rosettes accent the waist, a lavender hat adorned with an extravagant white marabou feather over her hair, 2001 line, $94.95.
Photo courtesy Alexander Doll Co.

Alexander Doll Co.

8" vinyl "Sweet Silk Victorian," blonde hair tied with a bow, blue eyes, hand-painted face, soft pink silk dress adorned with delicate pintucks, ribbons, and lace, white Mary Janes on her feet, 2001 line, $94.95. *Photo courtesy Alexander Doll Co.*

10" vinyl "Out For a Stroll," blonde upswept hair, blue eyes, hand-painted face, lavish gown of pink and ivory voile ending with a ruffle adorned with pink rosettes, details of the dress include delicate pleats, picot edging, and laces, matching short strolling jacket, carries a beaded purse, wears a straw hat with lace, ribbon and flower trim, 2001 line, $119.95. *Photo courtesy Alexander Doll Co.*

21" hard plastic "Black and White Ball" Cissy, black hair, blue eyes, long black sheath dress with white flared ruffle, floral trim, long black gloves, necklace, earrings, 2001 line, limited edition of 500, #28430, $450.00. *Courtesy Alexander Doll Company.*

21" hard plastic "Haute Couture" Cissy, black short suit, large feathered black hat, black purse, white gloves, black necklace, black and white high heel sandals, limited edition of 500, 2001 line, #28435, $500.00 retail. *Courtesy Alexander Doll Company.*

21" hard plastic "On the Avenue Yardley" Cissy, short green dress with straw hat, chiffon stole, dog on leash, white gloves, tan shoes, reproduction of Yardley 1950s ad, limited edition of 500, $500.00. *Courtesy Alexander Doll Company.*

21" hard plastic "Promise of Spring" Cissy, dark hair, long white embroidered dress with matching white hat, white long gloves, necklace, earrings, carries rope of pink roses, limited edition of 500, #31235, retail $800.00. *Courtesy Alexander Doll Company.*

"A Day in the Life of Cissy Trunk Set" accessories includes red suit, black dress, leopard coat with jewel buttons, pink party dress, shoes, stockings, black gloves, petticoat, and pearl necklace, capri pants with sweater, three pairs of shoes, stockings, black gloves, limited edition of 500, #28420, 2001 line, $550.00 retail. *Courtesy Alexander Doll Co.*

Alexander Doll Co.

"Cissy Hatbox" set includes, shoes, handbag, stockings, gloves, hat, and earrings, #28425, 2001 line, $70.00 retail. *Courtesy Alexander Doll Co.*

"Cissy Shoe Package" includes six pairs of shoes, #28830, 2001 line, $70.00 retail. *Courtesy Alexander Doll Co.*

21" hard plastic "Society Stroll" Cissy, auburn hair, pink dress with dark pink floral pattern, spaghetti straps over shoulders, dark pink matching coat, white gloves, necklace, earrings, dark pink shoes, limited edition of 500, 2001 line, #28415, retail $500.00. *Courtesy Alexander Doll Co.*

8" vinyl "Eloise at Christmastime" in red Santa suit with fur trim and matching red hat, #27701, 2001 line, $42.95 retail. *Courtesy Alexander Coll Co.*

18" cloth "Eloise at Christmastime" in skirt with white blouse, red and white striped scarf, Santa hat, black Mary Jane shoes, white socks, #27581, 2001 line, $49.95 retail. *Courtesy Alexander Doll Co.*

18" cloth "Holiday Eloise" in red skirt with white blouse, red, green and white striped scarf, Santa hat, black Mary Jane shoes, white socks, #28680, 2001 line, $44.95 retail. *Courtesy Alexander Doll Co.*

8" vinyl "Loves to Dance Eloise" brown hair, brown decal eyes, in pink ballerina costume, black top with pink buttons, 2001 line, #30935, $34.95 retail. *Courtesy Alexander Doll Co.*

American Character

The American Character Doll Co. (1919+, New York City) made composition dolls; in 1923 the company began using "Petite" as a tradename for mama and character dolls, and later made cloth, hard plastic, and vinyl dolls. Sweet Sue, Tressy, Mary Make-up, and other dolls with high-heeled shoes and fashion-type figures reflect the focus on women as objects of beauty that remains an ongoing theme in dolls. The company closed circa 1963.

What to look for:

Composition American Character dolls should have good color, little crazing, and tagged original outfits or be appropriately dressed in copies of original costumes using natural or period fabrics.

Hard plastic and vinyl dolls should have great color, be clean, and should be dressed in original costumes, with tags, labels, and brochures intact. Again, the newer the doll, the more complete and mint it must be to command higher prices. Reject soiled or nude dolls unless they have wonderful color, and you have original clothes you can use to re-dress the doll.

Hard Plastic and Vinyl

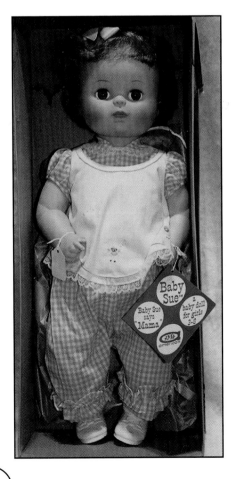

17" vinyl "Baby Sue," short curly synthetic hair, blue sleep eyes, real lashes, closed mouth, baby body, pink and white checked jumper, white shirt trimmed with lace, white shoes, hang tag reads "Baby Sue™//Baby Sue says 'Mama'//A baby doll for girls 3 – 8// American," circa 1954 – 1957, $200.00. *Courtesy Joan Radke.*

18" hard plastic "Annie Oakley," synthetic wig in original set, sleep eyes, closed mouth, jointed hard plastic walker body, original clothing, green vest and skirt with gold fringe, name embroidered on skirt, yellow blouse, black boots, black hat with gold trim, light yellow neckerchief, guns and holster, hang tag, circa 1954 – 1955, $675.00. *Courtesy Rita Mauze.*

24" hard plastic "Sweet Sue," synthetic wig in original set, blue sleep eyes, closed mouth, jointed hard plastic walker body, original satin floral print dress, socks, blue center-snap shoes, hang tag, mint-in-box, circa 1954, $595.00. *Courtesy Rita Mauze.*

24" hard plastic "Sweet Sue," synthetic wig in original set, hair adornment, sleep eyes, closed mouth, jointed hard plastic body, original blue formal with netting, hang tag reads "Sweet Sue//queen of//Dolls," circa 1956, $350.00. *Courtesy Rita Mauze.*

14" hard plastic "Sweet Sue," synthetic wig in original set, sleep eyes, closed mouth, jointed hard plastic walker body, original striped satin dress with violet bows, red sleeves, carrying wig box which reads "Sweet Sue's//Saran® Chignon//by Charles of the Ritz," circa 1952, $325.00. *Courtesy Rita Mauze.*

20" hard plastic "Sweet Sue Sophisticate," light brown synthetic wig in original set, sleep eyes, closed mouth, jointed hard plastic body, satin off-shoulder gown with pink netting, necklace, hairbow, high-heeled shoes, circa 1958, $350.00+. *Courtesy Rita Mauze.*

18" hard plastic "Sweet Sue," unmarked, blonde wig, sleep eyes, closed mouth, jointed hard plastic body, with "Sweet Sue" hang tag, blue organdy dress, white socks, blue shoes, mint-in-box, box reads "Petite Dolls," circa 1950s, $300.00. *Private collection.*

22" hard plastic "Sweet Sue" walker, curly wig, sleep eyes, real lashes, rosy cheeks, closed mouth, jointed hard plastic body, peach organdy dress with lace, blue velvet ribbon around waist, matching hat, white parasol, white socks, black shoes, all original with box and booklet, unplayed-with condition, circa 1953 – 1961, $595.00. *Courtesy Gay Baron.*

21" hard plastic "Sweet Sue," Saran hair, sleep eyes, real lashes, painted lower lashes, closed mouth, jointed hard plastic body, jointed elbows, wearing long formal with pink skirt and blue top trimmed with lace, circa 1950s, **$225.00.** *Courtesy Rose Pitzer.*

20" hard plastic "Sweet Sue," walker, Saran hair, blue sleep eyes, real lashes, painted lower lashes, closed mouth, jointed hard plastic body, jointed elbows, wearing pink nylon dress with blue netting trimmed with lace, pink velvet ribbon and pink roses, pearl beaded headband, circa 1954 – 1956, **$450.00.** *Courtesy Harlene Soucy.*

20" hard plastic "Sweet Sue," walker, Saran hair, blue sleep eyes, real lashes, painted lower lashes, closed mouth, jointed hard plastic body, jointed elbows, wearing "Sunday's Best," a blue and pink nylon dress trimmed with lace and blue flower accents, straw hat, white socks trimmed with pink, pink one-strap shoes, all original with box, circa 1954 – 1956, **$450.00.**
Courtesy Harlene Soucy.

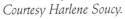

American Character

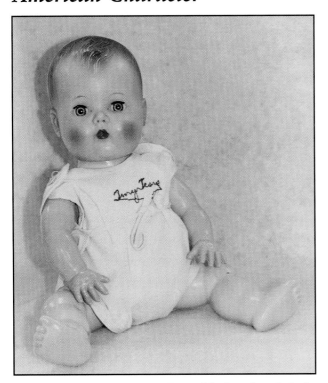

12½" vinyl "Tiny Tears," molded painted hair, blue sleep eyes, holes for tears, open mouth for bottle, rosy cheeks, five-piece bent leg baby body, white sunsuit, circa 1950s, $185.00. *Courtesy Sharon Kolibaba.*

14" vinyl "Toni," unmarked, reddish blonde wig, sleep eyes, closed mouth, jointed body with jointed ankles, original royal blue mid-length gown with full skirt and black lace trim at sleeves, replaced white high-heeled sandals, circa 1958, $275.00. *Private collection.*

20" vinyl "Toni Bride," marked "American//©//Character" in circle on back, "The//Toni//Doll//With Rooted Hair" on wrist tag, rooted hair in original set, blue sleep eyes, real lashes, light blue eyeshadow, closed mouth, pierced ears, jointed lady body, swivel waist, high heel feet, original wedding gown and veil, underclothing, nylon stockings, high-heeled shoes, unplayed-with condition in original box, circa 1958, $395.00. *Courtesy McMasters Doll Auctions.*

19½" vinyl Whimsie "Wheeler the Dealer," marked "Whimsies//19©60//American//Doll & Toy," one-piece stuffed vinyl body with molded head, molded painted slightly closed eyes, painted mustache, closed smiling mouth, black pants, red polka dot short sleeve shirt, red vest, black pants, circa 1961, $65.00. *Courtesy Joan Sickler.*

21" vinyl Whimsie "Lena the Cleaner," molded painted brown eyes, freckles across nose, synthetic reddish blonde rooted wig, one-piece stuffed vinyl body, closed smiling mouth, original costume with blue striped dress, white apron with plastic pockets, circa 1961, $60.00. *Courtesy McMasters Doll Auctions.*

Arranbee Dolls

Arranbee Doll Company, operating from 1922 until 1958 in New York, was sold to Vogue Doll Company who continued to use the Arranbee molds until 1961. Armand Marseille and Simon & Halbig made some of their bisque dolls. Arranbee also produced composition baby, child, and mama dolls; their early dolls have an eight-sided tag. They went on to make hard plastic and vinyl dolls, many carrying the R & B trademark. Some hard plastic and vinyl dolls (Littlest Angel and Li'l Imp) were made for Vogue by the Arranbee division and may be marked by either.

What to look for:

Composition dolls should have good color, only very fine crazing (preferably none), and original clothes or appropriate copies. Always look for mint-in-box and tagged dolls in excellent to mint condition.

Hard plastic and vinyl dolls should be clean with bright rosy cheek color, and tagged or labeled clothes, preferably with brochures and/or boxes to command higher prices in the future.

Composition

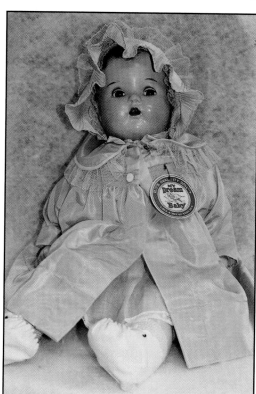

20" composition "My Dream Baby," tagged "RandB QUALITY DOLL//My//Dream//Baby//LIKE A TOT OF YOUR OWN," molded painted dark brown hair, blue sleep eyes, real lashes, painted lower lashes, open mouth with teeth, composition arms, legs, cloth body, blue baby dress and matching bonnet trimmed with lace and net, white shoes, circa 1927+, $475.00.
Courtesy Sandra Tripp.

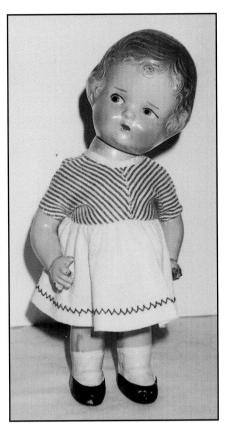

9" composition "Bo Peep," marked "ARRANBEE//DOLL CO." on body, molded painted hair, painted blue side-glancing eyes with lash line, closed mouth, molded painted socks and black shoes, jointed at neck and arms only, possibly original red and white dress with white skirt and red/white striped top, circa 1930s, $100.00.
Private collection.

8½" composition "Bo Peep," marked "R & B//Doll Co." on back, molded painted hair, painted blue eyes, single stroke brows, open/closed smiling mouth, five-piece composition body, original pink and flower print dress, pink hat with blue ribbon pinned to head, underwear with lace trim, socks, leatherette tie shoes, wire staff with ribbon, two 3½" and one 2½" papier-mache sheep with ribbons around necks, circa 1930s – 1940s, $155.00.
Courtesy McMasters Doll Auctions.

14" composition "Debu'Teen," blonde human hair wig, sleep eyes, eyeshadow, closed mouth, jointed compo body, all original in long pink satin gown trimmed with lace, fur jacket, with all original wardrobe including skis, riding boots, ski boots, long and short slips, jodhpurs, flower print dress, vest, shirt, jumpsuit, hats, doll and outfits near mint condition, circa 1939, $750.00. *Private collection.*

Arranbee Dolls

9" composition Storybook doll "Mary Had A Little Lamb," marked "R&B Doll Co." on body, molded painted brown hair, painted eyes, closed mouth, fully jointed composition body, red and white check dress, matching bonnet, white socks, shoes, all original except for lamb which has been replaced, circa 1930s, $150.00. *Private collection.*

15" composition "Nancy," brown human hair wig, brown sleep eyes, open mouth with teeth, fully jointed composition body, oval gold hang tag reads "This doll has a human hair wig," long peach formal, matching bonnet, rayon net cape, blue ribbon trim, all original, near mint, circa 1930s, $400.00. *Private collection.*

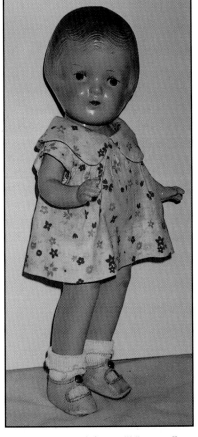

12" composition "Nancy," a Patsy look-alike, marked "ARRANBEE DOLL CO." on back, molded painted hair, painted blue eyes, painted lashes, closed mouth, jointed composition body, original tagged flower print dress, white socks, one-strap shoes, circa 1930, $200.00. *Private collection.*

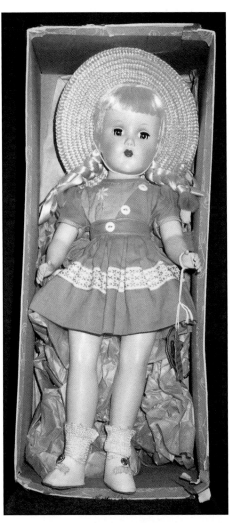

25" hard plastic "Nanette," blonde mohair wig, blue sleep eyes, closed mouth, jointed hard plastic body, light blue dress with fruit accents, white socks black one-strap shoes, hang tag, mint-in-box, circa 1949 – 1959, $795.00. *Courtesy Rita Mauze.*

14" hard plastic "Nancy Lee," blonde braided synthetic wig, sleep eyes, closed mouth, jointed hard plastic body, pink and blue dress with button trim, straw hat, white socks/shoes, hang tag, mint-in-box, circa 1949 – 1959, $460.00. *Courtesy Rita Mauze.*

17" composition "Nancy Lee," marked "R&B" on back of head, original human hair wig, brown sleep eyes, real lashes, painted lower lashes, single stroke brows, closed mouth, five-piece composition body, original brown flannel belted dress with white ruffle trim, original underwear combination, socks and brown suede shoes with fringe tongue, unplayed-with condition, circa 1939+, $300.00. *Courtesy McMasters Doll Auctions.*

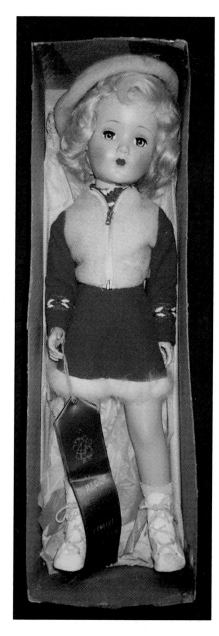

15" hard plastic "Nanette," auburn mohair wig, blue sleep eyes, closed mouth, jointed hard plastic body, multi-flowered print formal with matching purse, circa 1949 – 1959, $495.00. *Courtesy Rita Mauze.*

21" hard plastic "Nanette," blonde mohair wig, blue sleep eyes, closed mouth, jointed hard plastic body, red wool with fur trim skating outfit, white ice skates, 1987 UFDC Blue Ribbon, mint-in-box, circa 1949 – 1959, $900.00. *Courtesy Rita Mauze.*

Two 17½" composition "Debu'Teen" dolls; marked "R&B," human hair wigs, sleep eyes, closed mouths; doll on left is all composition, doll on right has composition shoulderhead on cloth body, composition arms and legs, all original clothing, circa late 1930s, $375.00 each. *Private collection.*

21" hard plastic "Nanette," marked "R&B" on head, Saran wig, blue sleep eyes, real lashes, painted lower lashes, single stroke brows, closed mouth, five-piece hard plastic body with walking mechanism, original red/white striped dress, red organdy sleeves/apron, blue vinyl wide belt, charms attached, curlers on card, comb, wrist tag reads "R&B//Nanette//Walks//Sits//Stands//Turns Her Head//R&B Doll Company//New York," circa 1957 – 1959, $700.00. *Courtesy McMasters Doll Auctions.*

14" hard plastic "Nanette Bridesmaid," mohair wig in original set, blue sleep eyes, real lashes, painted lower lashes, rosy cheeks, closed mouth, jointed hard plastic body, long pink and white bridesmaid gown, all original, circa 1949 – 1959, $400.00. *Private collection.*

Artist Dolls

While a hot debate goes on in some doll making and collecting circles as to the exact definition of an artist doll, we use this definition: original, one-of-a-kind, limited edition or limited production dolls of any medium (cloth, porcelain, wax, wood, vinyl or other material), made for public sale. Dolls may be considered works of art, and some collectors may wish to have just these in their collection. Other collectors define a doll as a play object and choose to collect them as such. You, as a collector, are free to make your own decision to suit yourself, and we can all appreciate the creativity that these talented artists exhibit.

What to look for:

One should remember with all collectibles, a well-made object of beauty will always be appealing. Well-made dolls by artists should appeal to you. Some, not all, will increase in value. Study the range of dolls to find what you like. Some may only be popular fads.

A doll that is artistically done and is in proper proportion stands a greater chance of increasing in value over time. You can enjoy such a doll as part of your collection, rather than acquiring it solely as an investment. With artist dolls, one may need six examples or more of the artist's work to show the range of his or her talents. The artist doll category offers something for everyone.

Alphabetically by Maker

14" porcelain Basketbabies "Mirta" (Peru), by Atelier Bets van Boxel, human hair wig, handcrafted crystal eyes, open mouth, teeth, blanket coat, hat, made from natural fibers authentic from the country of origin, limited edition of 10, circa 2000, $1,500.00. *Photo courtesy Atelier Bets van Boxel.*

14" porcelain Basketbabies "Lindsay" (North American Indian), by Atelier Bets van Boxel, human hair wig, handcrafted crystal eyes, closed mouth, maroon with black print hooded parka with fur trim, tan pants, made from natural fibers authentic from the country of origin, limited edition of 10, circa 2000, $1,500.00. *Photo courtesy Atelier Bets van Boxel.*

21" Prosculpt woman by Kathleen Campbell, red curly hair with black band around forehead, open smiling mouth with teeth, black outfit, gold bead necklace around neck, black one-strap shoes, holding wire with music notes, cloth and wire armature body, circa 2000, $385.00. *Photo courtesy Kathleen Campbell.*

24" porcelain Children of the World "Ji-na & Joo" (member of the H'Mong tribe from Vietnam), by Atelier Bets van Boxel, human hair wig, handcrafted crystal eyes, closed mouths, carrying child on her back, authentic hand embroidered fabric from Vietnam, jewelry is also originally from Vietnam, limited edition of 5, circa 2000, $4,800.00. *Photo courtesy Atelier Bets van Boxel.*

21" Prosculpt Wizard by Kathleen Campbell, long white hair and beard, black pointed wizard hat with gold star sequins, matching cape and black gown, carrying bent wood stick with glass ball, cloth and wire armature body, circa 2000, $485.00. *Photo courtesy Kathleen Campbell.*

21" Prosculpt juggler by Kathleen Campbell, orange hair, large molded nose, closed smiling mouth, small beady eyes, hands open with palms up as if he were juggling; gold, purple, and blue outfit, matching hat with bells, five balls in gold, silver, white, and purple, cloth and wire armature body, circa 2000, $500.00. *Photo courtesy Kathleen Campbell.*

18" Cernit "The Farmer's Daughter" by Stephanie L. Cauley, one-of-a-kind, auburn braided hair, brown eyes, closed mouth, white peasant shirt, flowered scarf tied around shoulders, standing barefoot with goat, circa 2000, $550.00. *Photo courtesy Stephanie Cauley.*

18" Cernit "Masquerade" by Stephanie L. Cauley, one-of-a-kind, girl and boy, dark hair, open smiling mouths with teeth, boy has painted black mask across brown side-glancing eyes, girl's eyes are closed, both wearing elaborate gold, red, white, and black costumes, circa 2000, $1,200.00. *Photo courtesy Stephanie Cauley.*

18" Cernit "The Snow Queen and Karl" by Stephanie L. Cauley, one-of-a-kind, handmade Karl, blonde hair, molded features, red vest, gray pants with fur cuffs, matching hat, white shirt, arms crossed at chest. The Snow Queen has white face, red lips, painted nails, intricate detailed white gown with silver and white embellishments, matching hat, fur collar, kneeling with arms out, circa 2000, **$1,200.00 pair.** *Photo courtesy Stephanie Cauley.*

18" cloth "St. Agnes Academy is Having a Fortieth Reunion" by Jane Darin, hand needle sculptured and painted faces made from 100% Swiss pima cotton knit, 14" x 18" wooden base; the figures are both self-portraits, wearing a combination of cottons and wools, glasses, charms, the mirror is a wire armature covered with batting, nylons, wooden beads, Fimo clay grapes, peacock, clock, and shasta mirror, inspired by the artist's 40th high school reunion, circa 1997, $5,400.00. *Courtesy Jane Darin.*

16" cloth "The Sweeper" by Jane Darin, hand needle sculptured and painted face made from 100% Swiss pima cotton knit, standing on a 12" square by 2½" wood base with a black floor tile polished to reflect her figure, gray mohair wig, broom is made from real Indian broom fiber, wears a traditional cotton East Indian sari, golden arm bangles, toe rings, all made by Jane Darin, circa 1999, $3,200.00. *Courtesy Jane Darin.*

22" resin "I Dream of Zebras" by Jacques Dorier, one-of-a-kind, made of paper and resin, circa 2000, $2,800.00. His art ranges in sizes 6" to 22" and is priced from $125.00 to $3,000.00. *Photo courtesy Jacques Dorier.*

12" polymer clay "Grace" by Marleen Engeler from the Netherlands, one-of-a-kind Art Nouveau doll, holding genuine solid silver antique button, lady with head leaning down toward shoulder, one arm extended up, circa 2000, $1,250.00. *Photo courtesy Marleen Engeler.*

24" paper clay "Dancing Mise" by Yvonne Flipse of Maskerade in Holland, one-of-a-kind, hand-made wig, mouse ears, open/closed with tongue sticking out, handmade outfit, paper clay and papier-mache body, tail, circa 2000, $3,300.00. *Photo courtesy Yvonne Flipse.*

16" paper clay "Honey with Bear" by Yvonne Flipse of Maskerade in Holland, one-of-a-kind, handmade wig, brown eyes, handmade outfit of blue and white, paper clay and papier-mache body, plush long-haired brown bear, circa 2000, $1,800.00. *Photo courtesy Yvonne Flipse.*

28" Polymer clay "A Christmas Waltz" by Marilyn Henke, 28" Santa and 24" Mrs. Santa, one-of-a-kind, glass eyes, acrylic white hair, foam rubber over wire armature bodies, Santa wears cranberry crushed velvet to match Mrs. Santa's outfit, fur trim on hat, and leather boots, Mrs. Santa has white rabbit and braid trim, circa 2000, $990.00. *Courtesy Marilyn Henke.*

Pictured with artist Lebba Kropp is a 21" Cernit "Virginia Blackman." Kropp's Cernit portrait dolls range in size from 18" to 26" and in value from $750.00 to $2,000.00. *Portrait doll photo courtesy Lebba Kropp.*

36" Cernit "Celeste," a boudoir doll by Lebba Kropp, short white wig, molded painted features, open smiling red mouth with upper and lower teeth, painted toenails, with a cigarette in a holder in one hand and a wine glass in the other, pearl necklace, circa 2000, $750.00. *Photo courtesy Lebba Kropp.*

18" Cernit "Surfing Santa" by Lebba Kropp, one-of-a-kind, white hair, beard, and mustache, sunglasses, arms out with red outfit trimmed in white fur, riding on surfboard, circa 2000, $650.00. *Photo courtesy Lebba Kropp.*

30" porcelain Mountain Babies "Michelle" by Denise Lemmon, limited edition of 15, each doll uniquely finished; wears all antique, handmade clothing and carries a small wooden doll made by the doll artist and her father, handpainted blue eyes, pure white long mohair wig, buckeye burl stand, circa 2000, $2,700.00. *Photo courtesy Denise Lemmon.*

30" polymer clay Mountain Babies "Reminisce" by Denise Lemmon, one-of-a-kind, dreamy little girl riding a frisky white horse sculpted by the artist and poured in resin. Reminisce is about the wonderful feeling of security and dreams every child should have, hand painted with alkyd oils, circa 2000, $2,800.00. *Photo courtesy Denise Lemmon.*

24" porcelain Mountain Babies "Roses" by Denise Lemmon, limited edition of 15, each doll uniquely finished; tawny mohair wig, blue eyes, open mouth, white dress of antique fabrics and laces, carrying a bouquet of antique roses, hat, hidden stand with a wooden base. "Roses" is from the mold of "Whisper," an original doll by the artist, circa 2000, $2,300.00. *Photo courtesy Denise Lemmon.*

15½" cloth "Titanic Evening Gown" by Diane Little, hand-painted face, cloth body, black evening gown with red rose, matching red and black hat with feather plume, black shoes, original pattern, circa 2000, $150.00. *Photo courtesy Diane Little.*

15½" cloth "Titanic Walkingsuit" by Diane Little, hand-painted face, cloth body, black suit with gray collar, matching black hat with black feather plume, gloves, original pattern, circa 2000, $175.00. *Photo courtesy Diane Little.*

15½" cloth "Victorian Afternoon Dress" by Diane Little, hand-painted face, cloth body, maroon dress with bustle, patterned jacket with maroon cuffs and trim, original pattern, circa 2000, $200.00. *Photo courtesy Diane Little.*

24" Porcelite resin "Carrie" by Pat Moulton, blonde human hair wig, painted blue eyes, closed mouth, holding golden plush bear, plaid pleated skirt, white sweater, matching cap, white stockings, black shoes, limited edition of 20, circa 2001, $600.00. *Courtesy Pat Moulton.*

16" Porcelite resin "Christa" by Pat Moulton, blonde mohair wig, painted blue eyes, closed smiling mouth, white antique fabric dress with matching bow in hair, one-of-a-kind, circa 2001, $900.00. *Courtesy Pat Moulton.*

20" Super Sculpy and Cernit "Tanner" by Pat Moulton, newborn, human hair wig, closed eyes, open/closed mouth, holding teddy bear, blue sleeper and matching cap, one-of-a-kind, circa 2001, $1,195.00. *Courtesy Pat Moulton.*

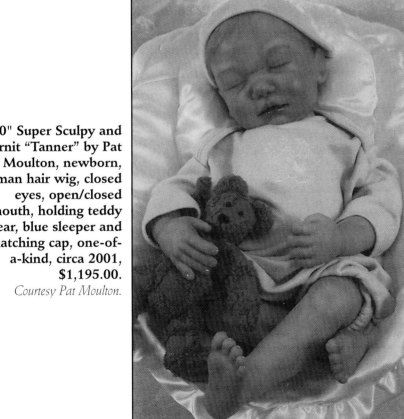

24" porcelain "Christ Has Risen" by W. Harry Perzyk, fully sculpted, anatomically correct, hand-made glass eyes, silk hair fastened to the head by individual hairs, hand-made clothing, one-of-a-kind, circa 1999, $1,500.00. *Courtesy W. Harry Perzyk.*

24" carved wooden "Hideyyoshi Toyotomi" by W. Harry Perzyk, a Japanese warlord and warrior of the late 15th to early 16th century, handmade glass eyes, silk hair fastened to the head by individual hairs, handmade clothing, the helmet is 24 carat gold-filled, one-of-a-kind, circa 1990, $9,500.00. *Courtesy W. Harry Perzyk.*

42" carved wooden "Nobukatsu" by W. Harry Perzyk, a Japanese warrior of the late 16th century, sitting on a white horse, handmade glass eyes, silk hair fastened to the head by individual hairs, handmade clothes, one-of-a-kind, circa 1993, $9,950.00. *Courtesy W. Harry Perzyk.*

36" solid wood carved "Stallion" by W. Harry Perzyk, anatomically correct, handmade glass eyes, silk hair fastened to the head by individual hairs, handmade clothing, one-of-a-kind, circa 1987, $30,000.00. *Courtesy W. Harry Perzyk.*

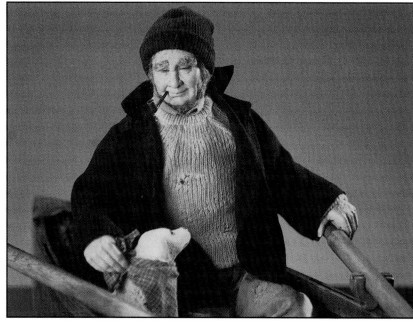

12" stone clay "Salty Dogs" by Myra Sherrod of Born Yesterday Art Dolls, old man seated in a boat with a dog, sweater and pants with holes, black jacket, molded painted features, dark gray beard, hair, and eyebrows, with a pipe in his mouth, holding an oar in one hand and patting his dog with the other, circa 2000, $1,600.00. *Photo courtesy Myra Sherrod.*

23" porcelain "Anya's Garden" by Linda Lee Sutton, limited to 10 worldwide, dark blonde hair, blue paperweight eyes, open smiling mouth with teeth, poseable body, flower print dress, white pinafore with embroidered flowers and trim, blue bonnet, carrying baskets of flowers, circa 2001, $825.00. *Courtesy Linda Lee Sutton.*

Artist Dolls

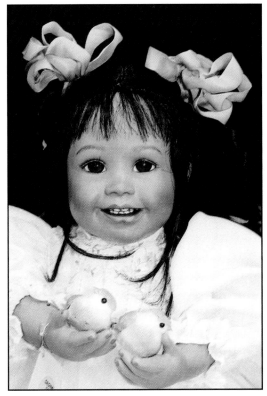

22" porcelain Linda Lee Sutton Black "Ipsy," limited to 12 worldwide, black hair with bangs, brown paperweight eyes, open smiling mouth with teeth, holding two birds, white dress with puff sleeves, embroidered flowers on bodice, ribbons in hair, circa 2001 Photo #, $850.00. *Courtesy Linda Lee Sutton.*

22" porcelain "Flutter-Bi" by Linda Lee Sutton, limited to 12 worldwide, black hair parted in middle, plaited down back, brown paperweight eyes, open/closed mouth, Native American girl holding flowers she has picked in her family's meadow, sitting in awe of a butterfly, suede leather costume of blue fringed top and white fringed skirt, circa 2001, $725.00. *Courtesy Linda Lee Sutton.*

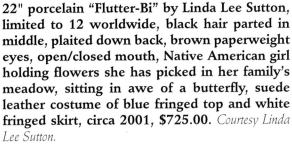

30" porcelain "Snow White" by Linda Lee Sutton, black curly hair, blue intaglio eyes, closed mouth, holding a bird on her fingers, black beaded gown with white organdy sleeves, yoke, and collar, white petticoat, necklace, limited to 10 worldwide, circa 2001, $1,095.00; with the seven 13" porcelain "Seven Dwarfs," intaglio eyes, all in multicolored leather suede and velour outfits, circa 2001, $1,985.00 for 8-doll set.
Courtesy Linda Lee Sutton.

Bisque "Alice in Wonderland" set, 27½" Alice, 30" White Rabbit, 31" Mad Hatter, 27" Queen of Hearts, 25½" Cheshire Cat, 27" Duchess with Pig Baby by Faith Wick, all with bisque character heads, cloth bodies with wire armatures for posing, bisque lower arms and legs, each with labeled wooden stand, marked "W.//©Silvestri®1985 Limited Edition" on heads, "Faith Wick//©Silvestri®//Doll Crafter Classics//©1985 Silvestri Corp." on tags on backs, circa 1985, $1,450.00. *Courtesy McMasters Doll Auctions.*

26" porcelain "Airy" by Goldie Wilson, detailed and hand-painted by the artist, black handmade human hair wig, glass paperweight eyes, organdy and lace two-piece dress, handmade leather shoes, comes with porcelain rabbit, porcelain arms and legs, cloth and wire armature body, limited edition of 20, circa 2000, $695.00. *Photo courtesy Goldie Wilson.*

26" porcelain "Osa" by Goldie Wilson, detailed and hand-painted by the artist, black handmade wig, glass paper-weight eyes, elaborate white dress, handmade choker necklace with rhinestone dangles, matching earrings, handmade leather shoes, porcelain arms and legs, cloth with wire armature body, limited edition of 20, circa 2000, $995.00. *Photo courtesy Goldie Wilson.*

26" porcelain "Osa" by Goldie Wilson, detailed and hand-painted by the artist, black handmade wig, glass paperweight eyes, one-of-a-kind outfit, handmade leather shoes, porcelain arms and legs, cloth with wire armature body, limited edition of 20, circa 2000, $995.00. *Photo courtesy Goldie Wilson.*

Barbie Dolls

First produced by Mattel, Inc. in Hawthorne, California, Barbie doll remains the top collectible doll at the dawn of the new century and is becoming stronger and stronger as twentieth century children grow up and become avid collectors of their childhood dolls. Of interest to collectors too is the reflection of fashion trends as they view Barbie doll's seemingly endless wardrobe.

Marks:
1959-62: BARBIE ™/PATS. PEND.// ©MCMLVIII//by//Mattel, Inc.
1963-68: Midge ™/©1962//BARBIE®/ ©1958//BY//Mattel, Inc.
1964-66: ©1958//Mattel, Inc. //U.S. Patented//U.S. Pat. Pend.
1966-69: ©1966//Mattel, Inc.//U.S. Patented//U.S. Pat. Pend//Made in Japan

Description of the first five Barbie dolls:
Number One Barbie™ 1959
11½" heavy vinyl solid body, faded white skin color, white irises, pointed eyebrows, soft pony-tail, brunette or blonde only, black and white striped bathing suit, holes with metal cylinders in balls of feet to fit round-pronged stand, gold hoop earrings.

Number Two Barbie™ 1959 – 1960
11½" heavy vinyl solid body, faded white skin color, white irises, pointed eyebrows, but no holes in feet, some with pearl earrings, soft ponytail, brunette or blonde only.

Number Three Barbie™ 1960
11½" heavy vinyl solid body, some fading in skin color, blue irises, curved eyebrows, no holes in feet, soft ponytail, brunette or blonde only.

Number Four Barbie™ 1960
11½", same as #3, but solid body of skin-toned vinyl, soft ponytail, brunette or blonde only.

Number Five Barbie™ 1961
11½", vinyl head, now less heavy doll, has hard plastic hollow body, with firmer texture Saran ponytail, some now redheads, has arm tag.

What to look for:
It is still possible to assemble outfits from loose wardrobe pieces and sell or trade your extras. The under 2,000 production limited edition dolls are the ones that will go up in price — or the fad doll that hits the collector's fancy, such as the Harley-Davidson Barbie. Check out *Miller's Price Guide,* PO Box 8722, Spokane, WA 99203, 1-800-874-5201 (orders only), a must-have if you are a hard-core Barbie fan. This is one category that is so broad you are sure to find a niche that will keep you happy.

Barbie Dolls

11½" heavy vinyl #1 "Ponytail Barbie," re-set blonde hair, white irises, pointed eyebrows, holes in feet, painted fingernails and toenails, in black and white striped knit swimsuit, hoop earrings, in box with black plastic pedestal stand, pink cover booklet, black open-toe shoes, white rimmed glasses, marked "Barbie™//Pats. Pend.//©MCMLVIII//by Mattel//Inc.," circa 1959, $4,100.00. *Courtesy McMasters Doll Auctions.*

11½" vinyl #5 "Ponytail Barbie," straight leg, blue painted eyes, blue eyeshadow, nostril paint, red lips, brunette hair in original top-knot, original black/white striped one-piece strapless swimsuit, white rimmed glasses with blue lenses, black open-toe shoes, pink cover Barbie/Ken booklet in cellophane bag, replaced cardboard box liner, black wire stand, pearl earrings taped in box, near-mint-in-box, circa 1961, $450.00. *Courtesy McMasters Doll Auctions.*

11½" vinyl #6 "Ponytail Barbie," honey blonde hair, blue painted side-glancing eyes, blue eyeshadow, coral lips, fingernail and toenail paint, straight legs, pink square neck sweater with sewn-on waistband, pink sheath skirt with pocket accent, #0819 "It's Cold Outside" red coat with button accent, fur trim and belt, matching hat with fur pompons, red open-toe shoes, circa 1962, $270.00. *Courtesy McMasters Doll Auctions.*

11½" vinyl "Bubblecut Barbie," straight leg, blue painted side-glancing eyes, blue eyeshadow, brunette hair, red lips, nostril paint, pearl earrings, fingernail and toenail paint, original black/white striped swimsuit, wrist tag, in box with black wire stand, cardboard neck and leg inserts, pink cover Barbie/Ken booklet in cellophane bag, white rimmed glasses with blue lenses, black open-toe shoes, near-mint-in-box, circa 1961, $375.00. *Courtesy McMasters Doll Auctions.*

11½" vinyl "Bubblecut Barbie," marked "Midge™ //©1962//Barbie®//©1958//by//Mattel, Inc.//Patented," platinum hair, light pink lips outlined in white, straight leg, painted fingernails and toenails, wearing Japan market Garden Tea Party satin print floral dress with white lace panel and ribbon bow accent, white nylon short gloves, olive green open-toe shoes, near-mint-in-box, circa 1962 – 1967, $275.00. *Courtesy McMasters Doll Auctions.*

Barbie Dolls

11½" vinyl "Swirl Ponytail Barbie," blonde hair, gold lips with tint of peach, blue irises, fingernail and toenail paint, straight legs, wearing #917 Apple Print Sheath, black #1 open-toe shoes with holes, hair has been reset, marked "Midge™// ©1962//Barbie®// ©1958//by//Mattel, Inc.//Patented," circa 1964 – 1965, $175.00. *Courtesy McMasters Doll Auctions.*

11½" vinyl "Bubblecut Barbie," blonde hair, blue painted side-glancing eyes, blue eyeshadow, pink lips, nostril paint, pearl earrings, fingernail paint, toenail paint, straight legs, original black/white striped swimsuit, in box with black wire stand, black open-toe shoes, near-mint-in-box, marked "Barbie®/Pats. Pend.//©MCMLVIII//by Mattel//Inc.," circa 1961, $220.00. *Courtesy McMasters Doll Auctions.*

11½" vinyl "Swirl Ponytail Barbie," titian hair in side-swept ponytail, tan lips, blue irises, nostril paint, fingernail and toenail paint, straight legs, wearing red nylon swimsuit, top of ponytail has been re-tied, circa 1964 – 1965, $240.00. *Courtesy McMasters Doll Auctions.*

11½" vinyl "Swirl Ponytail Barbie," honey blonde hair in side-swept ponytail, beige lips with hint of peach color, blue irises, fingernail and toenail paint, straight legs, wearing #1617 Midnight Blue gown with blue satin skirt and silver lamé bodice, matching long cape with fur trim, white nylon long gloves, medium blue open-toe shoes, silver clutch purse, pearl necklace, circa 1964 – 1965, $245.00. *Courtesy McMasters Doll Auctions.*

11½" vinyl "Montgomery Ward's Anniversary Barbie," Number One replica ponytail Barbie, brunette hair in original set, red lips, straight legs, wearing original black/white knit swimsuit, white open-toe shoes taped to her feet, wrist tag, mint condition, circa 1972, $355.00. *Courtesy McMasters Doll Auctions.*

11½" vinyl "Fashion Queen Barbie," molded painted dark brown hair with a blue vinyl headband, blue irises, light pink lips, eyeshadow, wearing original gold lamé and white striped swimsuit with matching turban, pearl earrings, white open-toe shoes, three interchangeable wigs and a white wig stand, marked "Midge™//©1962//Barbie®//©1958//by //Mattel, Inc.," circa 1963 – 1964, $95.00. *Courtesy McMasters Doll Auctions.*

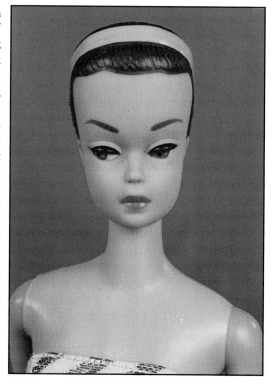

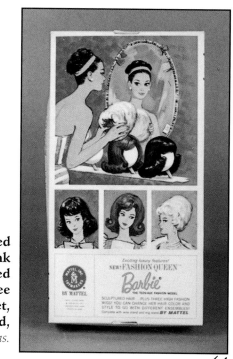

11½" vinyl Mattel "Fashion Queen Barbie," #870, molded painted dark brown hair with a blue vinyl headband, blue irises, light pink lips, eyeshadow, wearing original gold lamé and white striped swimsuit with matching turban, pearl earrings, wrist tag, three interchangeable wigs and a white wig stand, white cover booklet, and white open-toe shoes in cellophane bag, black wire stand, NRFB, circa 1963, $370.00. *Courtesy McMasters Doll Auctions.*

Barbie Dolls

11½" vinyl "Twist 'n Turn Barbie," brunette hair, pink lips, cheek blush, rooted eyelashes, fingernail paint, bendable legs, waist that twists back and forth, wearing #1453 Flower Wower print dress, wrist tag, clear plastic stand, circa 1968, $205.00. *Courtesy McMasters Doll Auctions.*

11½" vinyl "Growin' Pretty Hair Barbie," blonde hair, pink lips, cheek blush, rooted eyelashes, bendable legs, wearing pink satin dress, wrist tag, in box with pink high-top shoes in small cellophane bag, blonde braided hairpiece with pink metal barrette, blonde curly hairpiece with pink ribbon bow, metal hairpins, white plastic comb and brush, two pink flower hair accents, NRFB, circa 1971, $220.00. *Courtesy McMasters Doll Auctions.*

11½" vinyl "Twist 'n Turn Barbie," brunette hair, pink lips, cheek blush, rooted eyelashes, fingernail paint, bendable legs, waist that twists back and forth, wearing #1860 Smasheroo, The Collector's Request Limited Edition 1967 Doll and Fashion Reproduction, #18941, BD 1997, NRFB, $35.00. *Courtesy McMasters Doll Auctions.*

11½" vinyl "Living Barbie," brunette hair, pink lips, cheek blush, bendable arms and legs, wearing original one-piece swimsuit with orange net cover-up, wrist tag, clear plastic stand, in box with box insert, near mint, circa 1970, $200.00. *Courtesy McMasters Doll Auctions.*

11½" vinyl "Live Action Barbie," blonde hair, pink lips, cheek blush, rooted eyelashes, bendable arms and legs, wearing two-piece multi-colored pants and shirt with fringe trim, circa 1971, $55.00. *Courtesy McMasters Doll Auctions.*

11½" vinyl "Soda Fountain Sweetheart Barbie," #15762, Coca-Cola Fashion Classic Series First in Series, bendable legs, NRFB, with cardboard shipping box, circa 1996, $75.00. *Courtesy McMasters Doll Auctions.*

Barbie Dolls

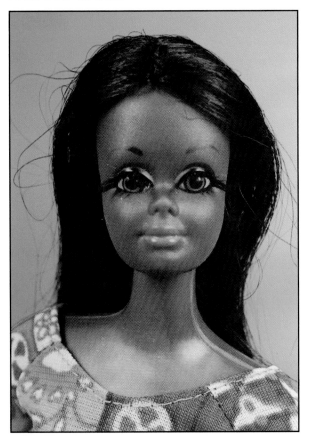

11½" vinyl "Walk Lively Miss America," #3200, brunette hair with attached crown, pink lips, cheek blush, rooted eyelashes, bendable legs, wearing original gown with gold bodice and white skirt, red cape with fur trim, Miss America sash, red flower bouquet with ribbon streamers, white high-tongue shoes, wrist band, near mint, circa 1972, $40.00. *Courtesy McMasters Doll Auctions.*

11½" vinyl "Live Action Christie," black hair, brown lips, rooted eyelashes, bendable arms and legs, wearing two-piece print pants with fringe accent and matching shirt with fringe trim, circa 1971, $135.00. *Courtesy McMasters Doll Auctions.*

11½" vinyl "Talking Barbie," #1115, non-working talker, blonde hair in original set, blue eyes, pink lips, cheek blush, bendable legs, wearing two-piece nylon swimsuit with net jacket, wrist tag, near mint, circa 1968, $170.00. *Courtesy McMasters Doll Auctions.*

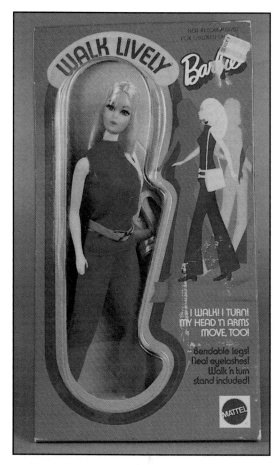

11½" vinyl "Walk Lively Barbie," #1182, blonde hair, pink lips, blush, rooted eyelashes, bendable legs, wearing red nylon shirt and pants, brown belt, shoes, yellow shoulder purse, wrist tag, in box with brown plastic stand, NRFB, circa 1972, $210.00. *Courtesy McMasters Doll Auctions.*

11½" vinyl "Hair Happenin's Francie," blonde hair with faded ribbon band, pink lips, cheek blush, rooted eyelashes, bendable legs, wearing original blue dress with white lace trim, three hairpieces: headband with blonde braid and two long twisted curls on both sides with rubberbands and pink yarn ties; blonde wiglet; headband with blonde short flip curls on both sides with rubberbands and orange ribbon ties, circa 1970, $105.00. *Courtesy McMasters Doll Auctions.*

11½" vinyl "Twist 'n Turn Francie," brunette hair with brown string attached to both sides of head, pink lips, rooted eyelashes, bendable legs, wearing #1207 Floating In dress, circa 1967, $95.00. *Courtesy McMasters Doll Auctions.*

11½" vinyl "Molded Hair Midge," painted titian hair with orange plastic headband, orange lips, fingernail and toenail paint, straight leg Midge/Barbie body, wearing Dinner at Eight hostess coat, circa 1965, $65.00. *Courtesy McMasters Doll Auctions.*

11½" vinyl "Francie," bendable legs, brunette hair with attached string and plastic cover, pink lips, cheek blush, rooted eyelashes, wearing original print nylon swimsuit, white soft pumps, white plastic comb, pink plastic eyelash brush, in box with gold wire stand, Francie booklet, near mint, circa 1966, $190.00. *Courtesy McMasters Doll Auctions.*

11½" vinyl "Midge," titian hair, painted blue eyes, pink lips, freckles, finger and toe paint, straight legs, wearing #951 Senior Prom green satin gown with tulle panels, green open-toe shoes, circa 1963, $85.00. *Courtesy McMasters Doll Auctions.*

11½" vinyl "Twist 'n Turn P.J.," blonde hair in original set with beaded accents, pink lips, cheek blush, rooted eyelashes, fingernail and toenail paint, bendable legs, wearng original pink one-piece swimsuit, wrist tag, attached lavender glasses, near mint, circa 1970, $115.00. *Courtesy McMasters Doll Auctions.*

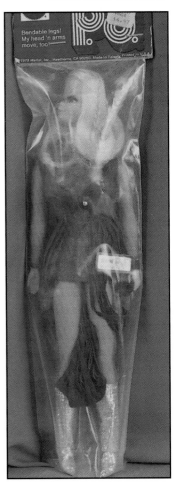

11½" vinyl "Baggie P.J.," blonde hair, pink lips, cheek blush, rooted eyelashes, bendable arms and legs, wearing original orange outfit with attached gold boots, purple fringe vest, wrist tag, in bag with cardboard top, NRFP, circa 1973, $110.00. *Courtesy McMasters Doll Auctions.*

11½" vinyl "Walk Lively Steffie," brunette hair, light peach lips, cheek blush, rooted eyelashes, bendable legs, wearing original nylon print jumpsuit, circa 1972, $85.00. *Courtesy McMasters Doll Auctions.*

9¼" vinyl "Skooter," titian hair in original set with ribbon ties, pink lips, cheek blush, straight legs, wearing original red and white two-piece swimsuit, red flat shoes, wrist tag, white cover Skipper booklet, cardboard box insert, gold wire stand, near-mint-in-box, circa 1965, $165.00. *Courtesy McMasters Doll Auctions.*

9¼" vinyl "Skipper," brunette hair, pink lips, straight legs, wearing red and white swimsuit, metal headband, in box with cardboard insert, gold metal stand, near-mint-in-box, circa 1964, $105.00. *Courtesy McMasters Doll Auctions.*

6¼" vinyl "Tutti" in "Cookin' Goodies," brunette hair in original set, pink lips, cheek blush, bendable arms and legs, wearing orange dress with ribbon accent, apron, white nylon socks, orange shoes, pink and white plastic stove with black burners, black plastic pan with two eggs, pink plastic brush and comb in small cellophane bag attached on box liner, in box with plastic window lid, circa 1967, $225.00. *Courtesy McMasters Doll Auctions.*

6¼" vinyl "Tutti Night-Night Sleep Tight," blue painted side-glancing eyes, light brown brows, pink lips, cheek blush, red waist-length ponytail with pink ribbon tie, bangs, dressed in pink floral robe with solid pink nightgown, pink felt slippers with white lace trim, white plastic bed with pink floral bedspread, bed attached to box liner, near mint, circa 1965, $125.00. *Courtesy McMasters Doll Auctions.*

Irwin Corporation plastic "Barbie's Sports Car," Austin Healy peach-colored with turquoise interior, plastic windshield, silver plastic steering wheel, near-mint-in-box, circa 1962 – 1964, $245.00. *Courtesy McMasters Doll Auctions.*

Miner Industries "Knitting for Barbie," kit #8013, Skirt and Sleeveless Blouse, includes blue, red, yellow, and green yarn, red plastic darning needle and small silver thimble attached to pink card, two large red plastic knitting needles, basic instruction booklet, also includes a metal thimble and darning needle, hard-to-find, box date 1962, $135.00.
Courtesy McMasters Doll Auctions.

Standard Toycraft Industries "Barbie Luncheon Embroidery Set," includes napkins to embroider with accessories, plastic windows; box is discolored, scuffed, and worn along edges and corners, plastic window is scuffed, edges of plastic window torn, needle is missing, lower right box bottom seam is split, circa 1962, $135.00.
Courtesy McMasters Doll Auctions.

11½" vinyl #1 Ponytail Barbie, #850, white irises, dark eyeliner, red lips, arched eyebrows, brunette, soft hair with ringlet bangs, holes in feet, heavy solid body, circa 1959, $7,100.00.
Courtesy McMasters Doll Auctions.

11½" vinyl #2 Barbie, #850, brunette, soft hair, ringlet bangs, white irises, dark eyeliner, red lips, arched eyebrows, same as #1 but no holes in feet, mint-in-box, circa 1959, $6,350.00.
Courtesy McMasters Doll Auctions.

Betsy McCall Dolls

Ideal

Betsy McCall is based on the 1951 May *McCall's* magazine paper doll. First licensed to Ideal Doll Company, 1952 – 1953, this 14" Betsy was designed by Bernard Lipfert. She has a vinyl head, rooted Saran wig, watermelon smile, and a strung hard plastic Toni body. She is marked on the back of her head, "McCall Corp. ®" and "IDEAL DOLL//P 90" on her back torso. She came with a McCall's pattern for an apron.

Uneeda

In 1964, Uneeda produced an 11½" vinyl Betsy McCall with rooted hair, rigid vinyl body, brown or blue sleep eyes, and slim pre-teen body and costumed her in mod style outfits. She did not strongly resemble the paper doll Betsy McCall and was unmarked.

Rothchild

In 1986, 35th anniversary 8" and 12" hard plastic Betsy McCalls were produced by Rothchild. She had sleep eyes, painted lashed below the eyes, single stroke eyebrows, a tied ribbon emblem on her back, and a hang tag.

What to look for:

Vinyl Betsys should be clean, retaining color in their cheeks, and wearing original clothes. The large size can still be found in good condition. If you can't find an old one, try the new ones from Robert Tonner.

Ideal

14" vinyl, marked "McCall Corp®" on head, "Ideal Doll//P-90" on body, designed by Bernard Lipfert, black rooted hair, brown sleep eyes, watermelon smile, strung hard plastic Toni body, original gray and white checked dress with red front, original black shoes, circa 1952 – 1953, $165.00.
Courtesy Judie Conroy.

American Character

In 1957, American Character introduced an 8" hard plastic Betsy McCall with rigid vinyl arms, sleep eyes, single stroke eyebrows, molded eyelashes, and metal barrettes in her hair. The first-year production dolls had a mesh-based wig that was glued on and plastic peg-jointed knees. The second-year and later production dolls had rooted Saran hair in a rubber-type skullcap, metal pin-jointed knees, and were marked in a circle on the back waist, "McCall © Corp." Advertising proclaimed 100 ready-made costumes were available. They later introduced other sizes, 14", 19", and 36" in 1959, and a 22" and 29" in 1961. Betsy had a family with her cousin Linda and brother Sandy McCall in 1959.

8" hard plastic, with synthetic wig, sleep eyes, metal barrettes on each side of head, and more translucent skin tone, in original dress, circa 1958, $150.00.

7½" vinyl, marked "McCall//©//Corp" in circle on back, blonde wig with barrettes, sleep eyes, single stroke brows, closed smiling mouth, jointed knees, original pink dress with pink and white checked top, white rick-rack, white socks, black shoes, with box, circa 1957 – 1963, $200.00. *Courtesy Barbara Hull.*

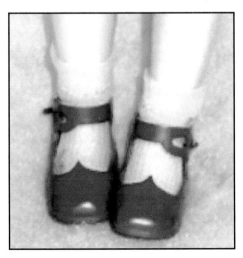

Red vinyl shoes for an 8" hard plastic American Character "Betsy McCall," circa 1958, $25.00.

14" vinyl, marked "McCall// 19©58" on head, rooted hair, sleep eyes, vinyl jointed body with swivel waist, black body suit, rayon socks, one black strap shoe, tied in bottom of original box, Betsy McCall trunk with extra clothing and accessories, trunk marked "Betsy McCall" in star designs on trunk, original cardboard insert marked "trunk and clothing made exclusively for your 14" Betsy McCall Doll," circa 1958, $400.00. *Courtesy McMasters Doll Auctions.*

Left: 36" vinyl "Betsy McCall," marked "McCall Corp//1959" on head, rooted hair, sleep eyes, closed smiling mouth, Patti Playpal style jointed body, re-dressed in size 3T child's red dress, black jacket, red cap, black stockings, and shoes. Right: 39" vinyl "Sandy McCall," marked "McCall 1959 Corp," molded painted hair, sleep eyes, re-dressed in size 3T childs striped overalls, red shirt, red cap, and sandals, $175.00 each, circa 1960. *Private collection.*

Tiny Betsy — Then and Now!

One of the nice things that is happening in today's marketplace is the reproduction of many of dolls that were popular during our childhood. One of those that is being reproduced is the 8" Betsy McCall that was originally introduced by American Character in 1957. Today, the Robert Tonner Doll Company is making Tiny Betsy for a delighted group of collectors. Today's collectors, to distinguish it from the other Betsys that have been made in other sizes, call it Tiny Betsy. But, are there any differences? How can we tell the difference between the reproductions and the old ones?

Looking at the face coloring, the old 8" Tiny Betsy has a more translucent look to the hard plastic, while the new Tiny Betsy has a more realistic skin tone. In 1957, the first year of issue, the wigs on the American Character Tiny Betsy were glued-on mohair. In 1958, the wigs on the old Tiny Betsys were rooted into a vinyl skullcap and had one metal barrette holding the hair on each side. The bangs may be much shorter on the old Tiny Betsy as compared to the new Tiny Betsy.

The old Tiny Betsy usually has looser stringing and may not stand; Tonner's Tiny Betsy can stand alone. The old Tiny Betsy is known for breakage in the crotch and problems with knee joints. The new Tiny Betsy seems to have a better body design. Both lower back torsos have a "Y" with two dots above it. The old Tiny Betsy, however, also has a round copyright mold mark above the "Y" that reads "MCCALL CORP." This mark might seem the best way to distinguish the old Tiny Betsy from the new, but some unmarked Betsys were versions sold through catalogs like Sears and Montgomery Ward.

The new Tiny Betsys do not have vinyl shoes — yet! It is hard to find the old Tiny Betsy vinyl Mary Jane shoes because they were small and easy to lose when children played with them. A pair of red vinyl ones like these on our old Tiny Betsy with their distinctive v-shaped cut above the toe are easy to distinguish from the soft cloth-like shoes on the new dolls.

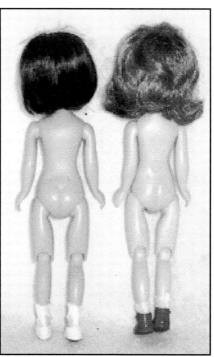

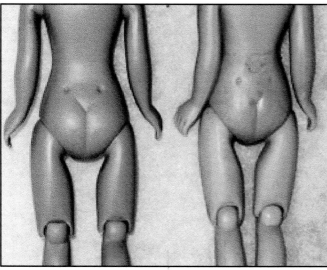

These photos compare 8" Tiny Betsys. On left is the new Robert Tonner Doll Company "Betsy McCall." On the right is the old hard plastic Amercian Character Betsy McCall from 1958. Note loose stringing on old Betsy and back round mark that reads "MCCALL CORP."

Betsy McCall Dolls

The boxes too are different. The old American Character boxes were white with blue starburst pattern and some with a graphic of Betsy holding a bouquet of flowers. Tonner's box has a blue and white overall check pattern with red printing. While the differences may seem very distinct in the dolls right now, in a few years when the new dolls have been played with, the differences may be less clear. Since the old Tiny Betsys are selling at record prices, it is nice to make sure you are not paying old prices for the more affordable new Tiny Betsy.

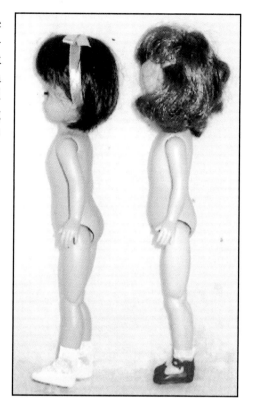

Robert Tonner

8" rigid vinyl "Betsy McCall" with more realistic skin tone, longer bangs, no barrettes in hair, in pale yellow dress with lace trim, white shoes, carries basket of flowers, souvenir of the Betsy McCall Spring Luncheon at the Tonner Convention, 2001, $125.00.

In 1996, the Robert Tonner Doll Company produced a 14" vinyl Betsy McCall that immediately reminded collectors of the original paper doll character. She had rooted hair, rigid vinyl body, plastic eyes, closed smiling mouth, and is marked on the back "Betsy McCall//by//Robert Tonner//©Guner & Jarr USA PUB." There were also porcelain editions. In 2000, the Robert Tonner Doll Company introduced the 8" vinyl Betsy McCall, a replica of the 1957 version, and plans a larger version Betsy.

Shoes to fit 8" Betsy McCall are made of clothlike synthetic material.
Ccourtesy Marilyn Ramsey.

76

8" vinyl "Tiny Betsy McCall," Tosca, Brown, and Blonde, rooted hair, plastic sleep eyes, real lashes, painted lashes below, closed smiling mouth, jointed vinyl body, jointed knees, white one-piece outfit with pink flower print, lace trim, white socks, black one-strap shoes, circa 2001, $39.99 each. *Courtesy Robert Tonner Doll Company.*

8" vinyl "Tiny Betsy McCall's Sundress," style #BM CL 1102, rooted hair, plastic sleep eyes, real lashes, painted lashes below, closed smiling mouth, jointed vinyl body, jointed knees, white sundress with yellow flower print on skirt, trimmed in yellow, matching bolero, matching white hat with yellow trim, black purse, black one strap shoes, white socks, circa 2001, $54.99. *Courtesy Robert Tonner Doll Company.*

8" vinyl "Tiny Betsy McCall Takes A Ballet Class," style #BM CL 1101, rooted hair, plastic sleep eyes, real lashes, painted lashes below, closed smiling mouth, jointed vinyl body, jointed knees, pink tutu with pink flower trim, pink ribbons in hair, pink tights, pink ballet shoes, circa 2001, $49.99. *Courtesy Robert Tonner Doll Company.*

Betsy McCall Dolls

8" vinyl "Tiny Betsy McCall Goes to the Theatre," style #BM CL 1104, rooted hair, plastic sleep eyes, real lashes, painted lashes below, closed smiling mouth, jointed vinyl body, jointed knees, white organdy dress with full skirt and shorter skirt overlay with flower trim ribbon, matching flower barrettes in hair, white socks and white plastic one-strap shoes, circa 2001, $54.99. *Courtesy Robert Tonner Doll Company.*

8" vinyl "Tiny Betsy McCall," rooted hair, plastic sleep eyes, real lashes, painted lashes below, closed smiling mouth, jointed vinyl body, jointed knees, wearing "Betsy McCall Writes a Letter to Grandpa," style #BM CL 8101, gray corduroy coat, white collar trimmed in lace, matching white hat, white gloves, white stockings, black one-strap shoes, outfit only, circa 2001, $23.99. *Courtesy Robert Tonner Doll Company.*

8" vinyl "Tiny Betsy McCall Sails a Boat," style #BM CL 1103, rooted hair, plastic sleep eyes, real lashes, painted lashes below, closed smiling mouth, jointed vinyl body, jointed knees, blue checked dress with button and red ribbon trim, full skirt, red hat, white socks, red one-strap shoes, circa 2001, $54.99. *Courtesy Robert Tonner Doll Company.*

8" vinyl "Tiny Betsy McCall," rooted hair, plastic sleep eyes, real lashes, painted lashes below, closed smiling mouth, jointed vinyl body, jointed knees, wearing "Betsy McCall Has A Happy Holiday," style #BM CL 1105, red party dress with white organdy underskirt, white sheer collar with red flower, red ribbon headband, white stockings, white gloves, red shoes, dressed doll, circa 2001, $49.99. *Courtesy Robert Tonner Doll Company.*

8" vinyl "Tiny Betsy McCall," rooted hair, plastic sleep eyes, real lashes, painted lashes below, closed smiling mouth, jointed vinyl body, jointed knees, wearing "Betsy McCall Goes Sleigh Riding," style #BM CL 8102, navy blue coat with red trim and wooden buttons, red pants, red shoes, wooden sleigh, outfit only, circa 2001, $23.99. *Courtesy Robert Tonner Doll Company.*

14" vinyl "Betsy McCall," long rooted brown hair, brown plastic eyes, closed smiling mouth, style #BMC 3103, "Betsy Style 1970s," multicolored flowered long sleeve shirt, fringed vest with appliqued flower, bell bottom jeans, belt, brown crocheted handbag, sandals, circa 2001, $89.99. *Courtesy Robert Tonner Doll Company.*

Betsy McCall Dolls

14" vinyl "Betsy McCall," rooted brown hair, brown plastic eyes, closed smiling mouth, style #BMC 3104, "Betsy Style 1980s," gray, white, and pink striped aerobic outfit with matching leggings, white stockings, white shoes, pink band in hair, and jump rope, circa 2001, $89.99. *Courtesy Robert Tonner Doll Company.*

14" vinyl "Betsy McCall," rooted brown hair, brown plastic eyes, closed smiling mouth, style #BMC 3101, "Betsy Style 1950s," red full-skirted dress with black flower print and black rick-rack trim, white collar and front panel trimmed with black rick-rack and black buttons, white slip with lace trim, white socks, black one-strap shoes, circa 2001, $89.99. *Courtesy Robert Tonner Doll Company.*

14" vinyl Betsy McCall as "Cinderella," style BMC 1103, rooted brown hair, brown plastic eyes, closed smiling mouth, and 14" vinyl Sandy McCall as "Prince Charming," rooted brown hair, blue plastic eyes, closed smiling mouth. Both Betsy's gown and Sandy's suit are coordinated in coral velvet with exquisite embroidery touches and gold ribbon embellishment, slippers, and velvet pillow, circa 2001, Cinderella, $99.99, Prince Charming, $79.99. *Courtesy Robert Tonner Doll Company.*

10" porcelain "Betsy McCall" in pink taffeta dress with white trim, pink slippers, pink bows in hair; souvenir of the 2001 Robert Tonner Doll Co. Convention Betsy Happy Birthday, celebrating 50 years of Betsy McCall, $125.00.
Courtesy Marilyn Ramsey.

Horsman

In 1974, Horsman produced a 12½" vinyl Betsy with rigid plastic body and sleep eyes, and packaged her in a Betsy McCall Beauty Box with extra hairpiece, brush, bobby pins on a card, eye pencil, blush, lipstick, two sponges, mirror, and other accessories. Marked on the head, "Horsman Doll Inc.//19©67" and "Horsman Dolls Inc." on the torso. This was a generic type doll with little resemblance to the paper doll, the same as their walking 29" Betsy.

28" vinyl "Betsy McCall," marked "12//Horsman Dolls, Inc.//1974," painted eyes, molded lashes, open/closed mouth, painted teeth, blonde rooted hair with side part, white eyelet blouse, black shirt with "BMc" in red on front belt, black slip-on shoes, circa 1974, $125.00.
Private collection.

Black Dolls

A great collectible category is black dolls. Because fewer were made, black dolls almost always place over white dolls in competition. Fewer of these survived their owners' childhoods and finding a doll in mint condition is difficult. These come in many different mediums, offering a wide range of collecting possibilities in cloth, composition, hard plastic, porcelain, rubber, and vinyl.

What to look for:

Condition is still the number one factor in great collectible dolls. From a Leo Moss papier-mache/composition to a modern vinyl one, black dolls can be an intriguing part of your collection. Almost any out-of-production black doll mint-in-the-box will remain a good collectible and may also increase in value. Check for marks to find those Shindana dolls — these included the infamous O.J. Simpson as well as other celebrities. Do not overlook black dolls at garage sales, flea markets, and other sales.

Golliwogs, circa early 1900s to present

Florence Kate Upton, born 1873 in Flushing, New York, to English immigrant parents, was a struggling young artist who drew book illustrations to finance her art studies. Her first book, *The Adventures of Two Dutch Dolls and a Golliwogg,* was first published in England. Florence did the simple illustrations, and her mother, Bertha Upton, composed a poem to tell the story of the illustrations. The characters were two "Dutch" German (Deutsch) wooden dolls named Peg and Sarah Jane who live in a toyshop. During the night when the shop is closed, the dolls come alive and make themselves a dress out of an American flag, Peg in red and white stripes and Sarah Jane in blue with white stars. During the evening they meet a congenial black character with fuzzy hair wearing a blue jacket and red trousers who announces that he is "The Golliwogg," spelled with two "g's." Florence wrote 12 books about these characters but retained no copyright, and like the teddy bear, they soon were widely copied.

The story and Golliwog character became a staple in England but did not receive the same warm reception in the U.S. as it may have been perceived as a desecration of the American flag. With the passage of time and perhaps to avoid copyright infringements, the Golliwog spelling dropped the last "g." Even later in the 1960s, when "wog" was used as a racial slur in Europe, the name was shortened to Golli or Golly. With racial tension in the U. S. during this period, a black doll with fuzzy hair was not politically correct. After 100 years have passed since the introduction of the Golliwog character, interest has been revived with collectors — even if it is no longer the staple with English children.

Deans, Hermman, Merrythought, and Steiff are some of the well-known companies that made Gollies during the early 1900s. In addition, seamstresses could create their own rendition at home from commercial patterns. Robertson's, who produced jam in England, took the Golly image as their logo and has used it continually, producing a series of pins and other memorabilia. The pins, or brooches as they are also called, can be a collecting field in itself. Gollies remain a charming collectible and can be found at several sites on the Internet including the International Golliwog Collector's Club and Golliwogs.com — just type "Golliwog" into your search engine.

Shindana, 1968 – 1983, Los Angeles, California

After the Watts riots in Los Angeles, Shindana Toys was formed in 1968, the first major manufacturer of high-quality black dolls with ethnically correct features, covering a wide selection of babies, children, and adults. Shindana was a division of Bootstrap Inc., a non-profit black community organization founded by Lou Smith and Robert Hall. Its motto was "Learn Baby, Learn!" and the company presented positive images of black children. It ceased production in 1983 and because of the short 15-year span of operation, only a few of these dolls are still available. Dolls may be marked "Div. Of//Operation Bootstrap, Inc, USA//©1968 Shindana" or have other Shindana marks.

Golliwog

8½" felt Steiff "Golliwog," holding small 4" Steiff teddy bear, both with Steiff buttons in ears and labels, limited edition of 1,500, hang tag reads "Golli G & Teddy B//Travel the World//Festival of Steiff//Steiff Button in Ear," red felt pants, blue jacket, white shirt, black shoes, teddy bear has red ribbon bow, circa 1995, $325.00. *Courtesy Debra Adorni.*

9" cloth American Black Sambo, black yarn hair, painted features, cloth body, red shirt with big white buttons, blue shorts, felt shoes, carrying green umbrella, belonged to owner since new, politically incorrect now, circa 1948 – 1950, $50.00 – $100.00. *Courtesy Stephanie Thomson.*

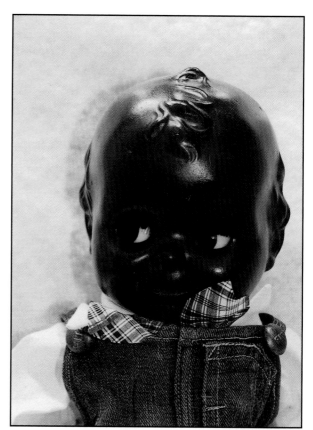

16" cloth unmarked black handmade doll, stockinette head with needle sculptured nose, ears, and chin, painted eyes and mouth, wire earrings, yarn "braids" attached to head, black cloth body with no indication of fingers on hands, feet shaped with light wire and stitched, dressed in original clothing with red/white polka dot dress, black shoebuttons on front, white apron, original underclothing, painted brown shoes, completely hand stitched, circa 1900+, $425.00. *Courtesy McMasters Doll Auctions.*

16" composition unmarked black boy, molded hair in tufts on top and sides, black side-glancing sleep eyes, real lashes, closed smiling mouth with red painted lips, jointed composition body, wearing white shirt, denim overalls, circa 1920s – 1930s, $2,300.00. *Courtesy Anita Ladensack.*

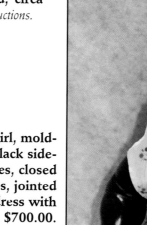

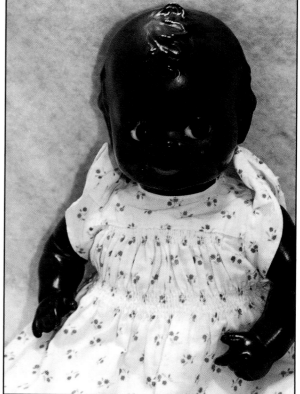

16" composition unmarked black girl, molded hair in tufts on top and sides, black side-glancing sleep eyes, real lashes, closed smiling mouth with red painted lips, jointed composition body, original white dress with flower print, circa 1920s – 1930s, $700.00. *Courtesy Anita Ladensack.*

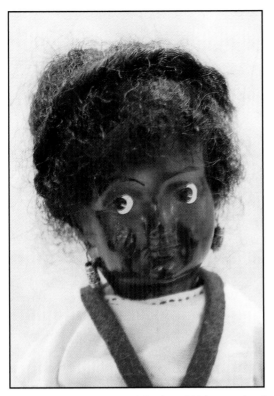

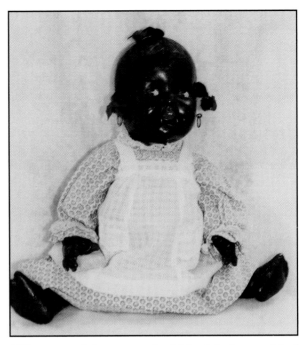

17" composition unmarked black baby, molded brown hair with three braided tufts, one on top and two above ears, painted side-glancing eyes, closed mouth, hoop earrings, composition baby body, pink print dress with white apron, circa 1920s, $350.00. *Courtesy Sharon Kolibaba.*

10" papier-mache black child marked "Germany," brown painted side-glancing eyes, red painted mouth and nostrils, black synthetic wig, red skirt, white blouse, red crocheted booties, circa early 1900s, $200.00. *Courtesy Dorothy Bohlin.*

13" composition Cameo Brown "Scootles," molded painted brown hair, painted brown eyes, closed mouth, dimples, fully jointed brown composition head and body, original peach striped romper and blue shirt, circa 1930s, $975.00. *Courtesy Sharon Kolibaba.*

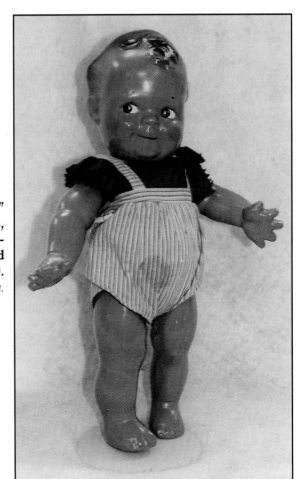

Black Dolls

12½" composition black woman, unknown maker, apron skirt is marked "Souvenir of New Orleans," painted features, composition hands and feet, cloth body, white dress with blue and red flower print, white apron with red rick-rack, red bandana in hair, circa 1940s, $25.00. *Courtesy Betty Strong.*

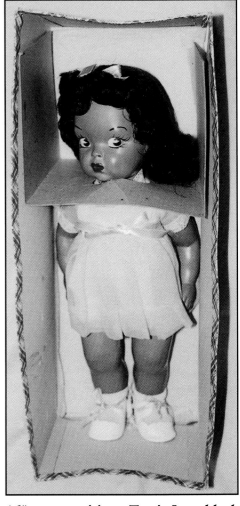

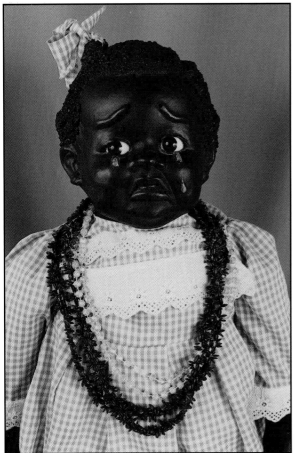

32" black composition-type artist compound "Genevieve" by R.Q., Leo Moss-type doll, cloth body, composition-type arms and legs, circa 1988, $625.00. *Courtesy McMasters Doll Auctions.*

16" composition Terri Lee black "Bonnie Lou," chestnut brunette hair evenly curled around head, mannequin wig style, black single stroke brows, brown eyes/white highlights, five painted lashes above, three painted lashes below, red accent dots in nose, all original, mint, in pink outfit, satin bows, red and white plaid Terri Lee Toddler box with porthole lid. This doll would date circa 1947, before Jackie Ormes began painting the Patty Jo faces on black Terri Lee dolls, $3,800.00. *Courtesy Pat Rather.*

18" vinyl Royal Black "Emma Sue," unmarked, rooted black Saran hair, brown sleep eyes, real lashes, painted lower lashes, closed mouth, fully jointed brown hard plastic walker body, long white dotted Swiss gown with pink ribbon and rose at waist, circa 1950s, $55.00. *Private collection.*

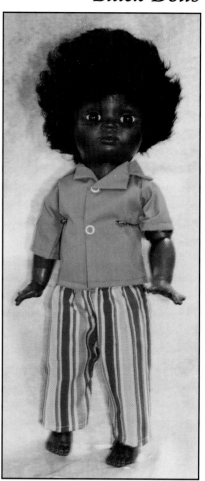

20" vinyl Beatrice Wright black child, marked "B. Wright" on neck, black rooted afro, brown sleep eyes, closed mouth, jointed rigid vinyl body, blue shirt, striped pants, circa 1967, $30.00. *Courtesy Judi Domm.*

Shindana

15" vinyl Shindana "Kim – Jeans 'n things" with painted eyes, closed mouth, long black hair, jointed vinyl body, wears blue jumpsuit, red striped knit dickey and cap, ©1969//Shindana Toys//Division of Operation Bootstrap USA, circa 1975, $75.00. *Courtesy Cornelia Ford.*

Cameo Dolls

Joseph L. Kallus's company operated from 1922 to 1930 in New York City and Port Allegheny, Pennsylvania. They made composition dolls with segmented wood or cloth bodies as well as all-composition ones.

What to look for:

Seek out composition with little crazing, no cracks, no peeling paint, good cheek color, and original costumes that are tagged; costumes should not be faded or soiled. When looking for vinyl, look for clean dolls with good color, and costumes that are clean and bright. Wood segmented dolls are a great collectible and are sometimes overlooked by collectors focusing on better-known dolls.

10½" vinyl Jesco Cameo "Snow White," dark brown wig, brown sleep eyes, closed mouth, gold/white hang tag in shape of open book reads "Cameo's//Storybook// ™//JESCO," jointed body, white gown with white lace overlay, matching shawl that ties at neck, mint-in-box, circa 1983, **$100.00.** *Private collection.*

Celebrity Dolls

Celebrity dolls must represent real people — they cannot be a literary, comic or cartoon character. They must represent someone who lived. To still be considered a celebrity doll, the doll may represent the person who plays the character on television, in the movies or in a play. Abraham Lincoln was a live person so the Lincoln doll is entered in the celebrity doll category. Princess Diana was a live person, so again, the doll that represents her is considered a celebrity doll.

Charlie McCarthy was never alive — he was an object, and although he is famous as a ventriloquist dummy from the movies, he is not a celebrity doll and would be disqualified in competition if placed in that category. Dorothy of Oz fame is not a celebrity doll, but Judy Garland, who portrayed the Dorothy character in the Wizard of Oz film, is regarded as a celebrity doll. Mickey Mouse is not a live person; he is a Disney cartoon character and is not considered a celebrity doll.

This is an exciting, fun, and very interesting category of collecting. While Shirley Temple is a celebrity, she is so collectible and so famous, the doll usually has its own category. The same is true for the Dionne Quints. Avid Quint and Shirley fans usually collect all sorts of accessories, ephemera, and related memorabilia as well as the dolls. You can collect just television or movie celebrities, athletes, black dolls, or whatever catches your fancy.

What to look for:

Condition and originality greatly influence the collecting status of these dolls as well as associated boxes, labels, brochures, and other paper products. Look for clean dolls with original tagged or labeled costumes, good color, and related items that enhance the collector's knowledge of the doll.

Sonja Henie — Skating Star of the Century

An angel on the ice, this vibrant, gifted, capable, hard-working, talented woman had another side — a tragic life plagued with marital problems, alcoholism, and illness and some considered her miserly. Is it too much to have it all? Gold medals, awards, fame, and riches did little to bring happiness and healing to this early ice skating athlete.

Stars may not be born — but sometimes you wonder when you see the tremendous talent that is exhibited by those who become stars in athletics, movies or television. Sonja Henie was one of those persons who was born with athletic abilities, a drive to succeed, and the perseverance to focus on her goals. Driven to win on the athletic field, she attained her goals, and her championship records have not been surpassed today. Unfortunately, success in one field does not guarantee success in other parts of your life. While we can applaud her capabilities on skates, her life-style left little to admire and she has become a tragic character when viewed overall.

Born in Oslo, Norway, on April 8, 1912, she was indulged, but also encouraged by her affluent parents to study ballet, skiing, and skating. At age 12, Sonja participated in her first Olympic games in figure skating. She won the World Woman's Ice Skating Championship each year from 1927 – 1936. She loved to dance and was inspired by the talented Russian ballerina Pavlova. Sonja used a choreographed form of ballet on the ice. She won three Olympic gold medals for figure

17" composition Madame Alexander "Sonja Henie," marked "Madame Alexander//Sonja//Henie" on head, human hair wig in original set, brown sleep eyes, real lashes, painted lower lashes, single stroke brows, open mouth, six upper teeth, five-piece composition body, original red skating dress with white bodice, red taffeta panties, white skates, circa 1939 – 1942, $625.00.
Courtesy McMasters Doll Auctions.

skating in 1928, 1932, and 1936. She was the European Woman's Ice Skating Champion from 1931 through 1936. Sonja gave up her amateur standing and came to the United States in 1936, becoming a citizen in 1941, and participated in traveling ice shows, bringing brilliant choreography and great costumes to her performances. The petite five-foot two-inch, 105-pound skater also starred in nine films. In 1939, she was right behind Shirley Temple and Clark Gable in box office draw. Besides being a great athlete, Sonja also had great business sense, earning as much as $50 million a year by producing and starring in the Ice Revue shows.

Sonja's personal life was not fulfilling. Sonja married three times: Dan Topping (1941 – 1946), Winthrop Gardiner (1949 – 1956), and Niels Onstad (1956 until her death in 1969 from leukemia). She seems to have found happiness with her last husband, who possibly was as selfish and controlling as she was — or at least is so portrayed by her brother.

Sonja's autobiography, *Wings on My Feet*, was published in 1940 by Prentice Hall in New York (now out of print). Her brother Leif Henie teamed up with Raymond Strait to write a tell-all *Queen of the Ice; Queen of the Shadows* by Scarborough House in 1990, still available at amazon.com. Leif reveals that Sonja cursed like a construction worker, was friendly to Hitler and his regime, and had torrid love affairs — one with Tyrone Power. She also drank heavily during her later years and was very stingy — doing nothing to help Norway during World War II, but was generous with co-workers, family, and friends that she liked. The A&E network produced a video biography of her, also available through Amazon, as are many of her old movies.

While Sonja's personal life may have more in common with the skater Tonya Harding, whose career was tainted with scandal, Sonja cannot be denied her outstanding skating ability. Sonja was notable for several reasons — not only for winning World Championships and Olympic gold medals at a young age, but also for her production capabilities with the ice shows using choreography and costuming to enhance the performances. Her success in the business world was unusual for women of her era. Several sites on the Internet feature Sonja, including www.zianet.com/jjohnson/sonja/ which contains a variety of information about her.

The brief notoriety of fame brings with it the attention of others who hope to capitalize on the passing fancies of the moment. Doll manufacturers were no exception. Madame Alexander Doll Company won the license to make the composition celebrity "Sonja Henie" doll in 1939. Her entry in the doll world soon sparked look-alike skating dolls from other manufacturers who were forbidden by law to infringe on the name, and the copycat makers were often sued, perhaps not only to keep the copyright, but also for the accompanying publicity thought to make the doll more desirable. Effanbee hotly contested infringements of copyright in the 1930s for Patsy and Dy-Dee look-alikes. Ideal threatened Shirley Temple look-alikes and Alexander the Dionne copycats. The rise of popularity of Sonja Henie as an Olympic skater and star of the movies and ice-skating shows broadened the appeal of the ice-skating doll.

In the 1940s, Reliable produced a composition skating doll of Barbara Ann Scott, the Canadian Olympic gold medal skating star, some 16 years younger than Sonja. Producers of the Ice Capades dressed dolls from various manufacturers such as Alexander's Cissy and Jacqueline to be used as visual aids for relating colors in set design and lighting during the 1960s. Some of the ice show dolls reportedly were sold; others were tossed into the trash.

Madame Alexander had a 15" composition Sonja Henie advertised in the 1941 and 1942 Sears catalogs. Alexander offered a vinyl Sonja version in 1951 and a late 1940s composition "Babs Skater" also made in hard plastic. Alexander also had other dolls in skating costumes in their line throughout the years. Vogue had a skating costumed 8" "Ginny" included in their production line.

Arranbee clad their "Nancy Lee" dolls in skating costumes in the 1940s. One R&B skater was advertised in 1949 in *Toys and Novelties*, a toy trade publication. Arranbee skaters were typical of the look-alike skaters produced to take advantage of the popularity of skating stars and shows.

In 1948, an 18" hard plastic "Skating Girl" with mohair wig was shown in the Ward catalog with white flannel skating outfit and red trim. Mary Hoyer offered knitting and crochet patterns for skating costumes for her popular 14" composition and hard plastic dolls in the 1940s and 1950s. Ice skating dolls continue to be popular, as Peggy Fleming (1968) and Dorothy Hamill (1976) became Olympic gold medal skaters. In 1978 Ideal

20" composition Madame Alexander "Sonja Henie," brown sleep eyes, real lashes, feathered brows, eyeshadow, painted lower lashes, open mouth, six teeth, dimples, blonde human hair wig in original set, five-piece composition body, pink taffeta skating dress with pink marabou trim, pink panties, gold skates, all original, tag on dress reads "Genuine 'Sonja Henie'//Madame Alexander//N.Y. U.S.A.; All Rights Reserved," circa 1939 – 1942, $900.00. *Courtesy McMasters Doll Auctions.*

offered a 11½" vinyl Dorothy Hamill skating doll. Mattel's ever-present Barbie was presented in numerous ice-skating costumed versions. Less favorable publicity was made when skater Tonya Harding became involved in a scandal to harm skater Nancy Kerrigan.

At any time, several hundred skating-related items turn up on eBay auctions (www.ebay.com) under the listing for dolls. Televised ice skating competitions and traveling shows like the Ice Capades popularize ice skating events, assuring that skating dolls continue to be desirable and sought after by collectors.

14" composition Madame Alexander "Sonja Henie," marked "Madame Alexander//Sonja Henie" on back of head, brown sleep eyes, eyeshadow, open mouth with four upper teeth, blonde mohair wig in original set, five-piece composition body, tagged blue flowered taffeta skating dress, gold skates, blue ribbon in hair, original trousseau case with red ski jacket, blue pants, striped shirt, knit cap, wooden skis, ski poles, pink nightgown, bra, girdle, circa 1939 – 1942, $3,100.00. *Courtesy McMasters Doll Auctions.*

15" vinyl Madame Alexander "Sonja Henie" (Madeline), marked "ALEXANDER" on head, blonde wig, sleep eyes, closed mouth, rosy cheeks, jointed hard plastic body, white lined skating outfit, red shirt, skates, all original, missing hat, circa 1951, $750.00. *Private collection.*

18" composition Madame Alexander "Sonja Henie," marked "Sonja Henie," human hair wig with pink roses, brown sleep eyes, open mouth with teeth, dimples, tagged pink dress trimmed in white fur, ice skates, circa 1939 – 1942, $900.00. *Courtesy Donna Hadley.*

14" Madame Alexander composition "Sonja Henie," tagged original outfit, plus wardrobe in suitcase, $695.00. *Courtesy Sally DeSmet.*

18" composition Madame Alexander "Sonja Henie," brown sleep eyes, open mouth, dimples in cheeks, blonde wig, jointed composition body, satin outfit, flower ring in hair, white skates, all original, circa 1939 – 1942, $950.00. *Courtesy Flo Burnside.*

18" Madame Alexander composition "Sonja Henie," modeled after the actress/skater, sleep eyes, open mouth with teeth, human hair wig, excellent condition, original outfit, $995.00.
Courtesy June Algeier.

Alphabetically by Celebrity

22" cloth Applause "The Beatles," licensed by Apple Corps. Limited, yarn hair, painted features, attached booklet on each doll tells history of each, metal adjustable stand says "Beatles Forever," John Lennon #15111, George Harrison #15113, Ringo Starr #15112, and Paul McCartney #15110, holding guitars with names signed on guitars, Ringo Starr holding drum sticks, missing cardboard drum set, circa 1987, $400.00 set. *Courtesy Merlyn and Tina Richards.*

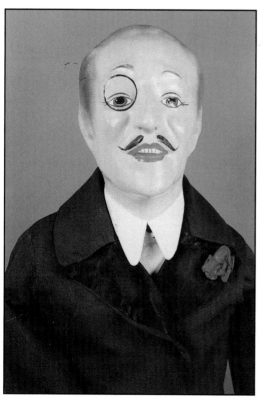

32" composition unmarked "Adolph Menjou," a 1930s actor, molded painted hair/mustache, painted brown eyes, molded monocle on right eye, feathered brows, open/closed mouth with seven upper teeth, molded white shirt collar with hole, presumably for a tie, excelsior-stuffed cloth body with long limbs, compo white hands as gloves, compo lower legs as socks and shoes, original black two-piece suit with satin lapels, circa 1930s, $725.00. *Courtesy McMasters Doll Auctions.*

25" composition Ideal "Deanna Durbin," marked "Deanna Durbin//Ideal Doll" on back of head, "Ideal Doll//25" on back, human hair wig, hazel sleep eyes, remnants of real lashes, painted lower lashes, single stroke brows, open mouth, six upper teeth, five-piece composition body, original flower print dress, underclothing, replaced socks and shoes, circa 1938 – 1941, $400.00. *Courtesy McMasters Doll Auctions.*

10" vinyl Mattel "Grizzly Adams" action figure, molded painted hair and beard, painted eyes, molded painted smiling mouth, brown pants, white shirt, suspenders, mint-in-box, circa 1971, $65.00. *Courtesy Sharon Kolibaba.*

11½" vinyl Mattel "Twist 'n Turn Julia," as portrayed by Diahann Carroll, the first black performer who was the star of a regular TV series, oxidized red hair, pink lips, rooted eyelashes, cheek blush, bendable legs, wearing two-piece nurse's outfit with attached pin and button accents, cap, circa 1969, $95.00. *Courtesy McMasters Doll Auctions.*

12" composition Madame Alexander "Jane Withers," sleep eyes, closed mouth, brown hat, original tagged flower print dress, Jane Withers pin, white socks, black shoes, repaired, circa 1937, $1,000.00. *Courtesy Bruce Endersbe.*

28" vinyl Ideal "Lori Martin," marked "©Metro Goldwyn Mayer Inc.//Mfg by//Ideal Toy Corp//80" on head, "©Ideal Toy Corp.//6-30-5" on back, rooted hair, blue sleep eyes, real lashes, painted lower lashes, closed smiling mouth, body jointed at shoulders, waist, hips, and ankles, tagged plaid shirt "National Velvet's//Lori Martin//©Metro Goldwyn Mayer, Inc.//All Rights Reserved," jeans, vinyl boots with horses, circa 1961, $550.00. *Courtesy McMasters Doll Auctions.*

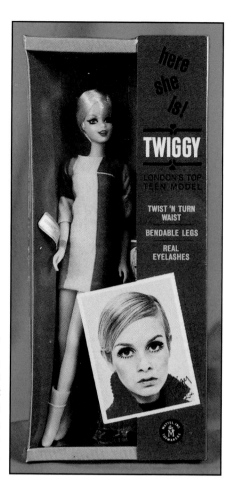

11" vinyl Mattel "Twist 'n Turn Twiggy," blonde hair, pink lips with painted teeth, rooted eyelashes, painted eyeliner, bendable legs, wearing knit dress, yellow boots, wrist tag in box with clear plastic stand, box says "Here she is//Twiggy//London's Top Teen Model," NRFB, circa 1967, $350.00. *Courtesy McMasters Doll Auctions.*

8" vinyl Mego "Mom & Pop Walton," from the TV drama series "The Waltons," all vinyl, painted features, fully poseable, marked "©1974//Lorimar Productions," mint-in-box, circa 1975, $40.00.
Courtesy Sharon Kolibaba.

14" composition Uneeda "Rita Hayworth," wrist hang tag reads "The Carmen Doll// ©W. I. Gould & Co. Inc.// Mfrd. By Uneeda Doll Do., Inc.// Inspired by Rita Hayworth's Portrayal of Carmen//'The Loves of Carmen'// Made in U.S.A.," blue sleep eyes, eyeshadow, real lashes, closed mouth, red mohair wig, five-piece composition body, red taffeta dress, gold rick-rack trim and black overlay, black net mantilla with rose trim, gold paper shoes, all original, circa 1948, $275.00. *Courtesy McMasters Doll Auctions.*

Chalkware Dolls

Carnival chalkware production started in the early 1900s in the United States, but the material really isn't chalk at all, but plaster of Paris. Chalk is a soft limestone while plaster of Paris is calcined gypsum or burned limestone that sets up hard with the addition of water. Carnival dolls emerged after the big Columbia Exposition in Chicago in 1893. There may be a link between chalkware and Pennsylvania chalkware, a gaudy pottery made almost 100 years earlier. The Pennsylvania Dutch word for lime is "kalk." With the popularity of Rose O'Neill's Kewpie figures, carnival dolls were frequent give-aways, and production costs were cut with the advent of the use of the airbrush for painting.

Carnival dolls are not dolls at all as we normally think of children's jointed play dolls, but correctly called figurines with only a few having jointed arms. Early chalkware dolls had a pink tint until the mid 1920s, and some have mohair wigs and crepe paper dresses. At first glance, collectors may find these figures too garish to suit their taste, but after looking at a number of them, this interesting part of twentieth century Americana can be quite intriguing.

Because they are easily broken and not highly valued, many of them have been discarded. Some have been copywritten by J.Y. Jenkins (June Yates Jenkins of Venice, California) 1923 – 1950, William Rainwater (Seattle, Washington) 1925+, and J. T. Gittins.

Carnival dolls were usually given as prizes for games, and many have added glitter and feathers. Thomas G. Morris of Medford, Oregon has published two volumes on *The Carnival Chalk Prize* with photos identifying many of the dolls.

What to look for and where:

Many chalkware dolls are politically incorrect, so figures such as Ku Klux Klan and black characters may be quite rare. Early dolls with wigs or clothing are desirable. The quality of these objects really has a huge range — some are well done, and some are quite garish. The challenge is to find those items which are well-painted with an appealing overall quality. You can run the gamut and find something to suit everyone's taste, from Shirley Temple look-alikes to the early vamps. Look for them at garage sales and flea markets, junk shops, and on the Internet. On an average day, your online search can find 10 chalkware dolls out of over 1,000 chalkware items on eBay. These make a fun collectible and are a fascinating category.

4" copper painted Shirley Temple-type, marked "Shirley" on base, molded curly hair, side-glancing eyes, holding out skirt of dress, large molded painted legs and feet on base, all copper-colored, circa 1934+, $20.00. *Courtesy Tom Morris.*

Chalkware Dolls

10" girl, marked "Bert," heavily molded and painted blonde hair, really black eyeshadow around dark eyes, white bow and collar on green dress, circa 1920s, $165.00.
Courtesy Tom Morris.

10" girl, heavily molded and painted hair, really black eyeshadow around black eyes, black bow on blouse, circa 1920s, $165.00.
Courtesy Tom Morris.

7" girl, molded painted blonde hair, painted eyes, holding out skirt of dress, yellow and pink painted dress, uranium oxide (glows in the dark), circa 1930s, $65.00.
Courtesy Tom Morris.

14½" Shirley Temple-type "Lil Colonel," molded painted blonde hair with molded painted red cap, painted blue eyes, rosy cheeks, long eyelashes on top, in Little Rebel red jacket, white pants, circa 1930s, $190.00.
Courtesy Tom Morris.

9" Carnival doll, marked "©1935," molded painted blonde curls, black painted side-glancing eyes, heavily painted upper eyelashes, rosy cheeks, black dress with gold dots, circa 1935, $120.00.
Courtesy Tom Morris.

12½" Carnival doll, marked "©1935," heavily molded painted blonde curls, red bow on metal loop, painted side-glancing eyes, long painted upper eyelashes, rosy cheeks, molded painted pink dress with red polka dots and white collar, pink molded painted shoes with white socks, circa 1935, $185.00.
Courtesy Tom Morris.

Cloth Dolls

Cloth dolls have recently gained immensely in popularity. Because the doll is made of soft cloth, children have always favored them for their soft, cuddly appearance. This category again presents a wide variety for the collector, and while prices have skyrocketed in the past 10 years, there are still good buys to be found in some of the lesser-known dolls that collectors have overlooked in their pursuit of more well-known examples.

What to look for:

Clean dolls with high color on the cheeks, not soiled, ripped or torn, with original labels, tags, brochures, or boxes. A worn, dirty doll will retain little value, so the buyer should consider again that main factor, the condition, before purchasing. Do not pay huge prices for dolls that have rips, soil, fading, or other flaws — even if you do love it.

Alphabetically by Manufacturer

18" Georgene Averill "Teardrop Baby," tagged "A Georgene Doll// Teardrop Baby//Georgene Novelties, Inc.//New York, N.Y.//Made in U.S.A.," painted blue eyes, open-closed frowning mouth with painted teeth, one teardrop painted on cheek, white bonnet and baby dress, all original, circa 1940, $225.00.
Courtesy Joan Sickler.

13" Georgene Averill "Dutch Pair," mask faces, yellow yarn hair, painted side-glancing eyes, both tagged "A Genuine//Georgene//Doll," wooden shoes, circa 1930s – 1940s, $75.00 each.
Courtesy Sandy Johnson Barts.

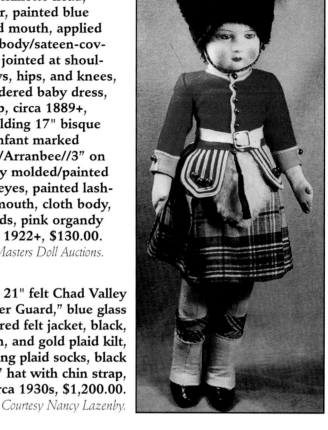

27" Martha Chase Baby, oil painted stockinette head, painted hair, painted blue eyes, closed mouth, applied ears, cloth body/sateen-covered torso, jointed at shoulders, elbows, hips, and knees, old embroidered baby dress, sweater/cap, circa 1889+, $385.00 holding 17" bisque Arranbee infant marked "Germany//Arranbee//3" on head, lightly molded/painted hair, sleep eyes, painted lashes, closed mouth, cloth body, rubber hands, pink organdy dress, circa 1922+, $130.00. *Courtesy McMasters Doll Auctions.*

21" felt Chad Valley "Grenadier Guard," blue glass eyes, red felt jacket, black, brown, and gold plaid kilt, matching plaid socks, black "bearskin" hat with chin strap, boots, circa 1930s, $1,200.00. *Courtesy Nancy Lazenby.*

13" Dollywood Studios "Miss Catalina," unmarked except for printed ribbon around neck, large painted blue eyes, brown yarn embroidered hair on forehead, painted upper lashes and eyebrows, red heart-shaped lips, red dots for nose, gussets under arms, firmly stuffed body, blue soled shoes sewn on feet, thumbs on cloth mitt hands, wears floral print bathing suit and red bandana on head, seam open in crotch, circa 1946, $100.00. *Courtesy Carol Van Verst-Rugg.*

Cloth Dolls

18½" Gorham "Taffy" from Sweet Inspirations, molded face mask, brown curly hair, blue button eyes, closed mouth, cloth body, white dress with flower print, trimmed in lace, matching hair ribbon, blue stockings, white one-strap shoes, tagged body, all original, circa 1985, $50.00. *Private collection.*

19" Kamkins, "Kamkins//A Dolly Made to Love//Patented by L.R. Kampes//Atlantic City N.J." stamped on back of head and bottom of front of torso, cloth swivel head, painted blue eyes, single stroke brows, closed mouth, original mohair wig, cloth body tab-jointed at shoulders, stitch-jointed at hips, dressed in blue/white flowered dress, matching romper, cotton socks, replaced leather shoes, gold coat and matching hat, circa 1919 – 1928, $575.00.
Courtesy McMasters Doll Auctions.

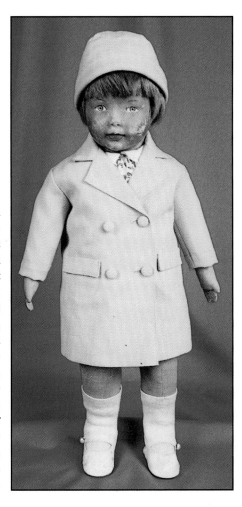

18" Kathe Kruse "Hella," painted hair, painted blue eyes, closed mouth, swivel head, Hampelchen body with loose legs, stitched fingers, three vertical seams on back of head, button and band on back to make legs stand, signed and numbered on foot, Doll I head, made in US Zone, white dress with blue flower print, hang tag and wrist tag, all original, mint, circa 1940s, $2,100.00.
Private collection.

19" Lloyderson "Nelly" from Prairie Sisters, made in Spain, all original with wrist tag, circa 1986, $40.00.
Private collection.

13" – 14" Molly'es "Susette of France," hang tag says "Susette of France," mask face, painted blue side-glancing eyes, black yarn hair, cloth body, red/white/black dress, white apron, black hat, black shoes, circa 1940s, $75.00.
Courtesy Sandy Johnson Barts.

13" Molly'es-type child, mask face, blue painted side-glancing eyes, closed mouth, mitt hands, all cloth body, green shirt, dark green pants, red belt, red boots, red hat, circa 1940s, $35.00. *Courtesy Carol Van Verst-Rugg.*

6½" "Raggedy Doodle," marked "Raggedy Doodle// U.S.//Parachute//Trooper design//pat.," painted blue side-glancing eyes, yellow cloth eye mask, camouflage body, sheepskin collar around neck, parachute, circa 1940s, $125.00. *Courtesy Art Mock.*

Cloth Dolls

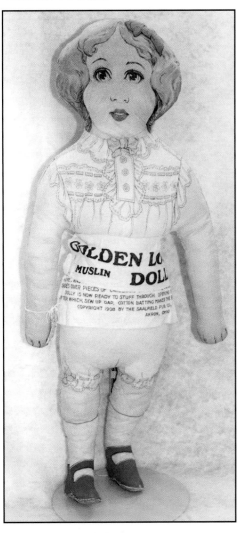

24" Saalfield Publishing Co. "Golden Locks Girl," marked on fabric tied around middle "Copyright//1908// by the Saalfield Pub. Co.//Akron, Ohio," lithographed cloth, painted blonde hair, with red bow on side, painted smiling mouth, painted white ruffled blouse, red leather shoes, circa 1908, $165.00.
Courtesy Elizabeth Fielding.

12" Shipstead & Johnson "Ice Follies," "Shipstead & Johnson" printed in silver on white ribbon, white fake fur, red eyes, pink ears, embroidered nose and mouth, white shoes with ice skates. Small children were picked up and skated with and later put in a small carriage in Los Angeles at Shipstead's and Johnson's Winter Ice Follies. Afterwards, each child was given a white rabbit with ice skates. Circa 1962 – 1963, $75.00 – $125.00. *Courtesy Celeste Pestlin.*

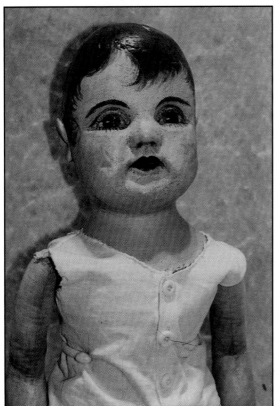

21" all cloth J.B. Sheppard & Co. "Philadelphia Baby," shoulder-type pressed oil painted head and lower limbs, brown hair, well molded and painted facial features, blue eyes, heavy molded eyelids, molded ears, stockinette body, closed mouth, stitched fingers and toes, white shirt and pants, circa 1900, $750.00.
Courtesy Joan Radke.

10½" Norah Wellings doll with molded painted features, painted blue eyes, smiling mouth, red velvet pants for legs, matching red velvet hat, black sewn-on shirt with white buttons and cuffs, black shoes for feet, circa 1926+, **$100.00.** *Courtesy Stephanie Thomson.*

4½" thread-wrapped Tiny Town Doll, white wig, painted features, blue eyes, pink thread-wrapped arms and legs, pink gown with lavender and pink floral overlay, lace cuffs, painted metal feet, circa 1940s, $35.00.
Courtesy Carol Van Verst-Rugg.

Comic Dolls

Comic characters are great collectibles, and this category too presents a huge potential for the collector who is looking for something away from the mainstream. Not only characters from the comic pages of the newspapers, but comic books, movies, and television cartoon characters are included. These may come in many different mediums, and the collector may wish to include associated paper goods or other accessories with the dolls.

What to look for:

Again, condition is king when choosing collectibles. Dolls should be clean, with good color, little crazing if composition, and preferably with tags, boxes, labels, and original clothing all intact. Have fun looking for these dolls at garage and estate sales, on eBay, or thrift shops. Comic characters are a great collectible that men seem to like.

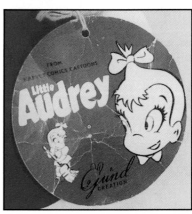

17" vinyl Gund "Little Audrey," tagged **"From//Harvey Comics Cartoons//Little Audrey//Gund (rabbit mark)//Creation"** molded painted brown hair with topknot, molded painted features with large blue eyes, sideways closed smiling mouth, white cloth arms and legs, red dress, black shoes, circa 1950s, **$225.00.** *Courtesy Sharon Kolibaba.*

13" cloth Georgene Averill comic characters "Nancy & Sluggo," marked **"A Georgene Doll//Sluggo// GeorgeneNovelties, Inc. New York//N.Y. Made in U.S.A."** on Sluggo's wrist tag, cloth swivel heads, molded mask faces, painted black eyes, closed smiling mouths; Sluggo has applied ears, Nancy has curly floss hair, cloth bodies stitch-jointed at shoulders/hips, gold flannel feet for shoes, both in original clothing, unplayed-with condition, circa 1944 – 1951, **$825.00.** *Courtesy McMasters Doll Auctions.*

Composition Dolls

Composition dolls have been made from the 1890s and possibly earlier. Cold press composition describes the method of putting a mixture of ingredients (composition) into molds. The recipe for composition varied with each manufacturer, but at first, glue was used to bind together such substances as wood flour, shredded cardboard or paper, rags, and then later wood pulp as manufacturers learned how to bake the composition in multiple molds in the hot press method. The mixture was soupier when poured into molds than when pressed, and the ingredients also differed somewhat.

These doll heads were first described as "indestructible" or "Can't Break 'Em" as compared to the bisque and china heads that were easily broken. The dolls were dipped in tinted glue baths to give a flesh tone, and later the features and coloring were airbrushed. Humidity made it difficult for the dolls to dry correctly in early production procedures, but later techniques were refined to reduce this problem. The big problem with composition dolls was their glycerin and glue base; when the surface became saturated with water, it would disintegrate. Extremes of heat and humidity cause bacteria to grow on the surface and destroy the painted finish.

Collectors need to keep composition dolls clean and away from direct sunlight, avoid extremes of temperature, and keep a gauge in their cases to monitor the relative humidity. When the relative humidity exceeds 85%, bacteria have prime conditions to grow and destroy the painted surfaces. Composition dolls should not be stored in plastic, but wrapped in cotton fabric that has been washed and rinsed well to remove any soap or conditioner that may be present. However, collectors who

had this type of doll as a plaything in their childhood can, with a little caution, enjoy some of the wide variety of dolls still available. Included in this category are composition dolls by unknown makers or little-known companies.

What to look for:

Great composition dolls should have no crazing, cracking, peeling or lifting of paint, with rosy cheek color, original wig and clothes. They may have blush on knees, hands, and arms. Added incentives would be tags, labels, brochures, or labeled boxes. Consider purchasing dolls with major flaws only if they have pluses like tagged original costumes, brochures, hang tags, or boxes; flawed dolls should be priced accordingly.

18" Acme Toy Co. baby marked "Acme//Toy Co." on head, "Molly'es//Product// American Made" on tag on seam of right leg, molded painted hair, dark sleep eyes, real lashes, painted lower lashes, single stroke brows, closed mouth, pink cloth body, composition hands, original long organdy dress, slip, undershirt, diaper, and socks, tagged pink taffeta coat and bonnet, circa 1928+, $200.00.
Courtesy McMasters Doll Auctions.

Composition Dolls

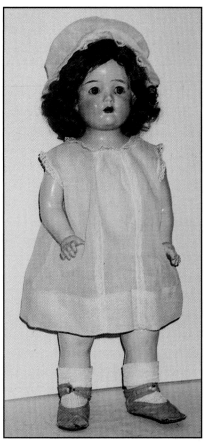

21" Century Doll Co. "Mama Doll," marked "CENTURY DOLL CO." on shoulder-plate, auburn wig, tin sleep eyes, cloth body with crier, swing legs and arms of compo, white dress with matching bonnet, white socks, tan one-strap shoes, all original, circa 1922+, $375.00. *Private collection.*

13" "Adam," marked "ADAM" on neck, painted blue eyes, closed mouth, painted hair, deteriorating composition, metal and cardboard joints, excelsior stuffed, dressed in khaki soldier outfit, with matching cap, found in grandmother's basement, circa 1910 – 1918, $75.00. *Courtesy Charlotte Beeney.*

11" Dream World Doll, blonde mohair wig, painted side-glancing blue eyes, painted upper lashes, closed mouth, jointed composition body, family doll in long white dress with red, white and blue trim, blue apron with white, stars, blue hat, all original, circa 1940s, $75.00 – $100.00. *Courtesy Michele Newby.*

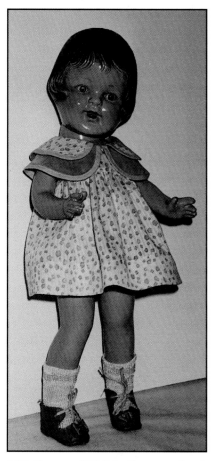

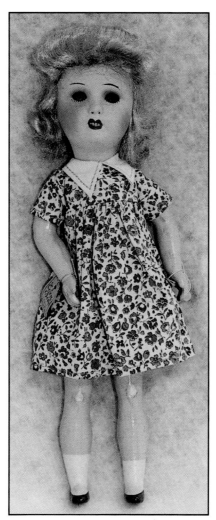

12" unknown French girl, "Eden//Bebe//Paris//Made in France" on hang tag, blonde wig, blue sleep eyes, open mouth with teeth, composition jointed body, painted socks and shoes, white dress with red and blue flower print, white collar, circa 1940s, $100.00. *Courtesy Carol Van Verst-Rugg.*

16" Eegee "Chikie," unmarked, molded painted hair, tin sleep eyes, closed mouth, jointed composition body, blue print dress, all original, circa 1930s, $200.00. *Private collection.*

11" La Madelon by Madeline Frazier, blonde mohair wig, blue painted side-glancing eyes, closed mouth, composition jointed body, tagged pink crocheted skating outfit, matching hat, white ice skates, circa 1940s, $350.00. *Private collection.*

Composition Dolls

5" Hollywood Doll, blonde mohair wig, painted features and shoes, blue eyes, closed mouth, jointed shoulders and hips, all original with box, circa 1940s, $25.00. *Courtesy Joan Radke.*

14" unmarked "Patsy-type," molded painted hair, painted side-glancing eyes, closed mouth, jointed composition body, homemade jumpsuit from old material with matching bonnet, circa 1928+, $175.00. *Private collection.*

13" Imperial Doll Co. girl, marked "IDC" on neck, molded painted hair, painted eyes, closed mouth, molded composition shoes over striped cloth legs/stockings, composition hands, cloth body, tan skirt with suspenders, tan and white print top, all original, circa 1919, $175.00. *Private collection.*

22" unmarked "Mama Doll," molded painted hair, sleep eyes, eyeshadow, open mouth with teeth, cloth body with swing legs, composition arms and legs, pink organdy dress and matching bonnet, circa late 1930s – 1940s, $200.00. *Courtesy Barbara Hull.*

16½" unmarked Patsy-type, molded painted bobbed hair, tin eyes, closed pouty mouth, jointed composition body, lavender dress with lace trim, socks, white shoes, circa 1928+, $100.00. *Courtesy Janet Hill.*

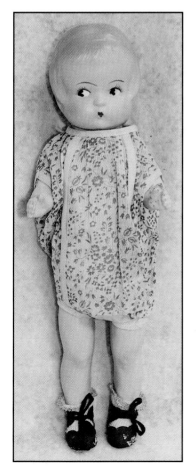

15½" unmarked girl, molded painted yellow hair with molded headband, painted side-glancing heart-shaped eyes, painted upper lashes, closed watermelon mouth, white muslin dress with brown flower print and yellow bias tape trim, white socks, black shoes, circa 1930s – 1940s, $100.00. *Courtesy Janet Hill.*

Composition Dolls

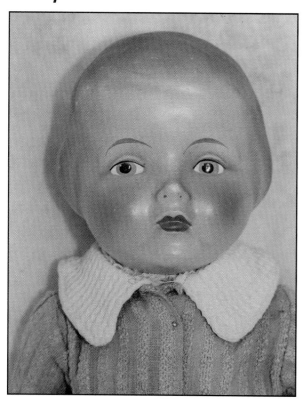

15½" child, unknown American maker, molded painted hair, painted blue eyes, molded painted features, closed mouth, excelsior stuffed joints, composition arms, circa 1910 – 1920, $100.00. *Courtesy Art Mock.*

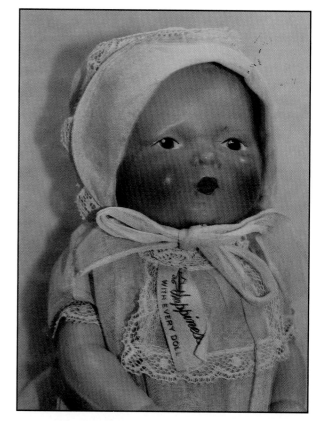

12" L.W. Co. "Happiness," advertising doll for Happiness Candy Stores, Inc., molded painted hair, painted blue eyes, closed mouth, rosy cheeks, wind-up doll, original tagged white baby dress, white bonnet, box says "L.W. Co.//Happiness//With Every Doll//Special Arrangement with Happiness Candy Stores, Inc.//No. 801," all original with box, circa 1920s, $400.00.
Courtesy Claudia Huber.

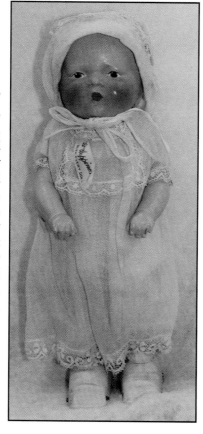

11½" Patsy-type, advertised in 1937 Sears ad, molded painted hair, painted side-glancing eyes, jointed composition body, probably re-dressed in red dress with white polka dots, trimmed in white bias tape, white socks, original shoes, circa 1928+, $175.00. *Private collection.*

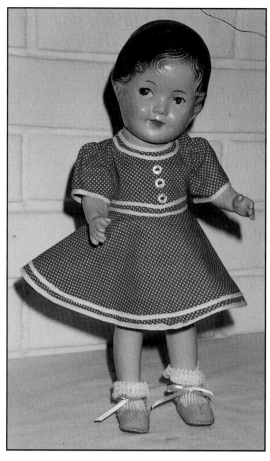

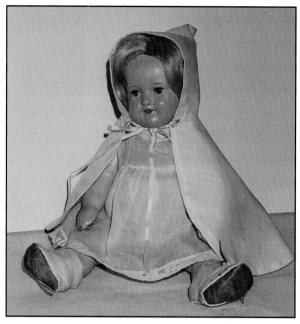

11½" Jesse McCutcheon Raleigh "Baby," unmarked, blonde mohair wig, brown painted eyes, open/closed mouth with two painted upper teeth, painted lashes, five-piece spring jointed composition baby body, original clothing, circa 1919, $450.00. *Private collection.*

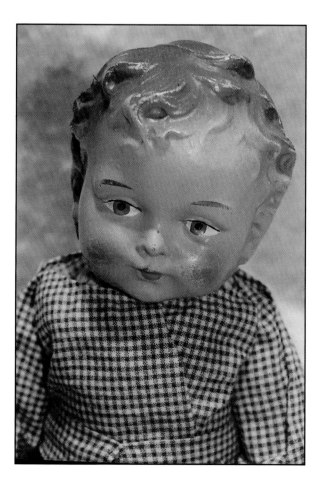

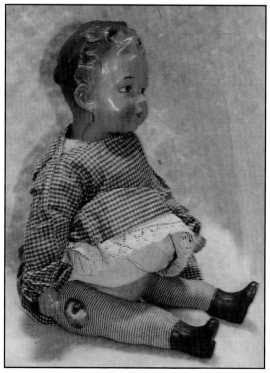

14" unmarked child, flange head, heavily molded and painted hair, painted blue eyes, closed mouth, composition lower arms, cloth body, brown and white striped cloth legs, jointed with outside disks, brown boots, brown checked dress, circa 1900 – 1910, $95.00. *Courtesy Barbara J. Andresen.*

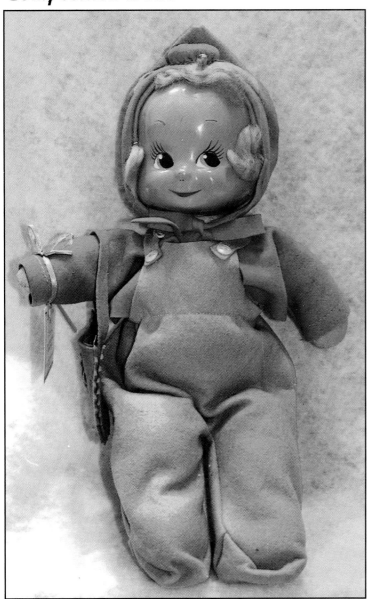

14" Three in One Doll Corp. "Trudy," with sleepy, weepy, and smiley faces, head turns by knob at top of head, painted eyes, yellow mohair wig, yellow overalls, green jacket with green and yellow hood, green purse, circa 1946+, $175.00. *Courtesy Harlene Soucy.*

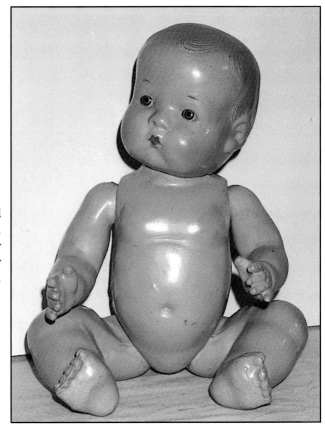

16" unmarked baby, molded painted hair, tin sleep eyes, closed pouty mouth, chubby composition bent-leg baby body, circa 1920s – 1930s, $125.00. *Private collection.*

Deluxe Reading Dolls

Deluxe Reading manufactured dolls circa 1957 – 65 that were sold as supermarket premiums, rewards for purchasing some item or for groceries totaling a certain amount. These dolls were marketed under several names: Deluxe Premium Corp., Deluxe Reading, Deluxe Topper, Deluxe Toy Creations Topper Corp., and Topper Toys. Often made of stuffed vinyl, jointed at the neck only, with sleep eyes and rooted hair, the dolls were inexpensively dressed, often as brides, in long formals or in street wear which included a hat in the 1950s and 1960s. Deluxe also made 8" "Penny Brite," a vinyl doll with side-glancing eyes and vinyl carrying case.

What to look for:

More and more of these dolls are showing up, often still packed in their original boxes. Unfortunately those that were played with often had problems with the stuffed vinyl rupturing at the neck. The costumes and accessories with some of these dolls make them an interesting and often overlooked collectible.

7" vinyl "Suzy Cute," marked "Deluxe Reading Corp.//©1964//229/4" on body, and "Deluxe Reading Corp.// ©1964 67//X" on head, rooted blonde hair, blue stationary eyes, drink and wet feature; push her arms down then press her chest and her arms come up "reaching for mommy," in a plastic yellow crib, mint-in-box with three boxed outfits, circa 1964, $400.00.
Courtesy Sharon Kolibaba.

Deluxe Reading Dolls

8" vinyl "Penny Brite" with ten MIP outfits, rooted blonde hair, painted side-glancing eyes, mint in plastic box, circa 1963+, $725.00 with extra outfits. *Courtesy Sharon Kolibaba.*

Disney Dolls

Walter Ellas Disney was born in 1902 in the Chicago area, grew up on a Missouri farm, and had his first art lessons at age 13. His family moved back to Chicago in 1917, and he entered the Chicago Academy of Fine Art and studied under cartoonist Leroy Gossitt. During World War I, at age 16 he was an ambulance driver in France. After the war, he worked for an advertising firm doing animation.

With his brother Roy, Disney came to Hollywood where they set up their own animation studio and in 1927 had his first character, Oswald the Lucky Rabbit, in a silent cartoon series. Finding he did not own the rights to his cartoon — they were held by the distributor — Disney determined he would not lose control of his own creations again. He then created a new mouse character, first named Mortimer, but changed to Mickey by his wife.

Charlotte Clark designed and made the first Mickey Mouse doll and won Disney's approval for this copyrighted character. The demand soon overcame her production capabilities, and the Disney brothers asked a major toy distributor, George Borgfeldt, in New York to mass-produce and market the doll. Unfortunately, these dolls proved inferior to Clark's dolls, so Disney got the idea for a pattern so that people could make their own. McCall's offered pattern #91 to make a stuffed Mickey Mouse in 1932.

After the Mickey and Minnie Mouse characters came Donald Duck, Pluto, Red Riding Hood, the Wolf and the Three Little Pigs and then, Snow White and the Seven Dwarfs, Cinderella, and Pinocchio. Some of the early firms who produced dolls for Disney include Lenci and Lars of Italy; Steiff; Chad Valley; Dean's Rag; Gund; Crown; Knickerbocker; Ideal; Horsman; Borgfeldt; Krueger; and Alexander. Because Disney retained the copyright for these dolls, he demanded high quality in the production and costuming of the dolls — and defended infringement on the use of his copyrights. Disney dolls are great collectibles, and their high quality has been appreciated over the years.

What to look for:

Because of the popularity of Disney theme parks and the related dolls sold in their gift shops, a collector could have a collection of just Disney dolls. The early cloth dolls should be clean and bright and have original clothing. Because early cloth dolls like Mickey Mouse were so loved, they are hard to find in excellent condition but even worn dolls have some value. These dolls still turn up in estate and garage sales — what child did not bring home a memento from their Disneyland visit?

23" bisque Kestner "Hilda" marked "Hilda//©// J.D.K.jr. 1914//ges.gesch.N.1070//made in 18 Germany" on head, lightly molded painted hair, blue sleep eyes, painted lashes, composition bent-limb Kestner baby body, white baby dress, bonnet, circa 1914, $4,000.00; holding 11" cloth Knickerbocker Mickey Mouse, swivel head, black oilcloth eyes, black nose, painted open/closed smiling mouth, black felt ears, unjointed cloth body, composition feet, shorts with buttons, circa 1930s, $650.00.
Courtesy McMasters Doll Auctions.

13" vinyl Gund "Jiminy Cricket," tagged "Jiminy Cricket//Copyright Walt Disney Prod.//Gund//(rabbit mark)," molded painted features, black felt jacket and hat, blue felt pants, yellow felt vest, carrying red umbrella, circa 1950s, $495.00. *Courtesy Sharon Kolibaba.*

12" composition Crown Toy Co. "Pinocchio," tagged "Walt Disney//Pinocchio//Ask for other Crown Toys//Complete Line//Walt Disney//Character Banks//Crown Toy Mfg. Co., Inc.//200 Fifth Ave. N.Y.," molded painted black hair, painted blue eyes, closed mouth, red felt hat, red felt short pants with suspenders, white shirt, black tie, molded painted white gloves, brown shoes, hang tag, all original, circa 1939, $400.00 – 500.00. *Courtesy Art Mock.*

Effanbee Dolls

Bernard Fleishaker and Hugo Baum formed a partnership, Fleishaker and Baum, in 1910 in New York City that eventually become Effanbee. They began making rag and crude composition dolls and had Lenox produce bisque heads for them. They developed a very high-quality composition doll with a high-quality finish, and this characterizes their dolls of the 1920s and 1930s, until after World War II when the company was sold to Noma Electric.

The company declined with the death of Hugo Baum in 1940, but had remarkable success with a series of dolls, including Bubbles, Grumpy, Lovums, Patsy, and Dy-Dee. Effanbee was a very entrepreneurial company during its prominent years using the talents of free-lance doll artist Bernard Lipfert who created Bubbles, Patsy, and Dy-Dee as well as Shirley Temple for Ideal, the Dionne Quintuplets for Alexander, and Ginny for Vogue. Effanbee Doll Company, with president Stanley and designer Irene Wahlberg, has reintroduced many of Effanbee's 1930s favorites in vinyl, painted to give a composition look.

What to look for:

Effanbee's early composition dolls are classics, and the painted finish was the finest available in its day. Unfortunately, the finish on played-with dolls was prone to scuffs and bumps, not to mention that these playthings will have been stored for 70 years or more and subject to varying degrees of heat, cold, and moisture. The biggest threat to composition dolls is changes in relative humidity. When the humidity is over 85 percent, conditions are ripe for the growth of bacteria that cause the paint to decompose, flake or peel. It is necessary to keep composition dolls clean and in a stable environment, avoiding high humidity. Also avoid direct sunlight to minimize fading.

Composition dolls should be clean, with rosy cheeks, and dressed in original or appropriate costume. These were some of the greatest dolls of the composition era and are a treasure when you find them.

Later hard plastic and vinyl dolls also have problems with cleanliness and high relative humidity that allows the growth of bacteria. You can, however, still find all-original dolls with labeled or tagged costumes, good color, and condition.

Composition

Three Effanbee American Children: 19", 17", and 19½", sleep eyes, real lashes, painted eyes on boy/painted lashes, multi-stroke brows, closed mouths, original human hair wigs, five-piece composition child bodies, girls dressed in blue/white striped zippered dresses, boy in blue wool two-piece suit, leatherette shoes, girls marked "Effanbee//American//Children" on head, "Effanbee Anne-Shirley" on back, boy unmarked, circa 1936 – 1939+, $650.00, $1,050.00, $1,500.00. *Courtesy McMasters Doll Auctions.*

Effanbee Dolls

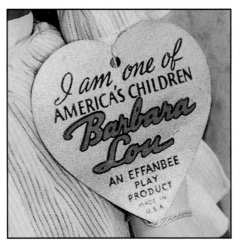

21" Effanbee "Barbara Lou" from the American Children collection designed by Dewees Cochran, marked "Effanbee//American//Children" on head, "Effanbee//Anne Shirley" on body, blonde human hair wig, brown sleep eyes, open mouth with four teeth, jointed composition body, separated fingers, red dress jumper with white shirt and apron, white socks trimmed with red, leather tie shoes, wrist tag reads "I am one of//AMERICA'S CHILDREN//Barbara//Lou," circa 1936 – 1939+, $1,000.00. *Courtesy Janet Hill.*

11" Effanbee Grumpy Cowboy, marked "Effanbee//Dolls// Walk – Talk – Sleep" on back of shoulderplate, molded painted hair, painted blue eyes to side, single stroke brows, closed pouty mouth, cloth body, composition arms and feet, dressed in rare cowboy outfit with plaid shirt, gold pants, green bandana, imitation leather chaps and holster complete with gun, felt hat replaced, circa 1915+, $475.00. *Courtesy McMasters Doll Auctions.*

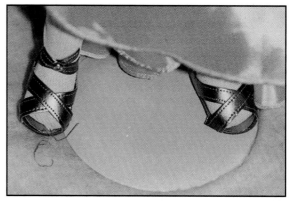

18" Effanbee "Little Lady," blonde human hair wig, sleep eyes, real lashes, painted lower lashes, closed mouth, jointed composition body, separated fingers, long pink nylon gown under long pink dotted organdy, matching shawl, pink ribbon in hair, white stockings, gold sandals, all original with box, circa 1940, $450.00. *Courtesy Harlene Soucy.*

9½" Effanbee "Suzette," marked "Effanbee// Made in//USA," molded painted hair, painted side-glancing blue eyes, painted upper lashes, closed mouth, fully jointed composition body, blue top with white stars, red rick-rack trim, red, white and blue jumper, red, white and blue ribbon in hair, white socks, black shoes, circa 1939, $425.00. *Courtesy Sharon Kolibaba.*

17" Effanbee "Little Lady," blue sleep eyes, real lashes, feathered brows, painted lower lashes, closed mouth, original human hair wig, five-piece body, original flowered dressing gown, nylon lace-trimmed panties and bra, replaced sandals, marked "Effanbee//USA," circa 1939; and Little Lady Lovely Beauty Kit, circa 1951, with beauty accessories, $450.00. *Courtesy McMasters Doll Auctions.*

Hard Plastic and Vinyl

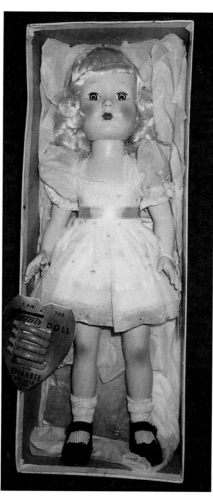

19" vinyl Effanbee "Champagne Lady," from Lawrence Welk's TV show, Miss Revlon-type, rooted hair, blue sleep eyes, lashes, pierced ears, vinyl arms, jointed hard plastic body, green taffeta dress, fur stole, hair adornment, jewel on dress, earrings, purse, silver high-heeled shoes, circa 1959, $385.00. *Courtesy Rita Mauze.*

15" hard plastic Effanbee "Tintair," made to compete with Ideal's Toni, blonde synthetic hair, blue sleep eyes, closed mouth, rosy cheeks, jointed hard plastic body, cream dress with pink ribbon trim, slip, panties, socks, black one-strap shoes, hairnet, ribbons, hang tag with hair curlers, mint-in-box, circa 1951, $795.00. *Courtesy Rita Mauze.*

14" hard plastic Effanbee "Honey Bridesmaid," marked "EFFANBEE" on body, elaborate hairstyle, sleep eyes, closed mouth, hard plastic jointed body, peach gown, matching hat with flower trim, all original, circa 1952, $500.00. *Private collection.*

The Patsy Family

Another one of Effanbee's great success stories was the Patsy doll designed by Bernard Lipfert and advertised in 1928. She almost was not named Patsy. Identical ads in *Playthings* magazines advertised her as "Mimi" late in 1927 and then as "Patsy" in 1928. Patsy was one of the first dolls to have a wardrobe manufactured just for her by Effanbee and other manufacturers. She was made of all composition, and her patent was hotly defended by Effanbee; what was actually patented was a neck joint that allowed the doll to pose and stand alone. She portrayed a 3-year-old girl with short bobbed red hair with a molded headband, painted side-glancing eyes, pouty mouth, bent right arm, and simple classic dresses closed with a safety pin. She had a golden heart charm bracelet and/or a gold paper heart tag with her name. Patsy was so popular she soon had several sisters, many variations, and even a boyfriend, Skippy.

Effanbee promoted Patsy sales with a newspaper, *The Patsytown News,* that went to a reported quarter million children. Effanbee also had an "Aunt Patsy" who toured the country promoting their dolls. In addition they formed a Patsy Doll Club and gave free pin-back membership buttons to children who wrote in or bought a Patsy doll. Effanbee tied their doll line to popular current events, such as producing George and Martha Washington for the bicentennial of George's birth. They costumed a group of dolls like the traveling troupe, the White Horse Inn Operetta. During the war years, they fashioned military uniforms for the Skippy dolls and also costumed dolls in ethnic dress (Dutch) or after characters in books like *Alice In Wonderland.*

The death of Hugo Baum in 1940 and the loss of income during the war years threw the Effanbee success story into a decline. In 1946, Effanbee was sold to Noma Electric, and they reissued a 1946 Patsy and later a new 17" Patsy Joan. Since that time, the company has changed hands several more times, until reaching new owners with Stanley Wahlberg as president and Irene Wahlberg as designer. Limited editions of Patsy Ann and Skippy were issued during the 1970s, and Patsy reappeared in vinyl in the 1980s. Effanbee reissued Patsy Joan in 1995, and continued in 1996, 1997, and 1998 with a new group of Patsy, Skippy, and Wee Patsy dolls in vinyl, painted to look like the old composition ones. These are already becoming collectibles for the modern collector.

8½" composition Effanbee "Patsy Babyette Twins," marked "Effanbee" on heads, "Effanbee//Patsy Babyette" on backs, molded painted hair, blue sleep eyes, real lashes, painted lower lashes, closed mouths, composition baby bodies, original matching blue and white baby romper and dress, bonnet on the girl, socks, white leatherette shoes, circa 1932, $500.00.
Courtesy McMasters Doll Auctions.

5¾" composition Effanbee "Wee Patsy," advertised only as "Fairy Princess," original striped beach pajamas with matching hat, doll castle box with peek-through window, circa 1935, $400.00.
Private collection.

9" composition Effanbee "Patsyette" in wardrobe box, painted brown eyes to side, painted upper lashes, closed mouth, molded painted hair, composition five-piece child body with bent right arm, blue check tagged dress, matching bonnet, leatherette tie shoes, original case with picture of Patsy-type dolls in lid, extra pink dress, red crocheted dress, matching panties and bonnet, flannel gown, marked "Effanbee//Patsyette Doll" on back, circa 1931, $375.00. *Courtesy McMasters Doll Auctions.*

8" composition Effanbee "Tinyette Toddler," marked "Effanbee" on head, "Effanbee Baby Tinyette" on back, Tyrolean girl, all original, with White Horse Inn pin, circa 1935, $375.00. *Courtesy Sharon Kolibaba.*

9" composition Effanbee "Patsyette," painted side glancing brown eyes, painted upper lashes, closed mouth, molded painted red hair, five-piece composition body with bent right arm, tagged original red dress, romper, socks, shoes, red ribbon bandeau, gold paper heart tag, metal heart bracelet, marked on back "Effanbee//Patsyette Doll," circa 1931, $500.00, 11" composition Effanbee "Patsy Jr., $300.00. *Courtesy McMasters Doll Auctions.*

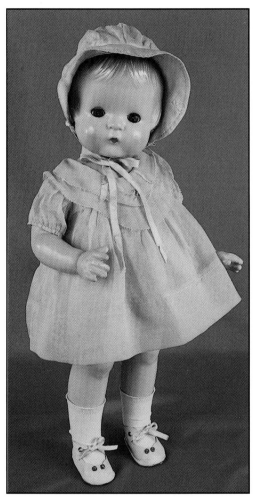

19" composition Effanbee "Patsy Ann" marked "Effanbee//'Patsy-Ann'//© //Pat. #1283558" on back, molded painted hair, brown sleep eyes, real lashes, painted upper and lower lashes, closed mouth, five-piece composition body with bent right arm, original tagged pink organdy dress and bonnet, original two-piece pink cotton underclothing, replaced socks and shoes, circa 1929, $370.00. *Courtesy McMasters Doll Auctions.*

19" composition Effanbee "Patsy Ann," marked "Effanbee//'Patsy Ann'//©//Pat. #1283558" on back, molded hair under human hair wig, blue sleep eyes, real lashes, painted lower lashes, single stroke brows, closed mouth, five-piece composition body with bent right arm, metal heart bracelet, original red/blue plaid dress, matching romper, original socks and red leatherette shoes, circa 1929, $450.00. *Courtesy McMasters Doll Auctions.*

17" composition Effanbee "Patsy Joan," marked "Effanbee" on back, molded painted hair, sleep eyes, closed mouth, jointed composition body, original blue and white check dress with white panel on bodice, red embroidered hearts on panel, matching hat, white socks, black one-strap shoes, circa 1946, $550.00. *Courtesy Ellen Sturgess.*

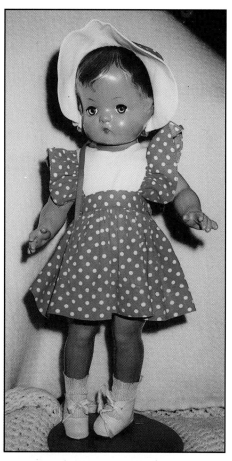

17" composition Effanbee Black "Patsy Joan," marked "Effanbee" on back, molded painted brown hair, green sleep eyes, closed mouth, jointed brown composition body, original red dress with white polka dots, white panel on bodice, matching hat, white socks and shoes, circa 1946, $675.00. *Courtesy Ellen Sturgess.*

Left: 14" composition Effanbee Patsy marked "Effanbee//Patsy," human hair wig over molded hair, sleep eyes, closed mouth, five-piece composition body, bent right arm, yellow print dress, matching panties, white organdy hat, circa 1928, $185.00; Right: 19" composition Effanbee "Patsy Ann" marked "Effanbee//'Patsy-Ann'//©//Pat. #1283558," molded painted hair, sleep eyes, closed mouth, five-piece composition body, original tagged flowered dress, teddy, leatherette shoes, circa 1929, $500.00. *Courtesy McMasters Doll Auctions.*

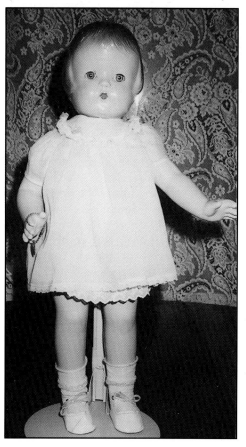

22" composition Effanbee "Patsy Lou," marked "Effanbee//Patsy Lou," molded painted red hair, green sleep eyes, closed mouth, jointed composition body, metal heart bracelet, old lace-trimmed dress, white socks and shoes, circa 1930, $475.00. *Courtesy Ellen Sturgess.*

11½" compostion Effanbee "Patricia-Kin" with trunk, marked "Patricia-Kin" on head, "Effan-bee//Patsy Jr." on body, blonde human hair wig, brown sleep eyes, jointed composition body, metal heart bracelet, red skirt with white polka dots, white top, red jacket with blue and white collar, matching hat, white socks and shoes, also has FAO Schwarz ad for this doll and trunk from 1938, blue trunk with pink lining and accessories, circa 1938, $1,900.00. *Courtesy Ellen Sturgess.*

26" composition Effanbee "Patsy Ruth," marked "Effan-bee//Patsy Ruth" on head, "Effanbee//Durable//Dolls" on dress tag and metal heart bracelet, original human hair wig, brown sleep eyes, real lashes, painted lower lashes, feathered brows, closed "rosebud" mouth, five-piece composition body, original peach silk dress, matching romper, socks, leatherette T-strap shoes, circa 1934, $800.00. *Courtesy McMasters Doll Auctions.*

22" composition Effanbee "Patsy Lou," marked body with Lovums head, blonde wig, brown sleep eyes, open mouth with teeth, jointed composition body, peach organdy dress, matching hat, circa 1928+, $650.00. *Courtesy Ellen Sturgess.*

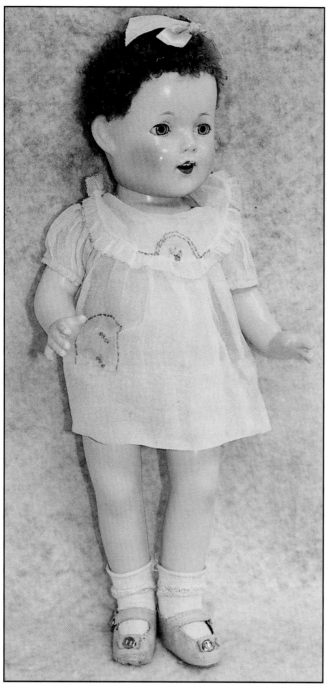

16½" composition Effanbee "Mary Lee," marked "©//Mary Lee" on head, "Effanbee//Patsy Joan" on body, caracul wig, blue sleep eyes, open mouth, teeth, jointed composition body, pink dress with lace trim on collar, pink ribbon in hair, white socks with pink trim, tan leather shoes, circa 1932, $350.00. *Courtesy Janet Hill.*

14" composition Effanbee Skippy Policeman, marked "Effanbee//Skippy//©//P.L. Crosby" on head, "Effanbee//Durable//Dolls//Made in U.S.A." on pants tag, molded painted hair, painted blue eyes to side, painted lashes, peaked brows, closed mouth, cloth body, compo arms/legs, molded painted socks/shoes, rare policeman outfit with tagged blue pants, light blue shirt, black ribbon tie, black belt with holster/original gun, cap/black oilcloth bill, button, circa 1929, $1,950.00. *Courtesy McMasters Doll Auctions.*

Ethnic Dolls

Collectors sometimes refer to dolls dressed in regional or national costumes as ethnic or tourist dolls. These were commonly available for sale in shops to tourists who wanted souvenirs of the country they visited. Dolls dressed in national costume were touted as "educational" by showing the costume or dress of that country.

Today some collectors are trying to identify many of these ethnic dolls that are often quite charming and passed over for the better-known collectible dolls. One doll club has taken on the project of researching certain groups of dolls. After one year's study efforts, they became so engrossed, they decided to continue for another year. This is an area with little research and worthy of continued interest. Dolls in national costume were made of many mediums, including bisque, cloth, composition, hard plastic, and vinyl. During the 1930s, 1940s, and 1950s and later, many dolls dressed in regional costumes could be purchased cheaply in different areas. A wide variety of these dolls are unmarked or made by little-known companies. This category is sometimes a catch-all for dolls that have little history and no category. Many were cheaply made and mass-produced for the tourist market, but some were extremely well made, are whimsical and charming, and make an interesting and eclectic collection.

What to look for:

The workmanship and the costuming make these dolls valuable. Look for clean, all original dolls with boxes, labels and or tagged clothing. Try for dolls with very well-made clothing that is clean, has bright colors, no fading or soil. This category had a big potential for collectors as it is not as popular with older collectors, who seek more conventional dolls in ethnic costumes, so the dolls of little-known or unknown manufacturers may be passed by. Acquire dolls that are appealing to you, but always look for well-made dolls of good color and original costume.

American Indian

9½" leather unmarked Native American, black braids, bead eyes, sewn mouth and nose, leather outfit with fringe, circa 1930 – 1940, $175.00 – 200.00. *Courtesy Carolyn Haynes.*

12" painted bisque Indian Brave, 11" Squaw with papoose, black mohair wigs, set pupiless eyes, painted lashes, open mouths, four upper teeth; Brave has composition body, cloth arms, felt hands, jointed at hips, flannel and felt outfit with string decoration, belt, bow, spear and shield; Squaw has five-piece composition body, striped clothing trimmed with red felt, carrying painted bisque baby head wrapped with blanket, near mint, original clothing, circa 1920s, $285.00. *Courtesy McMasters Doll Auctions.*

6" hard plastic Knickerbocker Brown "Indian Boy," painted black side-glancing eyes, painted black hair, yellow fringed leather top and pants with red and black designs, circa 1950s, $35.00. *Courtesy Carol Van Verst-Rugg.*

6" tree bark Seminole Indian, black head covering, painted features, string of blue beads and red beads around neck, blue, green, red, white, and yellow outfit, circa 1950s – 1960s, $25.00. *Courtesy Chelle Albonico.*

14" vinyl Hudson Bay Co. "Eskimo," marked "KOWEEKA©//HUDSON BAY CO." on head, "1-5//D&C" on lower back, rooted straight black hair, painted black eyes, open/closed mouth with four painted teeth, hard plastic five-piece jointed body, fur-trimmed parka, snow pants, and boots of white wool fleece, red and blue rick-rack trim, circa 1960, $50.00 to $75.00. *Courtesy Julie Ghavam.*

Skookums, 1914 – 1950+

Skookums was designed and patented by Mary McAboy in 1914 and the first doll heads were reported to be made of dried apples, made later in composition and plastic. They were manufactured first as a cottage industry for the Denver H.H. Tammen Company and then by Arrow Novelty Co. With side-glancing painted eyes, they had molded and painted features, horse-hair wigs, and padded cloth over stick bodies, formed by wrapping and folding an Indian blanket to suggest arms. The label on the bottom of the flat wooden feet reads, "Trade Mark Registered (Bully Good) Indian//U.S.A.// Patented." Later dolls had plastic molded feet. Dolls range in size from 6" to 36" store displays. Typical figures represent a chief, a squaw with papoose, and a child. The dolls were made for the tourist markets and sold through the Tammen Company catalogs and elsewhere and are a nostalgic piece of Americana tourist dolls.

10½" composition Skookum "Indian Squaw and Child," designed by Mary McAboy, black mohair wigs, painted features, painted side-glancing eyes, red headband, cloth figure wrapped in Indian blanket, folds representing arms, plastic feet, yellow beads around neck, left foot has oval paper tag reading "Trade Mark Registered//Skookum//(Bully Good)// Indian," circa 1940s – 1950s, $175.00. *Courtesy Carol Van Verst-Rugg.*

6½" composition Skookum child, designed by Mary McAboy, painted features, side-glancing eyes, black mohair wig, cloth figure wrapped in Indian blanket, plastic shoes, label "Trademark Reg.//Skookum// Bully Good// Indi-an//Patented U.S.A.," circa 1930s – 1940s, $40.00. *Courtesy Carol Van Verst-Rugg.*

13" composition Skookum "Indian and Child," designed by Mary McAboy, black mohair wigs, painted features, painted side-glancing eyes, red headband, cloth figure wrapped in Indian blanket, folds representing arms holding child, linen boots, beads around neck, circa 1940s – 1950s, $175.00. *Courtesy Carol Van Verst-Rugg.*

Austria

Baitz

The Baitz firm started in Germany in 1912. After World War II, the company moved to Austria where it became Camillo Gardtner and Company in 1963. They are still producing well-made dolls dressed in regional costumes.

Baitz dolls are good examples of attractive, well-made, nicely dressed dolls. They are 9" tall, and the head appears to be painted hard plastic but could also be described as composition; we are unsure of the material used. Since *Colemans' Collector's Encyclopedia of Dolls* refers to composition as "made of various ingredients," most collectors equate the term "composition" with heads made of sawdust or wood pulp mixtures.

Baitz dolls are very appealing with their side-glancing painted brown eyes, open round surprise or kissing mouths, and attractive costumes. They have single line painted eyebrows, two brown eyelashes painted from the upper corner of the eye, glued-on mohair wigs with curls or braids for the girls, and shorter hair for the boys. Their bodies are felt-over-wire armature with simple mitt felt hands with a red and black heart-shaped paper

9" painted hard plastic Baitz "Hansl" boy, painted features, mohair wig, side-glancing eyes, round open/closed mouth, felt-over-wire body, original regional outfit, Baitz heart tag, sticker "Made in Austria," circa 1970s, $75.00. *Private collection.*

hang tag marked BAITZ. On the back of the tag is a gold foil sticker that reads "Made in Austria" and the name of the doll or region it represents. Dolls come in cream floral pattern boxes, also with a gold foil sticker. Clothing is cotton with no fasteners or openings with felt accents and felt hats. All known dolls have head coverings. The feet have simple black gathered cloth shoes and white cotton knit stockings. They come dressed both as boys and girls.

Holland

10½" composition "Dutch Boy" from Volendam, Holland, molded painted hair, painted blue eyes, closed mouth, composition hands with painted fingernails, wooden shoes, red and white striped shirt, black wool pants, jacket and matching hat, circa 1940s, $75.00.
Courtesy Carol Van Verst-Rugg.

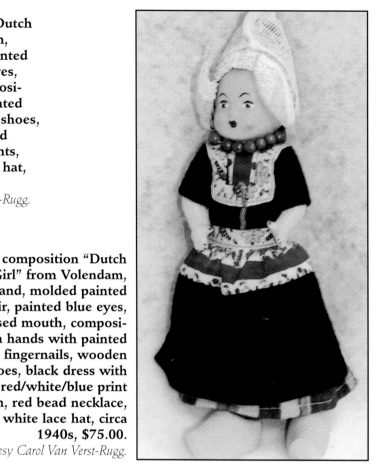

10½" composition "Dutch Girl" from Volendam, Holland, molded painted hair, painted blue eyes, closed mouth, composition hands with painted fingernails, wooden shoes, black dress with red/white/blue print trim, red bead necklace, white lace hat, circa 1940s, $75.00.
Courtesy Carol Van Verst-Rugg.

France

7" plastic Ethnic girl tagged "Marly//Maria Elizabeth//Perret//238 Rou de Rivoli//Paris," black wig, blue painted eyes, closed mouth, red felt skirt with gold trim, white apron with lace, blue paisley shawl, white hat, gold cross, circa 1950s, $25.00. *Courtesy Chelle Albonico.*

Germany

12½" silk-covered wood "Clown," painted eyes, painted round red nose, smiling mouth, marked "Dormstadt//Germany" on banner clown is holding, black pants, flower print shirt and clown hat, net ruffle collar around neck, bought in Germany in 1948 where they have a month-long clown festival, circa 1948, $35.00. *Courtesy Carol Van Verst-Rugg.*

Bavaria

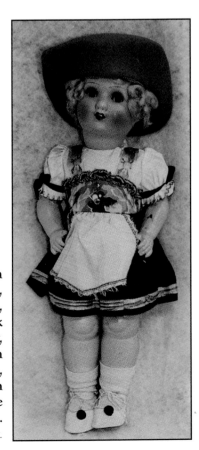

19½" painted hard plastic Bavarian Boy, blonde wig, blue sleep eyes, painted lashes, brown eyeshadow, open mouth with teeth, cheek blush, painted hard plastic body, jointed, chubby legs, dressed in ethnic costume of black jumper, matching hat, white shirt, white socks and shoes, circa 1948+, $100.00. *Courtesy Carol Van Verst-Rugg.*

19½" painted hard plastic Bavarian Girl, blonde wig, blue sleep eyes, painted lashes, brown eyeshadow, open mouth with teeth, cheek blush, painted hard plastic body, jointed, chubby legs, dressed in ethnic costume of green felt hat, red skirt, white top trimmed with red, white apron, socks, white shoes, circa 1948+, $100.00. *Courtesy Carol Van Verst-Rugg.*

Greece

12½" composition unmarked Greek Lady, mohair wig, painted blue eyes, closed mouth, cloth limbs, stuffed cloth torso, gold scarf, long white dress with brown print trim, gold apron, circa 1940s, **$100.00.** *Courtesy Carol Van Verst-Rugg.*

15" composition unmarked Greek Soldier, molded painted hair, painted blue eyes, closed mouth, cloth limbs, stuffed cloth torso, white outfit with pleated skirt, tan vest with yellow rick-rack, matching hat, circa 1948, **$100.00.** *Courtesy Carol Van Verst-Rugg.*

India

7" cloth "Indian Woman," marked "Made in India," black yarn hair, painted features, cloth body, fingers stitched separately, in multicolored ethnic costume, shawl over hair and around body, gold dangle earrings, matching jeweled headdress, circa 1950s, **$25.00.** *Courtesy Carol Van Verst-Rugg.*

Italy

7" composition Ethnic doll tagged "Made in Italy//Magis//roma// Napoli" in a triangle, black wig with hair pulled up on head, brown painted side-glancing eyes, blue eyeshadow, closed mouth, cloth body, ethnic clothing, holding blue tambourine, circa 1950s, $25.00. *Courtesy Chelle Albonico.*

7" composition Ethnic doll tagged "Magis made//in Italy," black wig, blue painted side-glancing eyes, blue eyeshadow, closed mouth, large hoop earrings, ethnic clothing, circa 1950s, $25.00. *Courtesy Chelle Albonico.*

7" composition Ethnic doll tagged "Magis//roma//made in Oslo" in a triangle, black wig, brown painted side-glancing eyes, blue eyeshadow, closed mouth, cloth body, regional dress, red felt dress with white trim, matching shawl over head, circa 1950s, $25.00. *Courtesy Chelle Albonico.*

10" composition girl from Florence, Italy, long blonde braided wig, curled bangs, tied with red ribbons, stuffed celluloid body, pink dress trimmed in green rick-rack, pink and white apron, white stockings, black shoes, circa 1940s, $75.00.
Courtesy Carol Van Verst-Rugg.

10" composition "Italian Lady" from Sorrento, Italy, black wig, painted blue eyes, painted lashes, closed mouth, rosy cheeks, painted red and white shoes, blue dress, white apron, circa 1940s, $75.00.
Courtesy Carol Van Verst-Rugg.

Lapland

13" composition unmarked Laplander, molded painted features, painted brown hair, closed smiling mouth, cloth body, felt hands, blue velvet shirt trimmed with red, matching hat, tan pants, circa 1940s, $160.00.
Courtesy Merilee Ellsworth.

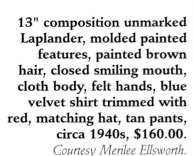

Mexico

10½" cloth unmarked "Mexican Lady," painted features, black mohair wig, cloth body, red dress with white lace apron, lace hat, elaborate embroidered blue bands on sleeves, red felt shoes, circa 1950s, $25.00. *Courtesy Carol Van Verst-Rugg.*

Peru

9" composition unmarked Peru ethnic couple, painted eyes and features, painted hair, woman has glued-on long black braids, ethnic costumes, circa 1975, $25.00. *Courtesy Bonnie Gvokas.*

Scotland

7" hard plastic Pedigree "Wee Lassie," blonde mohair wig, blue sleep eyes, closed mouth, jointed hard plastic body, molded white socks and black shoes, in Scottish outfit, red plaid skirt, black jacket, black tam with red pompon, in original box marked "Pedigree// Authentic Tartan//DRESSED DOLL//WEE LASSIE// ROYAL STEWART," circa 1950s, $35.00. *Courtesy Carol Van Verst-Rugg.*

7" hard plastic Pedigree "Highlander," blue sleep eyes, closed mouth, jointed hard plastic body, molded white socks and black shoes, in Scottish outfit, red plaid kilts, red jacket, black hat, carrying bagpipes, in original box marked "Pedigree//Authentic Tartan// DRESSED DOLL//HIGHLANDER//ROYAL STEWART," circa 1950s, $35.00. *Courtesy Carol Van Verst-Rugg.*

Spain

11¾" composition ethnic Spanish "Renaso Lady," black wig, painted features, closed mouth, rosy cheeks, composition arms with delicate fingers, painted fingernails, molded painted shoes, cloth body, red and white dress with flower embroidery, sombrero, circa 1953, $75.00. *Courtesy Carol Van Verst-Rugg.*

12" composition ethnic Spanish man, molded painted hair, painted features, closed mouth, rosy cheeks, composition hands, molded painted black shoes, cloth body, black outfit, white shirt, sombrero, circa 1953, $75.00. *Courtesy Carol Van Verst-Rugg.*

Switzerland

9" hard plastic Switzerland "Ethnic Lady," painted hair, painted blue eyes, closed mouth, rosy cheeks, earrings attached to maroon scarf around head, cloth body, long blue skirt trimmed with red, white top, maroon vest, white apron, red shoes, bought in Berne, Switzerland in 1948, $25.00. *Courtesy Carol Van Verst-Rugg.*

Fashion Dolls

One of the most interesting collecting trends recently is the comeback of the fashion doll. Collectors describe a fashion doll as having a narrow waist and adult proportions. From the early antique china dolls to the bisque and leather dolls of the latter 1800s, to the lady doll of the early 1900s, fashion dolls have been popular. There were dolls of movie stars of the late 1930s and pin-up girls of the World War II era when those pudgy little Patsys started to grow up and become "Little Ladies." When hard plastic dolls came along, there was Miss Revlon and even American Character's Sweet Sue got the grown-up look in the 1950s. Mattel changed everything with their introduction of the 11½" Barbie in 1959, and she has been the fashion queen for the last 42 years. That is a long run for one doll — but kids love her, her clothes, and her accessories.

Just when you think nothing will ever change, in 1995 a young magazine illustrator and designer, Mel Odom, created a new fashion doll, Gene, aimed at the collecting market. At 15½" tall, this vinyl creation with rooted hair, painted eyes, closed mouth, and a fashion body with defined waist (and bust) had something else — a history. Gene was Gene Marshall, an aspiring starlet, and we follow her career as she goes on to become a movie star during the 1930s and 1940s. This ingenious use of a nostalgic storyline with the doll and her outfits was a huge success. It was immediately followed by other companies' introductions of their own 16" fashion dolls with a story line. Here are a few of the new fashion dolls with their company-created histories.

Alexandra Fairchild Ford

Alexandra Fairchild Ford was born on March 9, 1973, in a suburb of Boston, the youngest of four children born to Annette and Peter Ford. As a child, Alex first developed an abiding interest in fashion that was fostered by an aunt who encouraged her to seek a summer internship at *Madame* magazine.

Madame, well-known for its pervasive influence on the fashion and beauty industry, was a tough proving ground but an ideal environment in which to learn the fashion magazine business. Fascinated and enthusiastic, Alex was well-liked and returned for her remaining three high school summers, catching the eye of powerful editor-in-chief, Odile Maxwell. Impressed by Alex's drive and innate feel for the business, Maxwell cultivated Alex's talent by giving her protégée small writing assignments. Pleased with Alex's effort and fashion perspective, Maxwell encouraged her to attend the Fashion Institute of Technology to pursue a degree in fashion journalism. Alex did so and continued working part-time at *Madame* while attending classes.

After earning her degree in 1994, Alex went to work at *Madame* full-time and was given a column called "The Clothesline." Geared toward young professional women, the column focused on hot trends, fashion forecasts, and emerging designers, as well as offering insight and a behind-the-scenes glimpse of the industry, written from a hip and edgy perspective. "The Clothesline" was a hit with a wide spectrum of readers, crossing all age demographics to become the most popular, must-read column in the magazine.

After several successful years spent attending the showings and writing "The Clothesline," Alex began to feel the need for a greater challenge. In 1998, this unspoken desire was answered when she was approached by publishing magnate Richard Sebastian about serving as editor-in-chief of *Élan*, a new fashion magazine to be launched in 2000. Sebastian's vision for *Élan* was a fashion and beauty book with a fresh perspective, deconstructing fashion to separate the real from the runway and

Fashion Dolls

defining the point where the two converge to make wearable fashion. The magazine would offer features on issues both timely and relevant to women in the new millennium. With the blessing of mentor Maxwell, Alex accepted and prepared to fulfill her duties at the top of a new masthead.

Madame Alexander's Alex Fairchild Ford, Editor-in-Chief of Hip Fashion Magazine Élan, Wins Coveted Woman of the Year Award
Ford Names "Paris" as New Entertainment Editor

It's been a very good year for Alexandra Fairchild Ford. Editor-in-chief of *Élan*, the hottest fashion magazine on the street, Alex has made media headlines and quickly earned respect among both the fashion cognoscenti and the publishing world since the launch of the magazine just one year ago. Since then, *Élan* has become the #1 must-read among savvy women with style, cutting across a broad range of demographics. Circulation and subscription rates have tripled. Advertising revenues have gone through the roof. And this astonishing success has not gone unnoticed.

This is the story behind Madame Alexander's 16" fashion doll, Alexandra Fairchild Ford. Currently the benchmark by which all other fashion dolls are measured, Alex is characterized as a versatile young woman with many talents, many looks, and unerring fashion instincts. Alex's identity as a powerful young editor creates the opportunity for varied costuming possibilities — attending fashion shows, black-tie galas, Hollywood premieres, charity events, award ceremonies, and fashion shoots all around the globe. This year, Alex's hectic itinerary will take her to Berlin for a New Year's celebration, to New York to receive Women in Media's Woman of the Year Award, to Miami to shoot the South Beach collections, to L.A. for a film premiere and a Music Video Awards show, and to Europe to shoot the fall collections. And those are just a few of the stops that Alex will make as she spans the globe and crosses the International Dateline for *Élan*!

Madame Alexander® is also pleased to continue to chronicle Alex's fast-paced, exciting life and to expand the Alex line with hip new fashions by both costume designer Tim Alberts and the Alexander Doll design team. More big news is that Madame Alexander is also premiering a new line of outfit and accessory packs for 2001 which will be utterly indispensable for the numerous wardrobe changes necessary in Alex's busy life. In addition, fresh new makeup looks and hairstyles ensure that Alex is absolutely "of the moment" while new bent-knee versions of Alex render her poseable and camera-ready at any moment.

And introductions are also in order: Alex has just named long-time friend Paris as the new Entertainment Editor for *Élan*, giving Madame Alexander® the chance to showcase fabulous new fashions that reflect the cutting-edge style of the newest player on Alex's team. With extensive experience in both the fashion and music industries, Paris is a known personality among, and has easy access to, a large cadre of celebrities and style-makers. She was born for this job. Media pundits are projecting that together, Alex and Paris will build on the fledgling success of *Élan*, confirming its status as the top consumer beauty book in the country.

Introducing Paris

Once *Élan* was off and running like a runaway train, Alex realized that an important part of her formula for continuing success would be to surround herself with good people who had a passion for their chosen profession and the talent to be successful within it. When the time came to engage a new Entertainment editor, she knew without hesitation that her long-time friend Paris was the only choice. When students at FIT, they both studied fashion journalism, became roommates and close friends, establishing a bond that held despite the fact that their careers often carried them to different ends of the globe. Hip, savvy, knowledgeable, well-liked, and very connected, Alex knew that Paris would be an indispensable asset for *Élan* and was delighted that the new position would have them circulating in the same orbit again — at least some of the time.

142

16" vinyl Madame Alexander "Alexander Fairchild Ford" #30630 – red hair and blue eyes, #30620 – blonde hair and green eyes, and #30625 – brunette hair and brown eyes, limited edition of 2,500, bent-knees, wears a metallic gold and white swimsuit with a sheer gold and white print sarong cover-up, white beach towel, sunglasses, hot pink straw hat and beach bag, 2001 line, $79.95 each. *Courtesy Alexander Doll Co.*

Left: 16" vinyl Madame Alexander "Alex" wearing "Soleil," #31195, shimmering gold blouse of moire silk, cream punched leather skirt, gold chain belt, "snakeskin" mules and shoulder bag, glittering earrings, gold sunglasses, outfit only, $59.95; right: "Laguna" #30805, sleeveless patterned midriff top, black halter top under, turquoise silk clamdiggers, cloth hat, black slides, denim shoulder bag, sunglasses, earrings, leather ponytail accessory, 2001 line, outfit only, $54.95. *Courtesy Alexander Doll Co.*

Left: 16" vinyl Madame Alexander "Alex" wearing "Sensual Essentials Accessory Pack," includes camisole, panties, teddy, stockings, slip, robe, and mule slippers, all in red and black, 2001 line, $39.95; right: wearing "Misty Magic Accessory Pack," includes mirror, brush, teddy, stockings, camisole, and panties, 2001 line, $29.95. *Courtesy Alexander Doll Co.*

16" vinyl Madame Alexander "Alex" wearing "Mardi Gras," auburn hair, blue eyes, pale pink strapless dress with skirt and collar of pale pink ostrich feathers, graduated crystal drop necklace, glittering evening sandals; rather than wearing a mask, pink and lilac makeup simulates the wings of a butterfly, the edges outlined with iridescent glitter, limited edition of 1,000, 2001 line, $229.95. *Courtesy Alexander Doll Co.*

Left: 16" vinyl Madame Alexander "Alex" wearing "Newport Drive," a pair of form-fitting jeans, matching short jacket, a cropped argyle sweater, black boots, and gold hoop earrings; right: wearing "Cape Cod," a heather blue six-button jacket, gray trousers, white blouse, white silk scarf with a bird motif and gray high-heeled ankle boots, 2001 line, outfits only, $49.95 each. *Courtesy Alexander Doll Co.*

16" vinyl Madame Alexander "Alex" wearing "Sugar Mountain," includes an ice blue turtleneck sweater with stretchy, deep sapphire ski pants, zip-front pale blue parka has a quilted lining and waist embellished with a band of blue and silver snowflakes, white faux fur trims the jacket hood and apres-ski boots, 2001 line, outfit only, $49.95. *Courtesy Alexander Doll Co.*

16" vinyl Madame Alexander "Alex" wearing "Book Tour," blonde hair, blue eyes, bent knees, black pants suit with skirt, red print sheer blouse and shirt, teddy, stockings, red faux fur collar, gold earrings, hair clip, black boots and heels, red handbag, black leather shoulder bag and matching satchel, 2001 line, $164.95. *Courtesy Alexander Doll Co.*

Left to right: 16" vinyl Madame Alexander "Alex" wearing "Dinner & A Movie," black twill trousers/floral embroidery, pink knit shirt, black leather jacket, high-heeled ankle boots, $49.95 outfit only; black "Alex" in "La Concorde," burgundy suede skirt, striped sweater, suede coat, burgundy faux fur collar, pumps, earrings, handbag, LE 1800, $89.95; "Pashmina" includes shawl, crocheted purse, sunglasses, $29.95 accessory pack, all 2001 line. *Courtesy Alexander Doll Co.*

Left: 16" vinyl Madame Alexander "Alex" wearing "Tropicana," #31205, hot pink wrap blouse/ruffled collar, pleated skirt with gold shapes, gold high-heeled sandals, hanging "Indian" earrings, chain necklace/pearl pendants, straw fan; right: wearing "Atlantico," a sequined aqua halter top with laced back that ties at waist, wide-legged aqua silk georgette trousers, dangling earrings, high-heeled sandals, beaded choker, shoulder bag, 2001 line, outfits only, $69.95 each.
Courtesy Alexander Doll Co.

16" vinyl Madame Alexander "Alexandra Fairchild Ford" wearing a Tim Alberts design, "Woman of the Year," #30640, limited edition of 2,500, a gold floor-length gown overlaid with a fine webbing of metallic gold lace accented with faceted crystal beads, strappy gold sandals and a beaded gold evening bag, a multi-strand pearl and crystal beaded necklace and matching earrings, includes a golden "WIMMY" award, 2001 line, $119.95. *Photo courtesy Alexander Doll Co.*

16" vinyl Madame Alexander black "Paris" fashion doll, #31170, black hair is worn in tumbling ringlets anchored with sapphire beaded hair pins, brown eyes, wearing "Grand Entrance," limited edition of 2,000, a ballgown of burnt orange silk with sapphire and burnt orange beads clustered within copper outlines to form embroidered blossoms on the skirt and bodice, lined in deep purple silk, matching wrap with beaded fringe, rhinestone purse, 2001 line, $189.95. *Photo courtesy Alexander Doll Co.*

Left to right: 16" vinyl Madame Alexander "Alex" in "Cyber Launch," LE 2500, sleeveless black slinky dress, leather turtleneck collar, black "alligator" boots, matching purse, $79.95; "Sunset Grille," LE 2500, low cut bronze vinyl pants, bronze organza tie shirt, beaded bra underneath, gold belly chain, sandals, beaded bag, $109.95; "Milano," LE 2000, cranberry wool trousers, turtleneck sweater, suede coat, black boots, leather tote, $99.95, 2001 line. *Photo courtesy Alexander Doll Co.*

Left: 16" vinyl Madame Alexander "Alex" wearing "New Year's Eve," moss green gown overlaid with iridescent bronze net, flower appliqués of bronze and iridescent green sequins cut a curved swathe around the neck and down the length of the gown, evening sandals, earrings, bracelet, LE 2200, $149.95; right: "Music Video Awards" Alex, black evening gown of simulated alligator, red and orange feathers on bodice, evening bag, black sandals, choker, 2001 line, $89.95, LE 2500. *Photo courtesy Alexander Doll Co.*

16" vinyl Madame Alexander "Santa Baby Gift Set" Alex, short black hair, blue eyes, two-piece holiday outfit of sleeveless dress of rich crimson satin, matching evening coat, jeweled wreath brooch; holiday scene reveals Alex's living room with walls, floor, fireplace and a table covered with green satin tablecloth, cranberry wreath, gold planters, carpet, small gifts, holiday cards, shopping bag, punch-bowl, andirons for the hearth, LE 1000 sets, 2001 line, $229.95. *Photo courtesy Alexander Doll Co.*

Gene Dolls

Created by magazine illustrator, Mel Odom, a North Carolina native now living in New York and marketed by Ashton-Drake Galleries, Gene is a 15½" vinyl fashion doll and comes complete with her own history. Making her debut in 1995 as Gene Marshall, an actress of the 1940s and 1950s, she is reminiscent of Betty Grable, Rita Hayworth, or Gene Tierney. Born in the East, Gene comes west to Hollywood and wins starring roles as well as performs on USO tours. Glamor and personality make Gene a favorite among collectors, but the well-made clothing, accessories, and presentations make her one of the hottest competitors for Barbie for the new millennium.

The Gene Team leader is Joan Greene who says the making of Gene is a labor of love — something few large corporations ever claim. Besides the excellent presentation of the doll, costumes, and accessories in 1996, the Gene Team came up with an inspiring new program, Young Designers of America. This concept encourages young high school students who receive a Gene doll and are challenged to create a scenario and costume. Each participant is honored with a special certificate of achievement and a sterling silver pin. Winners receive a cash prize and the possibility of seeing their design produced and collecting professional royalties. This program alone makes Gene a winner for collectors and young designers and also for Ashton-Drake. Fun to dress, fun to costume, and a great collectible, eight to 10 dolls are introduced annually and about the same number of new costumes. Dressed dolls retail for $79.95 and up, with "Simply Gene" offered for $54.95. It has been a long time since a doll created so much excitement in the doll-collecting world.

What to look for:

Check eBay, the Internet, doll shows, and your local doll shop for the latest dolls and costumes.

Gene Marshall

Her name was Katie Marshall. It was only after she was discovered by a famous Hollywood director that she adopted her beloved grandfather's name, Gene, because he had always urged her to follow her dream to Hollywood stardom.

Deeply inspired by Hollywood's greatest movie stars, Katie refined her natural abilities with after-school lessons in acting, dance, and music, and by performing in local community theatre. She quickly won the hearts and admiration of everyone who saw those early performances ... for even then, Gene was surely destined for stardom.

Still pursuing her dream, she made her way to New York City, becoming an usherette at a fashionable movie theatre frequented by celebrities.

On a night that changed her life forever, Gene led a tall, distinguished man to his seat in the darkened theatre. Her flashlight fleetingly revealed her lovely face to him. Astonished at her beauty and poise, the noted movie director declared her his latest discovery, whisked her to Hollywood, and helped polish Gene's shining star.

Madra Lord

Even when she was a kid in Milwaukee during World War I, Mabel Lorkovic knew a thing or two: that she loved the "flickers" and wanted to be a part of them, that she wanted to be famous, and that she was going to have to work hard to get her heart's desire.

Leaving the west coast of Lake Michigan for the West Coast of the country took a lot of moxie, but Mabel was up to it. And somewhere between the pines of Wisconsin and the palms of California, Madra Lord was born.

The road to stardom was uphill, but Madra was ready for the climb. She knew what she wanted and was going to take it, no holds barred.

She began as an extra in silent films — the "flickers" she had spent hours watching. And with the advent of "talkies" and color, Madra's distinctive husky voice and vivid beauty made her a natural for stardom, revered for her talent, and feared for a temper that made studio heads cringe, gave directors ulcers, and provided endless delight to her fans.

For many years, Madra Lord reigned as a queen of Hollywood. But into every queen's realm comes a princess; a shining light that can bring out the queen's jealous nature — so talented newcomers better beware!

Trent Osborn

The twentieth century had just made its debut, and its appearance also heralded the birth of one of Hollywood's favorite leading men, Trent Osborn.

He was born Theodore O'Bannion in Philadelphia, and young "Teddy" was quite the little neighborhood Romeo, stealing kisses from beneath the playground Pollyannas' pipe curls. He also always had a flair for the dramatic, prodding his playmates into staging elaborate pirate adventures on the bounding waters of the creeks in Philly's most prestigious park — much to the chagrin of the local police force!

After graduating from high school, he longed for adventure, even working as a truck driver to escape the city limits. But soon he discovered the local theater groups, where he was quickly spotted by a casting director for the Theatre Guild and whisked off to The Great White Way. His refined good looks, coupled with a certain aura of reckless abandon, brought him role upon role — and the attentions and intentions of an army of beautiful young actresses and debutantes.

After playing the gamut of juvenile roles on Broadway, Teddy, now known as Trent Osborn to the New York theater goers, was brought to Hollywood in 1935. A mainstay at Monolithic, he appeared in scores of films, and his most frequent leading ladies included Gene Marshall and Madra Lord.

As flamboyant a figure in Hollywood nightlife as he was on the screen, Trent Osborn broke countless hearts. But when he turned on those bedroom eyes, everyone from starlet to seasoned veteran melted at a glance.

Violet Waters

It was said that the only thing more beautiful than Violet Waters' face was her voice. It was a voice that perfectly suited her name, smooth and flowing, with a silver ripple that gave no hint of the rocks and turns hidden beneath the surface.

These rocks and turns had been a lifelong reality for Violet. But they were only things to conquer and overcome, because Violet was a girl with dreams — and a gift to share with the world.

Violet Waters was born amidst the 1920s roar. She was nurtured in the classics by her father, a literature professor at Central State College, a prestigious black school. And from the time she was a baby, her life was filled with music, listening to her grandmother play the church organ while her mother sang in the choir (and every waking minute of the day).

But, most importantly, her family filled her with a sense of pride and taught her always to be true to herself, no matter the odds.

With mixed emotions, Violet's close-knit family waved goodbye to their little flower as she went off to Chicago to fulfill her destiny. Soon she was playing smoky jazz clubs, electrifying the Windy City with her stylings.

Almost immediately, word of her talent began to travel through the jazz world, bringing gigs across the country and especially in Europe, where she was embraced as a true jazz star.

However, back in Hollywood, things were not quite as rosy. Major studios contacted her, but they only seemed to want her to play servants or to pass her off as a new South American bombshell. Violet would have none of it, however; her family had impressed upon her the importance of being true to her heritage.

Suddenly, a fan and friend brought Violet and Monolithic Studios together — and Hollywood and jazz history was made!

Fashion Dolls

15½" vinyl Ashton-Drake Gene in "Everything's Coming Up Roses," Annual Edition, marked "Gene ™//© 1995 Mel Odom" on head, painted eyes, brown rooted synthetic wig, jointed fashion type body, bendable knees, rose colored satin fitted jacket with glass bead buttons, beaded design, mid-calf skirt vented in back, lined in pink, matching feather trimmed beaded hat, purse, short gloves, hose, matching ribbon shoes, outfit designed by Jose Ferrand, circa 2001, **$99.95.** *Photo courtesy Ashton-Drake Galleries.*

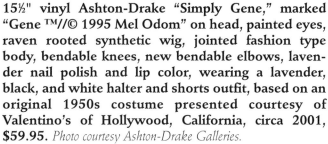

15½" vinyl Ashton-Drake "Simply Gene," marked "Gene ™//© 1995 Mel Odom" on head, painted eyes, raven rooted synthetic wig, jointed fashion type body, bendable knees, new bendable elbows, lavender nail polish and lip color, wearing a lavender, black, and white halter and shorts outfit, based on an original 1950s costume presented courtesy of Valentino's of Hollywood, California, circa 2001, **$59.95.** *Photo courtesy Ashton-Drake Galleries.*

15½" vinyl Ashton-Drake Gene in "My Heart's Song," marked "Gene ™//© 1995 Mel Odom" on head, painted eyes, red rooted synthetic wig, jointed fashion type body, bendable knees, in a dress of black and white striped georgette with an exposed back, a matching hat; the jacket is blue gabardine with matching black and white striped cuffs and collar, black gloves, purse, nylons, and black high-heeled sandals, circa 2001, **$89.95.**
Photo courtesy Ashton-Drake Galleries.

15½" vinyl Ashton-Drake Gene in "Batter Up!", marked "Gene ™//© 1995 Mel Odom" on head, painted eyes, rooted synthetic wig, jointed fashion type body, dressed in a softball uniform including jersey, skirt, shorts, socks, belt, hat, tennis shoes, and bat, Designers of America winner, created by Stephanie Iller-Drachman, a senior at Hanford High School in Richland, Washington, circa 2001, $44.95, costume only. *Photo courtesy Ashton-Drake Galleries.*

15½" vinyl Ashton-Drake Gene in "Little Blessings," marked "Gene ™//© 1995 Mel Odom" on head, painted eyes, rooted synthetic wig, jointed fashion type body, bendable knees, dressed in a maternity costume, white with black polka dots sleeveless sheath with a little swing coat in pink with black rollback cuffs and black bead trim, black hat with pink flower accents, white gloves, black high-heeled shoes, earrings, circa 2001, $49.95, costume only. *Photo courtesy Ashton-Drake Galleries.*

15½" vinyl Ashton-Drake Gene in "Blue Heaven," marked "Gene ™//© 1995 Mel Odom" on head, painted eyes, rooted synthetic wig, jointed fashion type body, bendable knees, dressed in a blue chiffon cocktail dress with pink accents, trimmed with a rhinestone pin and a sheer pink organza stole, nylons, blue high-heeled shoes, circa 2001, $44.95, costume only. *Photo courtesy Ashton-Drake Galleries.*

Fashion Dolls

15½" vinyl Ashton-Drake Gene in "Bonnie and Blithe," marked "Gene ™//© 1995 Mel Odom" on head, painted eyes, rooted synthetic wig, bendable knees, jointed fashion type body, dressed in a red and white striped black wool skirt softly pleated and hemmed just below the knee, red wool top with fringe trim around the jewel neckline, matching tam-style hat, black belt, purse, and open-toe high-heeled shoes, circa 2001, $49.95, costume only. *Photo courtesy Ashton-Drake Galleries.*

15½" vinyl Ashton-Drake Gene in "April Showers," marked "Gene ™//© 1995 Mel Odom" on head, painted eyes, rooted synthetic wig, bendable knees and elbows, jointed fashion type body, celebrating the Coca-Cola Calendar girls of the 1950s, maroon dress, with a pink rose at the neckline, pink short gloves, long white overcoat with buttons and belt, carrying a red and white umbrella, white open-toe high-heeled shoes, nylons, circa 2001, $125.00. *Photo courtesy Ashton-Drake Galleries.*

15½" vinyl Ashton-Drake Gene in "Garden Party," marked "Gene ™//© 1995 Mel Odom" on head, painted eyes, auburn rooted synthetic wig, jointed fashion type body, bendable knees, in a dress of cream silk charmeuse with colored silk ribbon, multi-colored beads and embroidered flowers as decorations, matching hat, purse, and high-heeled sandals, gloves, pearl necklace and bracelet, circa 2001, $120.00. *Photo courtesy Ashton-Drake Galleries.*

15½" vinyl Ashton-Drake Gene in "Crazy for Calypso," marked "Gene ™//© 1995 Mel Odom" on head, painted eyes, rooted synthetic wig, jointed fashion type body, bendable knees, dressed in a white blouse with frilly sleeves, toreador-style satin pants and multicolored sash, matching ribbon in hair, white stockings, black shoes, gold hoop earrings, circa 2001, $44.95, costume only. *Photo courtesy Ashton-Drake Galleries.*

15½" vinyl Ashton-Drake Gene in "Right in Step," marked "Gene ™//© 1995 Mel Odom" on head, painted eyes, rooted synthetic wig, jointed fashion type body, bendable knees, dressed in a gown of navy blue charmeuse, accented with navy and pink tulle and cloth roses, slightly longer in the back to suggest a small train, off-the-shoulder bodice has two straps that crisscross in the back, long gloves, circa 2001, $54.95, costume only. *Photo courtesy Ashton-Drake Galleries.*

Fashion Dolls

15½" vinyl Ashton-Drake Gene in "A Lady Knows," marked "Gene ™//© 1995 Mel Odom" on head, painted eyes, blonde rooted synthetic wig, jointed fashion type body, bendable knees, dressed in a black bouclé top with jewel neckline and a long skirt of dark blue taffeta and black chiffon, matching hat with black feather trim, black handbag and shoes, nylons, and a faux fur stole, circa 2001, $99.95. *Photo courtesy Ashton-Drake Galleries.*

15½" vinyl Ashton-Drake Gene in "Blue Fox," marked "Gene ™//© 1995 Mel Odom" on head, painted eyes, auburn rooted synthetic wig, jointed fashion type body, bendable knees, dressed in a light blue satin evening gown, the fitted bodice has a V-shaped pleat at the sweetheart neckline, matching wrap trimmed in faux fur, pearl necklace and earrings, circa 2001, $89.95. *Photo courtesy Ashton-Drake Galleries.*

15½" vinyl Ashton-Drake Gene in "Love in Bloom," marked "Gene ™//© 1995 Mel Odom" on head, painted eyes, rooted synthetic wig, bendable knees and elbows, jointed fashion type body, dressed in a pink silk sheath emblazoned with embroidered flowers gracing its train, with embroidered flowers over the bodice and one shoulder, long white gloves, open-toe high-heeled sandals, earrings, nylons, circa 2001, $120.00. *Photo courtesy Ashton-Drake Galleries.*

15½" vinyl Ashton-Drake "Ultimately Madra," painted eyes, rooted synthetic wig, bendable knees and elbows, jointed fashion type body, dressed in pink bra and panties, pink garter, nylons, pink high-heeled slippers, earrings, white fur stole, circa 2001, $69.95. *Photo courtesy Ashton-Drake Galleries.*

15½" vinyl Ashton-Drake Madra "Mad About Mitzi," painted eyes, rooted synthetic wig, bendable knees and elbows, jointed fashion type body, dressed in a black knit sheath dress with a white Peter Pan collar of sparkly white organza, big white hat, white gloves and purse, nylons, bracelet, white high-heel sandals, plush poodle "Mitzi" with rhinestone collar that matches Madra's bracelet, circa 2001, $59.95, outfit only. *Photo courtesy Ashton-Drake Galleries.*

15½" vinyl Ashton-Drake Madra "Coffee Klatch," painted eyes, rooted synthetic wig, bendable knees and elbows, jointed fashion type body, dressed in a vest-coat outfit popular in the '40s, the coat is navy with a cream-colored yoke, pockets, sleeve cuffs, and brocade trim, a sleeveless knit navy top and skirt, matching hat, brown gloves, purse and high-heeled shoes, circa 2001, $49.95, outfit only. *Photo courtesy Ashton-Drake Galleries.*

Fashion Dolls

15½" vinyl Ashton-Drake Madra "Anything But Nice," painted eyes, rooted synthetic wig, bendable knees and elbows, jointed fashion type body, dressed in a purple tailored shift-style dress with thin straps and a midriff-length top with a purple and green beaded pattern across the cowl neckline, black and silver beaded decoration on the back, beaded bracelet, white stockings, black high-heeled shoes, cigarette holder, circa 2001, $59.95, outfit only. *Photo courtesy Ashton-Drake Galleries.*

15½" vinyl Ashton-Drake Madra "Stormy Weather," painted eyes, rooted synthetic wig, bendable knees and elbows, jointed fashion type body, dressed in a raincoat and matching hat of metallic gold, lined with a maroon, gold, and green striped fabric, matching handbag and boots, under the raincoat is a sheath dress of green, brown, and copper brocade, circa 2001, $59.95, outfit only. *Photo courtesy Ashton-Drake Galleries.*

15½" vinyl Ashton-Drake Madra "Winter/Summer Set," painted eyes, rooted synthetic wig, bendable knees and elbows, jointed fashion type body; two beautiful outfits sold as a set, re-creations of sketches by renowned designer Jim Howard, one is a red skirt and jacket with fur collar and hat, brown high-heeled shoes, and brown gloves, the other is a black with white polka dot dress, white shawl, hat, gloves, and open-toe high-heeled shoes, circa 2001, $79.95, outfits only. *Photo courtesy Ashton-Drake Galleries.*

15½" vinyl Ashton-Drake Madra "Chocolate Truffle," painted eyes, rooted synthetic wig, bendable knees and elbows, jointed fashion type body, dressed in a cocoa brown dress and jacket combination, teal blue hat, white gloves, brown handbag, stockings, brown open-toe high-heeled scuffs, circa 2001, $59.95, outfits only. *Photo courtesy Ashton-Drake Galleries.*

15½" vinyl Ashton-Drake Madra "Scorned Woman" from the Costume Ball Series, painted eyes, rooted synthetic wig, bendable knees and elbows, jointed fashion type body, dressed in a lavish costume ball gown of black with multicolored trim, white net lace around neck and hem, large hat with mounds of pink feather trim, long white gloves, limited to 5,000 worldwide, circa 2001, $125.00. *Photo courtesy Ashton-Drake Galleries.*

15½" vinyl Ashton-Drake Madra "Scarlett Temptress," painted eyes, rooted synthetic wig, bendable knees and elbows, jointed fashion type body, dressed in a striking red gown with double-rose bodice, matching shawl, hat, long red gloves, bracelet, necklace, and earrings, nylons, red high-heeled shoes, circa 2001, $125.00. *Photo courtesy Ashton-Drake Galleries.*

15½" vinyl Ashton-Drake Madra "All About Eve," painted eyes, rooted synthetic wig, bendable knees and elbows, jointed fashion type body, dressed in a white evening gown and matching floor-length jacket with slits for arms, embellished with flower trim, long white gloves, earrings and necklace, circa 2001, $125.00. *Photo courtesy Ashton-Drake Galleries.*

15½" vinyl Ashton-Drake Madra "Rio Rumba," painted eyes, rooted synthetic wig, bendable knees and elbows, jointed fashion type body, dressed in a red and white striped cotton linen A-line dress with a V-neck and matching cap, red choker necklace and matching bracelet, red hoop earrings, holding guiro, circa 2001, $44.95, outfit only. *Photo courtesy Ashton-Drake Galleries.*

15½" vinyl Ashton-Drake Madra "Black Ice," painted eyes, rooted synthetic wig, bendable knees and elbows, jointed fashion type body, dressed in a classic '40s evening gown of black taffeta with a hint of pale yellow accent at the neckline, the fitted bodice rises over the right shoulder and is accented with a black bow lined in yellow, with a silver, black, and rhinestone decoration and a black collapsible fan, circa 2001, $99.95. *Photo courtesy Ashton-Drake Galleries.*

15½" vinyl Ashton-Drake Madra in "Cold Shoulder," painted eyes, rooted synthetic wig, bendable knees and elbows, jointed fashion type body, dressed in a sage green gown with a daring design that bares her left shoulder and has a provocative slit up the side of the skirt, brooch on gown, long "fur" stole, handbag, beaded necklace, ribbon shoes, earrings, circa 2001, $110.00. *Photo courtesy Ashton-Drake Galleries.*

15½" vinyl Ashton-Drake Madra "Stolen Moments," painted eyes, rooted synthetic wig, bendable knees and elbows, jointed fashion type body, dressed in an antique rose evening suit with a mermaid-style skirt, hooded jacket has an embroidered bead design across the front, fur muff, gloves, earrings, bracelet and necklace, matching high-heeled ribbon shoes, circa 2001, $99.95. *Photo courtesy Ashton-Drake Galleries.*

15½" vinyl Ashton-Drake Madra "Unsung Melody," and 16" Trent in "Formal Introduction," painted eyes, rooted synthetic wig on Madra, painted molded hair for Trent, bendable knees and elbows, jointed bodies; Madra dressed in a seafoam green satin gown with a black satin inset panel, matching wrap around neck, earrings, black purse, Trent dressed to the nines in a stunning set of tails, circa 2001, $110.00 each. *Photo courtesy Ashton-Drake Galleries.*

Tyler —
How New York's Grooviest Designer Hit the Runway

From an early age, Tyler Wentworth was destined to be a high flyer in the world of high fashion. During the 1950s, Tyler's great-aunt, Regina Wentworth, established the House of Wentworth in New York City and created innovative collections that set the standard for 7th Avenue fashion design. Years later, Tyler, who had always loved the glamour and excitement of her great-aunt's business, joined the prestigious house's design staff. She proved to be exceptionally talented, and it was not long until she was promoted to Regina's first assistant. With the House of Wentworth's reputation firmly established, Regina began to consider passing the reins to a new talent. Spurring her on was her relationship with Carlos, a young artist who had instantly fallen in love with the chic, elegant, older designer. Soon Regina made her decision to move with Carlos to the south of France, and she turned the company over to Tyler. Although young for the job, Tyler quickly showed that she was equal to her new responsibilities. With only a few short seasons of fashion experience, she confidently assumed leadership of the House of Wentworth and received rave reviews for her first collection. Tonner Doll Company is pleased to present the Tyler Wentworth collection. Tyler is a 16", vinyl/hard plastic doll with rooted hair and an extensive, stylish wardrobe.

Tyler is well-known on 7th Avenue for the no-nonsense professional look she's developed. Most mornings Tyler goes to work in her white cotton shirt and slim black wool skirt with tailored belt. Black sheer stockings and black pumps add a professional air. As a nod toward her aunt's own unique personal style, she wears a single strand of pearls. It's definitely Tyler's Signature Style!

Tyler creates her fashion dreams from flat pattern and draping methods. Her drafting table is where everything is drawn into cohesive designs ready for her sample makers. Exacting details such as polished drawer knobs and a brass drafting lamp complement the functional elements of this design center.

What to look for:
Check eBay, the Internet, doll shows, and your local doll shop for the latest dolls and costumes.

Esme

In a rare relaxed moment, Tyler went into a bookstore to browse. After making her selections, she noticed an incredibly beautiful young woman working behind the counter. Tyler introduced herself to the young woman and found out her name was Esme. She was a pre-med student who was at first very skeptical about Tyler's suggestion that she model in the upcoming fashion show. Although she had been approached to model before, she had never taken the suggestion seriously. But having heard of Tyler and the House of Wentworth, she thought she would give it a try. After a lengthy conversation with the Chase Modeling Agency, Esme was booked for her first show — The Tyler Wentworth Collection.

Sydney Chase

It was Sydney Chase's specific flair and independent style that told her good friend, Tyler Wentworth, that she was a mover and shaker … and an alliance was soon created between the fashion professionals. Madison Avenue immediately quaked over the report that the House of Wentworth and Chase Modeling would be a force to be reckoned with in the fashion industry. Tyler's business attire designs for Sydney were created to produce a professional and evocative look.

16" vinyl Robert Tonner "Tyler Wentworth," long brown rooted hair in a high ponytail, plastic eyes, closed mouth, hard plastic body, dressed in a white tailored cotton shirt, black slim skirt, black belt with gold buckle, earrings, black fish-net stockings, black shoes, circa 2001, $79.99; Drafting Table and Stool, polished drawer knobs, brass drafting lamp, circa 2001, $89.99. *Photo courtesy Robert Tonner Doll Company.*

16" vinyl Robert Tonner "Tyler Wentworth," red rooted hair, plastic eyes, closed mouth, hard plastic body, dressed in TW 1105 "Champagne and Caviar," limited edition of 2,000, multi-tiered, fan-pleated organza black cocktail dress, black fish-net stockings, jewelry, black high-heeled sandals, circa 2001, $99.99. *Courtesy Robert Tonner Doll Company.*

16" vinyl Robert Tonner "Tyler Wentworth," long blonde rooted hair in a high ponytail, plastic eyes, closed mouth, hard plastic body, dressed in TW 8104 "Metro Chic," limited edition of 2,000, pewter fabric adaption of the traditional trench coat cut to a new length, basic matching dress underneath, matching umbrella, knee-high boots, outfit only, circa 2001, $59.99. *Courtesy Robert Tonner Doll Company.*

Fashion Dolls

16" vinyl Robert Tonner "Tyler Wentworth," rooted hair, plastic eyes, closed mouth, hard plastic body, wearing TW 1103 "Precious Metal," mermaid-style burnished gold silk gown with tiny metallic sequins, belt and matching earrings, circa 2001, $169.99; and TW 8106 "Passion," pomegranate silk embellished with circular sequins, meticulous beadwork on the chiffon wrap, necklace, earrings, red high-heeled sandals, outfit only, circa 2001, $89.99. *Courtesy Robert Tonner Doll Company.*

16" vinyl Robert Tonner "Tyler Wentworth," long brown rooted hair, plastic eyes, closed mouth, hard plastic body, dressed in TW 8102 "Chill Chasers," limited edition of 2,000, satin parka with faux crystal fox, colorful sweater inspired by Alpine shapes and knits, fuchsia and tangerine with cocoa bean hues, topping a pair of velvet pants, mittens, snow boots, driving map, keys, outfit only, circa 2001, $74.99. *Courtesy Robert Tonner Doll Company.*

16" vinyl Robert Tonner "Tyler Wentworth" and "Esme," both with rooted hair, plastic eyes, closed mouths, hard plastic bodies, Esme in TW 8108 "Pretty Young Thing," fuchsia/gold cocktail ensemble, beaded gold handbag, gold high-heeled sandals, outfit only, $59.99; and Tyler dressed in TW 8103 "Uptown Paradise," limited edition of 2,000, mandarin/lime knit sweater set, silk pants, matching handbag, green high-heeled sandals, jewelry, outfit only, circa 2001, $69.99. *Courtesy Robert Tonner Doll Company.*

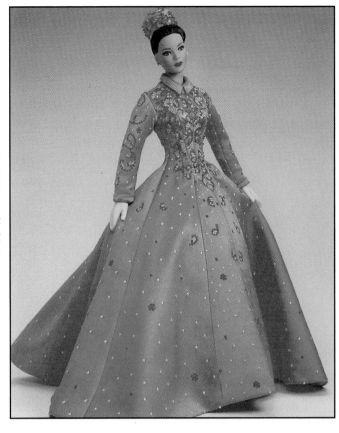

16" vinyl Robert Tonner "Tyler Wentworth," brown rooted hair, plastic eyes, closed mouth, hard plastic body, dressed in TDLM 003 "Framboise Robe du Grande Soir," limited edition of 3,000, extravagant shimmering raspberry gown, tiny collar and narrow sleeves contrast against the full skirt with delicate embroidery, matching pillbox hat, white gloves, earrings, circa 2001, $199.99. *Courtesy Robert Tonner Doll Company.*

16" vinyl Robert Tonner "Tyler Wentworth," auburn rooted hair, plastic eyes, closed mouth, hard plastic body, dressed in TDLM 002 "Longchamp Fleuri," limited edition of 3,000, gray wool suit lined in mauve silk, embroidered violets on skirt and jacket, straw hat, gray handbag, gloves, nylons, open-toe high-heeled shoes, circa 2001, $189.99. *Courtesy Robert Tonner Doll Company.*

16" vinyl Robert Tonner "Tyler Wentworth," blonde rooted hair, plastic eyes, closed mouth, hard plastic body, dressed in TDLM 001 "Fleurs du Mal," limited edition of 3,000, black embroidered bodice in illusion with short cap sleeves above asymmetrical skirt of pink with pleated side back, black feather hat, pink heels, circa 2001, $189.99. *Courtesy Robert Tonner Doll Company.*

16" vinyl Robert Tonner "Tyler Wentworth," brown rooted hair, plastic eyes, closed mouth, hard plastic body, dressed in TW 1104 "Midnight Garden," limited edition of 1,000, black silk gown embroidered in flowers and trimmed in velvet, earrings and necklace, circa 2001, $189.99. *Courtesy Robert Tonner Doll Company.*

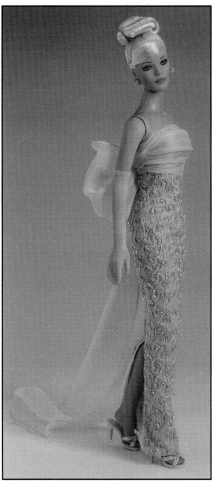

16" vinyl Robert Tonner "Tyler Wentworth," blonde rooted hair, plastic eyes, closed mouth, hard plastic body, dressed in TW 1105 "Champagne and Caviar," limited edition of 1500, pink beaded and embroidered column gown wrapped in floating silk chiffon, pink earrings, long gloves, pink high-heeled sandals, circa 2001, $149.99. *Courtesy Robert Tonner Doll Company.*

16" vinyl Robert Tonner "Esme," long black rooted hair, plastic eyes, closed mouth, hard plastic body, bendable knees, wearing TW 2001 "Basic Esme," red dress with mid-length sleeves, matching belt with gold buckle, black handbag, black fishnet hose, black high-heeled shoes, earrings, sunglasses, circa 2001, $79.99. *Courtesy Robert Tonner Doll Company.*

16" vinyl Robert Tonner "Esme Cover Girl," long black rooted hair pinned up, plastic eyes, closed mouth, hard plastic body, bendable knees, dressed in a Tyler Wentworth original gown style TW 2002, peach and gold lace dress with jewel neckline, lined in sparkle net and chiffon, sash on the dress ties in back to make a luxurious chiffon train, earrings, limited edition of 2,000, circa 2001, $149.99. *Photo courtesy Robert Tonner Doll Company.*

16" vinyl Robert Tonner "Esme," long black rooted hair, plastic eyes, closed mouth, hard plastic body, bendable knees, wearing TW 2101 "Boston Bound," white bodysuit, cream tights, button vest, brown corduroy skirt, coral diamond-quilted coat with large pockets, ankle boots, and printed scarf, circa 2001, $99.99. *Courtesy Robert Tonner Doll Company.*

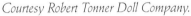

16" vinyl Robert Tonner "Sydney Chase," black rooted hair, plastic eyes, closed mouth, hard plastic body, bendable knees, dressed in TW 3101, silk tweed suit and silk crepe blouse/scarf combination, high-top black boots, circa 2001, $99.99. *Courtesy Robert Tonner Doll Company.*

16" vinyl Robert Tonner "Sydney Chase," blonde rooted hair pinned up, plastic eyes, closed mouth, hard plastic body, bendable knees, dressed in TW 3102 "Black and White Ball Sydney," limited edition of 2,000, couture gown with a double teardrop train in black satin over a dramatic contrast of black and white stripes in a bold chevron, jet choker, matching earrings, black opera gloves, circa 2001, $149.99. *Courtesy Robert Tonner Doll Company.*

Girl Scout Dolls

Pidd Miller of Houston, Texas, has been instrumental in promoting doll collecting for Girl Scouts and helped the San Jacinto Girl Scout Council (SJGSC) establish a Girl Scout doll-collecting patch in 1989. The patch may be earned by any Girl Scout — Daisy to Senior. Pidd Miller has researched Scouting and provided the following information on the Scout movement. Girl Scouting was established in the United States in 1912 by Juliette Gordon Low in Savannah, Georgia, for ten- to seventeen-year old girls, and Brownie Scouts began in 1926 for seven- to nine-year-old girls.

Englishman Robert Baden-Powell, who started the Boy Scouts and Girl Guides, bestowed the Brownie name. He derived the name "Brownie" from an English tale of little people, "brownies," who helped with chores when the family was asleep. The first Brownie uniform was a tan one-piece dress with two breast pockets, with or without matching bloomers showing. The peaked cap was of the same material. A recent article in *Newsweek* revealed there have been 175 modifications to the uniform since 1912. The Girl Scout camp uniform is pictured in the 1920 Girl Scout Hand Book. The uniform is gray-green with a skirt and bloomers below the knee. The tie is red. The socks are green with darker green — turned down on top. Her shoes are black with a small heel, and they tie at the ankle. In 1985 the Brownie uniform changed from an A-line jumper to a jumper with a two-button big top. A short-sleeved blouse has the Brownie emblem and brown stripes with an orange tie.

New Effanbee Brownie and Junior Girl Scout dolls are now available in Girl Scout shops. The Brownie doll wears a brown vest with a brown patch on the left side suggestive of the Brownie logo and brown skirt with two box pleats and brown leather belt. Her short-sleeve blue shirt has a white embroidered Brownie logo design on the left sleeve with two white buttons, white tie, and white panties. Her knee-high socks are blue with brown tie shoes and brown beanie. The Junior Girl Scout is dressed in the same design uniform with green material. Her white short-sleeve shirt has green trim on the sleeve cuff and green embroidered GS design on shirt. Her knee socks are white, and her brown shoes have brown ties. She wears a green baseball type cap.

The 8¼" doll is all-vinyl with rooted hair, inset eyes, and an open/closed mouth. She is jointed at neck, shoulders, waist, and hips. The doll is unmarked. The shirt has a label in left shirt seam "Effanbee Doll Co." She is available in white (#11863), African-American (#11864), Asian (#11865), and Hispanic (#11866).

The Effanbee 2000 Brownie and Junior Girl Scout dolls are the seventeenth dolls to be found in the Official Girl Scout Catalog since the first one by Effanbee in 1936. These are the first vinyl dolls since Effanbee's Pun'kin, an 11" vinyl dressed in Brownie and Junior Girl Scout jumper-type uniforms in 1974. In 1985 a pre-printed cloth one-piece Brownie doll was found in the catalog. This doll was unmarked. There were no Scout dolls offered in the catalog for the next 10 years.

In 1995, Bow Tie Co. made a cloth 12" Brownie and in 1997, a Junior Girl Scout green uniform was made and sold separately. In 1998 Bow Tie made a cloth Daisy "Color Me," 20" tall.

In 1999 Well Made Toy Manufacturing Corp. made an 11" cloth Daisy and 11" cloth Brownie. In 1998 Brownie, Junior Girl Scout and Senior Girl Scout uniforms were made to fit 17" – 19" dolls. These uniforms are still available.

The Effanbee 2000 handsome vinyl Brownie and Junior Girl Scout dolls are a dream come true for Girl Scouts and doll collectors. Dolls have a very important place in the history of Girl Scouts as they do in our culture. Dolls are made both for play and to reflect current events.

SJGSC has three established doll patches — Doll Collector, Share A Doll, and Dolly Goes to College. For more information on the Girl Scout doll collection patch, send an SASE to Pidd Miller, P.O. Box 631092, Houston, TX 77263.

14½" vinyl Effanbee Official Girl Scout (Patsy Ann) No. 629, rooted Saran hair, sleep eyes with lashes, freckles across nose, jointed vinyl body, dressed in authentic Girl Scout green fabric dress, yellow tie, marked on head "Effanbee//Patsy Ann//© 1959," circa 1960, $350.00. *Courtesy Grace Steuri.*

18" porcelain Juliette Gordon Low "Girl Scout," by doll artist Ruth Elena George. Juliette Gordon Low, founder of the Girl Scouts, shown in her official 1919 uniform; careful attention to detail has been given to authenticate the outfit from her hat on which she sports the Girl Scout insignia, to her strapped walking shoes that she so frequently wore. She proudly wears her Silver Fish Award affixed to a crisp blue and white ribbon, circa 2001, $49.95. *Courtesy Pidd Miller.*

16½" porcelain "Daisy" by doll artist Ruth Elena George who designed a replica of Juliette Gordon Low, called Daisy by friends and family, who started Girl Scouting in the United States. This doll in her pink ball gown was designed for the 1996 Summer Olympics, circa 1997, $129.95. *Courtesy Pidd Miller.*

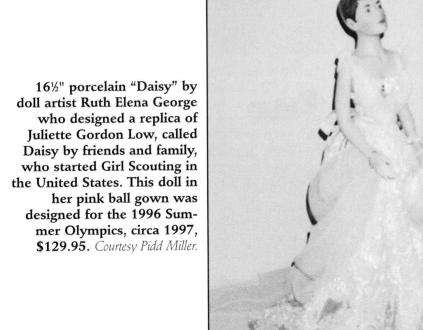

11½" cloth Brownie on pre-printed cloth, one-piece, unmarked, brown hair in pigtails tied with red ribbon, printed brown Brownie Scout beanie, brown and white striped shirt, brown outfit, printed brown socks, and black shoes, circa 1985 – 1986, $11.00. *Courtesy Pidd Miller.*

14" vinyl "Junior Girl Scout" sold by Avon, approved by the Girl Scout office, rooted hair, set eyes, painted lashes, closed smiling mouth, white with green pattern shirt, green Scout vest and matching skirt with pleat, green hat with Scout insignia, green knee-high socks, loafers, holding a Girl Scout cookie box in right hand, circa 1995 – 1996, $39.85. *Courtesy Pidd Miller.*

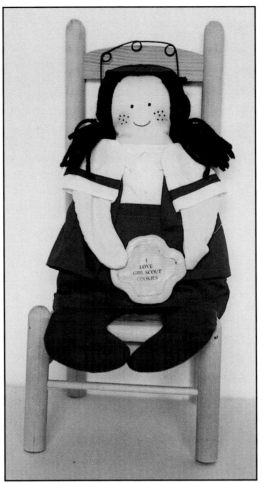

13" cloth Bow Tie Co. "Junior Girl Scout" door knob hanger, holding a cookie printed with "I Love Girl Scout Cookies," painted features, yarn hair, wire hanger attached to back, circa 1997, $15.00. *Courtesy Pidd Miller.*

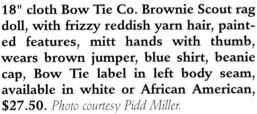

18" cloth Bow Tie Co. Brownie Scout rag doll, with frizzy reddish yarn hair, painted features, mitt hands with thumb, wears brown jumper, blue shirt, beanie cap, Bow Tie label in left body seam, available in white or African American, $27.50. *Photo courtesy Pidd Miller.*

20" cloth Girl Scout "Color-Me Daisy," non-toxic, water soluble markers included, wash in machine and color again, full Daisy Girl Scout uniform in black graphics, back pocket with Velcro® closure for storing markers, circa 1998, $13.00. *Courtesy Pidd Miller.*

Girl Scout Dolls

9" vinyl Effanbee "Brownie Scout" or "Junior Girl Scout," both come in Hispanic, African-American, Asian, and white, synthetic wigs, glass eyes, painted lashes, closed smiling mouths, vinyl bodies with twist-and-turn waists, dressed in full uniforms, cloth Effanbee label in left shirt seam, stands included, circa 2000, $25.00. *Courtesy Pidd Miller.*

Five wooden Nesting Girl Scout Dolls, starting at 5" tall, stack inside each other, include Cadette, Junior, Brownie, Daisy, and Girl Scout, with logo, painted features and hair, circa 2000, $22.00. *Courtesy Pidd Miller.*

Above and below: 11" cloth Well Made Corp. Whimsical Brownie Scout and Daisy Scout dolls, red yarn hair in ponytails, embroidered mouth, button eyes, elastic loop on head for attaching to a backpack or school bag or hanging on a door, circa 2000, $11.00 each. *Courtesy Pidd Miller.*

Two 7" cloth Mary Meyer dolls, yarn hair, cloth bodies, in white shirts and Girl Scout green or brown shorts, removable outfits, two fuzzy teddy bears, two nylon sleeping bags, a tent with zipper and flap closure in front, pretend window in back, and "Girl Scouts" printed on the side, soft, packable pieces store inside the tent, circa 2000, $26.00. *Courtesy Pidd Miller.*

Hard Plastic Dolls

Plastics came into use during World War II. The war and shortages of some materials caused great upheavals in the toy industry since many plants had been converted to make items for the war effort. After the war, some companies began to use plastic for dolls. Hard plastic seems to have been a good material for doll use. Relatively unbreakable, it seems not to deteriorate with time, as had been the case with "magic skin" and other materials that were tried and discarded. The prime years of plastic use, roughly 1940 – 1950, produced a wide variety of beautiful dolls that Baby Boomers still remember fondly. With the advent of vinyl in the late 1950s and early 1960s, fewer hard plastic dolls were made, although occasionally some manufacturers today still use hard plastic.

What to look for:

Look for clean dolls with rosy cheek color, in original clothing, with labels, boxes, hang tags or brochures. Dirt on dolls may cause the plastic to change chemically with the growth of bacteria in high relative humidity. Another niche where collectors may find inexpensive dolls is dolls unmarked or those made by little-known companies.

17½" Eugenia Doll Co. Personality Playmate "Carolyn," made for Montgomery Ward, mohair wig, brown sleep eyes, closed mouth, jointed hard plastic body, may be re-dressed, circa 1948, $150.00. *Private collection.*

25" Paris Doll Company "Rita," Saran hair, blue sleep eyes, painted lashes below eyes, eyeshadow, open mouth with teeth, five-piece hard plastic body, long blue formal with net and lace trim, circa 1951 – 1953, $125.00. *Courtesy Diane Vigne.*

14" Roberta Doll Co. girl, dark brown mohair braided wig, blue sleep eyes, closed mouth, jointed hard plastic body, style 4236 blue dress with white and red trim, straw hat, red hair ribbons, mint-in-box, circa 1950s, $300.00. *Courtesy Rita Mauze.*

17" Welsh Morris Doll Co. girl, dark brown mohair wig in original set, sleep eyes, closed mouth, jointed hard plastic body, fuchsia colored satin formal with matching hat, label on box reads "Darling Daughter Doll," mint-in-box, circa 1950s, $550.00. *Courtesy Rita Mauze.*

17" brown "Hawaiian Girl" walker, black synthetic braided hair with bangs, brown sleep eyes, open/closed mouth with painted teeth, hard plastic jointed body, grass skirt, floral bikini top, lei, ankle bracelet, hang tag reads "Miss Hawaii with Dynel Hair," mint-in-box, circa 1950s, $375.00. *Courtesy Rita Mauze.*

8" unmarked Ginny-type Bride, brunette synthetic hair, blue sleep eyes, molded lash, jointed hard plastic body, non-walker, white bridal gown with net and lace skirt overlay, net and lace veil, circa 1950s, $175.00. *Courtesy Barbara Hull.*

14" "Marilyn," blonde Saran wig, blue sleep eyes, hard plastic jointed body, pink slip, socks, shoes, mint-in-box with pink outfit with matching hat, panties, blue blouse, yellow skirt, purse, straw hat, rollers, comb, brush, mirror, circa 1950s, $345.00. *Courtesy Rita Mauze.*

Hitty Dolls

Hitty is the major character in the book, *Hitty, Her First Hundred Years* by Rachel Field, published in 1929. It is a story of a 6" doll, Hitty, and her adventures through 100 years. The story remains popular with people who read it as children and gave the book to their children and grandchildren. It is charmingly illustrated with pen and ink drawings, and early editions also contain some color plates. The original Hitty makes her home in the Sturbridge, Massachusetts, library, while today's artists recreate Hitty for collectors. A *Hitty Newsletter* is published and Hitty get-togethers happen at doll conventions and conferences. See Collector's Network for information on the *Hitty Newsletter* to keep abreast of latest artist creations.

What to look for:

Reread the Hitty book to fix in your mind your ideal Hitty and then look for the many artist interpretations available today. You can find them nude or dressed, giving you options on price and the opportunity to make a wardrobe for your own Hitty. You may even wish to try carving your own.

Three 6¼" carved wood Hitty dolls handmade by Janci, in calico dresses; center one has antiqued look, black carved and painted hair, painted features, jointed arms and legs, painted shoes, each with coral necklace, circa 2001, $295.00. *Photo courtesy Jill Sanders.*

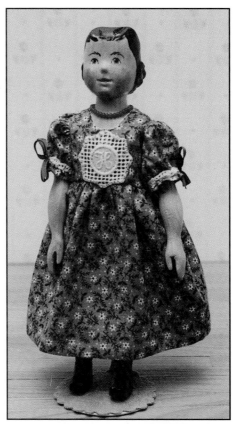

6¼" basswood Hitty, handmade by Judy Brown, with painted features, jointed arms and legs for independent movement, blue and white floral cotton dress, mother-of-pearl button and belt buckle in back, painted black boots and white knee socks, cross-stitched Hitty on bodice of petticoat, initial appliqué on bodice of dress, 2001, $325.00. *Courtesy Judy Brown.*

6¼" carved wood Hitty, handmade by Janci, black carved and painted hair, painted features, jointed arms and legs, painted shoes, dressed in fancy bridal gown with coral necklace, circa 2001, $395.00. *Courtesy Jill Sanders.*

6¼" wooden Albuquerque Hitty with "Hitty, an American Travel Doll" video, designed by Judy Brown with small cloth doll, produced in the Orient; dressed in her Navajo costume, she traveled to New Mexico to participate in the 2000 Sante Fe Doll Art Show, circa 2000, $185.00. *Courtesy Judy Brown.*

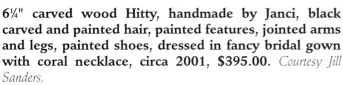

6¼" birchwood Hitty, handmade by Judy Brown, with painted features, jointed arms and legs for independent movement, gingham Western shirt and fringed denim skirt, carved and painted cowgirl boots, 2000, $425.00. *Courtesy Judy Brown.*

Horsman Dolls

Horsman was founded by Edward Imeson Horsman in New York City in 1865. The E.I. Horsman Company distributed, assembled, and made dolls, and in 1909 obtained its first copyright for a complete doll, "Billiken." Horsman later made hard plastic and vinyl dolls, many of which are unmarked; some have only a number or they may be marked Horsman. *Judd's* reports that painted inset pins on the doll's walking mechanism are one means of identification of these hard plastic dolls. Some of the hard plastic dolls had either a child or fashion type body.

What to look for:

Composition dolls should have minimal crazing, rosy cheeks, original clothing, and labels or tags when possible. Great characters like the Campbell Kids are always charming. Later dolls should be much more perfect and all original. This company offers a nifty collecting niche; collectors may find bargains, since Horsman's later dolls have not been as popular.

19" composition "Gold Medal Baby," tagged "GOLD//MEDAL//Baby//HORSMAN//SUPER QUALITY," blonde wig, blue sleep eyes, real lashes, painted lower lashes, eyeshadow, open mouth with teeth, tilting turning head, jointed toddler body, blue dotted Swiss dress, white coat and matching hat, white socks and white baby shoes, with Horsman box, circa 1939 – 1940, $300.00. *Courtesy Sandra Tripp.*

15" composition Horsman Toddler marked "E.I.H.//Co." on back, socket head, mohair wig, brown sleep eyes, single stroke brows, painted upper and lower lashes, jointed composition toddler body with straight wrists and diagonal hip joints, white organdy dress with lace trim, underclothing, socks, high-button boots, deep crazing on upper arms, circa 1930s – 1940s, $65.00.
Courtesy McMasters Doll Auctions.

10½" hard plastic Horsman "Cindy," blonde rooted hair, sleep eyes, closed mouth, pierced ears, painted fingernails and toenails, red and white check shirt, blue jeans with red and white check cuffs, mint-in-box, circa 1950s, $125.00.
Courtesy Sharon Kolibaba.

Mary Hoyer Dolls

Mary Sensenig Hoyer was born October 21, 1901, in Lancaster County, Pennsylvania, to Sallie Whitman and Daniel Sensenig, the youngest of 14 children. Her father had a general store and post office in Lancaster, but moved when Mary was six months of age to Mohnton, Pennsylvania, where her father again ran a store. When she was seven years old, the family moved to Reading, Pennsylvania, and she has lived in this area ever since. Her oldest sister, Alice, who did piece work and made cotton sunbonnets with brims of real straw, influenced her.

At age eight, Mary was hospitalized with appendicitis, and Alice told her to hurry and get well and she would buy Mary a beautiful doll. When she left the hospital, she went home to Alice's house, and the doll was waiting for her. Mary remembers the doll being the most beautiful doll she had ever seen. It had a bisque head with long, golden, finger curls of human hair, blue eyes, and a smiling mouth with little teeth. The doll was made in Germany, had a jointed body, and wore a dress Alice had made of blue China silk.

While Mary was recovering, Alice taught her how to knit and crochet and do some simple sewing. Alice eventually opened a store selling yarn, needles, and other related sewing items. Mary, at age 18, attended McCanns Business School and later worked for Alice, designing and writing knitting instructions.

Mary met William Hoyer in 1923, and they married in 1926, driving to their first home in Canada in 1926 in a Model T. The honeymooners lived in an apartment until they could build a house nearby in Springmont where daughter Arlene was born.

Mary's career began as a designer of knitted and crocheted fashions for children and babies. It seemed a natural outgrowth to extend her talents to designing fashions for children's dolls. She first made clothes for her daughter Arlene's doll, a 14" heavy composition of unknown maker. Mary soon began dreaming about having an artist make a doll to her own specifications, 14" tall and shaped like a little girl. She first used 13" dolls from Ideal Novelty and Toy Company. Her idea was to sell the undressed doll with accompanying instruction booklet with patterns for knit and crochet outfits.

About 2,000 of these unmarked Ideal 13" jointed composition dolls were sold before this model was discontinued by Ideal. They had sleep eyes and mohair wigs that came in three different shades, blonde, dark brown, and auburn. The composition bodies had a segmented torso joint just below the arms. The undressed doll sold for $1.50 or dressed for $3.00.

In late 1937 Mary met with doll sculptor Bernard Lipfert who had already designed Patsy, Shirley Temple, the Dionne Quintuplets, Ginny, and many other dolls. She said he did not want to sculpt the doll she wanted, but after some conversation and a glass of wine, they came to an agreement. The Fiberoid Doll Company in New York produced the Mary Hoyer doll, but Mary retained ownership of the molds. She estimates approximately 6,500 of the composition dolls were made before production was discontinued in 1946. The molds were later sold without the company's knowledge to someone in South America.

Mary Hoyer dolls were unmarked and had painted eyes, with mohair wigs in four shades. The next 5,000 dolls were incised with the mark "THE//MARY HOYER//DOLL." As soon as sleep eyes were available for the composition dolls, they were used, but painted eyes were used first.

With World War II and the use of plastic for the war effort, hard plastic became a popular material for use in dolls. It was new; it was different; it was *modern*! And it appealed to mothers and children. Hoyer began using this material on the new dolls. They were also 14" tall, had a walking mechanism, and were marked in a circle on the back, "ORIGINAL//MARY HOYER//DOLL." The walker body proved troublesome and was removed, leaving those models with two slits in the head.

A variation was introduced in 1950, an 18" Mary Hoyer named "Gigi" with the same hard plastic mark as the 14" dolls. The Frisch Doll Company made only about 2,000 of these dolls, and they never gained the popularity of the 14" dolls.

Another variant made in the middle 1950s by Ideal had a vinyl head, rooted hair in a ponytail, and high-heeled feet. This doll was discontinued after only one shipment was made. She originally sold for $6.95.

Mary placed ads in *McCall's Needlework and Crafts* magazine and by 1945, Mr. Hoyer quit his job as purchasing agent for Berkshire Knitting Mills to spend full-time managing the mail order business, opening a plant and shipping department. Mary also had a retail shop on Penn Street in Reading and another on the Boardwalk in Ocean City, New Jersey, where granddaughter Mary Lynne Sanders remembers playing under the Boardwalk in the summer as a little girl.

Another variation was the all-vinyl "Vicky" doll made in 1957 for Hoyer by Ideal. She came in three sizes, 10½", 12", and 14". The two larger sizes were discontinued, and only the 10½" was produced for any length of time. She was described as having a body that bent at the waist, sleep eyes, and rooted Saran hair and was a high-heeled doll. She came wearing a bra and panties, high-heeled shoes, and earrings.

The next year, 1958, the Unique Doll Company made Margie, an all-vinyl 10" toddler, with rooted hair and sleep eyes for Hoyer. In 1961 Hoyer added a 10" Cathy, an all-vinyl infant made by the same company. Next came an 8" vinyl baby, Janie. Hoyer continued her main marketing thrust with knitted and crocheted patterns, kits, and dressed dolls that came to be her trademark in the doll world as well as her custom-made costumes sold mail order and those sold in retail shops. The labels read "Mary Hoyer//Reading//PA."

In 1960, the Fiberoid Doll Company folded after producing approximately 72,000 of the 14" hard plastic dolls, Mary Hoyer's personal favorite of all her dolls. Hoyer next had the 14" doll copied in vinyl, with rooted hair and some face changes. She was called "Becky." Becky had long straight, curly or upswept hairstyles. The hair could be combed, washed, and set and came in four shades. The Becky doll was unmarked and was discontinued in 1968.

Granddaughter Mary Lynne Saunders continued the Mary Hoyer Doll Company in the 1980s with a vinyl play doll and characters from a fairy tale, "The Doll with the Magic Wand," written by Mary Hoyer. Her 1990s dolls are now more of a basic play doll with a variety of eye colors, hairstyles, and wardrobes. Some of the more intriguing pieces available include hiking boots, shorts, camping gear, and realistic accessories for the modern girls of today. The dolls, clothing, and accessories are forever popular.

A delightful, talented lady who turned her designing talents into a wonderful career, Mary Hoyer has given the doll world a treat with her designs, dolls, and patterns that will carry on for generations. The Mary Hoyer Doll Company and mail order business is still thriving: Mary Hoyer Doll Company, PO Box 1608, Lancaster, PA 17603, (717) 393-4121.

What to look for:

One of the hot collectible dolls has been the 18" hard plastic "Gigi" with the round Mary Hoyer mark on her back. Prices are high for dolls with original clothing in excellent condition. Mary Hoyer dolls are a great delight for knitters who can use all the patterns in Mary Hoyer pattern books that have been reissued. Mary Hoyer dolls are a great collectible to look for in composition and hard plastic, but do not pass up the new ones produced by the family business headed by Mary's granddaughter. Look for rosy cheeks, little crazing if composition, clean hard plastic, and original outfits when possible.

13" composition Mary Hoyer Skater, unmarked, blonde wig, sleep eyes, closed mouth, jointed composition body with twist waist, undressed to show body construction, crocheted skating outfit, white skates, circa pre-1937, $325.00. *Private collection.*

14" hard plastic Mary Hoyer, marked "Original Mary// Hoyer Doll" in circle, brown synthetic wig, blue sleep eyes, closed mouth, wearing cowgirl outfit, red shirt, brown skirt with fringe, vest, holster, brown hat, boots, also with wardrobe of 7 handmade outfit including commercially made roller skates, ice skates, dress shoes, bedroom slippers, etc., circa 1940s – 1950, $425.00. *Private collection.*

14" hard plastic Mary Hoyer doll, marked "Original//Mary Hoyer// Doll" in circle on back, blue sleep eyes, real lashes, dark eyeshadow, single stroke brows, painted lower lashes, closed mouth, original wig, five-piece hard plastic body, mauve knit outfit made from Mary Hoyer pattern, rayon socks, white leatherette center-snap shoes, first-place ribbon from 1953 show for Best Dressed doll, circa mid 1940s to 1950s, $335.00. *Courtesy McMasters Doll Auctions.*

14" hard plastic Mary Hoyer Doll, brown mohair wig, blue sleep eyes, closed mouth, rosy cheeks, jointed hard plastic body, aqua knitted skirt, matching hat, cream knitted sweater, white skates, mint-in-box, circa 1947 – 1950s, $695.00. *Courtesy Rita Mauze.*

14" hard plastic Mary Hoyer Doll, brown mohair wig, blue sleep eyes, closed mouth, rosy cheeks, jointed hard plastic body, cream formal with trim, pearl necklace, straw hat, mint-in-box, circa 1947 – 1950s, $850.00. *Courtesy Rita Mauze.*

Ideal Dolls

The Ideal Novelty and Toy Co., begun 1906 in Brooklyn, New York, produced their own composition dolls in their early years. Morris Michtom started the business by making "Teddy" bears in 1906 with his wife, Rose, after the incident in which President Teddy Roosevelt refused to shoot a bear cub during a hunting expedition. Michtom also began making composition "unbreakable" dolls about this time. His early comic characters were popular, and Ideal also produced licensed dolls for companies to help promote their products such as "Uneeda Kid" that carried a small box of crackers for the Uneeda Biscuit Company. Some of their big successes were Shirley Temple in composition, Saucy Walker and Toni in hard plastic, and Miss Revlon in vinyl. They also made dolls of cloth and rubber.

Marks: Various including IDEAL in a diamond; US of A; IDEAL Novelty and Toy Co., Brooklyn, New York, and others.

What to look for:

Look for dolls with minimal crazing in composition, good color, and original clothing. Hard plastic and vinyl dolls should be better, with very good color, clean, bright, and perhaps tagged original clothing. A wide variety of Ideal dolls are available since they were in business into the 1990s.

12" composition Fanny Brice as "Baby Snooks" and "Mortimer Snerd," Edgar Bergen's radio show dummy, marked "Ideal Doll" on back of head, character heads, painted blue eyes, open closed mouths with painted teeth, molded painted hair (molded loop for bow in Fanny's hair), wooden torso, flexy metal cable arms and legs, composition hands, wooden feet, both in original clothing, circa 1938, $405.00. *Courtesy McMasters Doll Auctions.*

13" composition "Snow White," marked "Shirley Temple//13" on back, tagged "Rayon//An Ideal Doll" on dress, original black mohair wig, green sleep eyes, real lashes, eyeshadow, painted lower lashes, single stroke brows, open mouth, six upper teeth, chin dimple, five-piece composition body, original dress with red velvet bodice, rayon skirt with red figures of Seven Dwarfs, red velvet cape, underclothing, socks and shoes, circa 1938, $300.00. *Courtesy McMasters Doll Auctions.*

12" vinyl "Tiny Pebbles," marked "©HANNA-BARBERA PRODUC-TIONS, INC.," rooted Saran hair with topknot and bone, painted side-glancing blue eyes, open/closed mouth, jointed vinyl body, leopard print outfit, circa 1964 – 1966, $75.00. *Courtesy Karen McCarthy.*

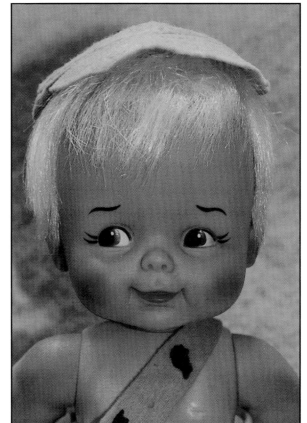

12" vinyl "Tiny Bamm-Bamm," marked "©HANNA-BAR-BERA PRODUC-TIONS, INC.," rooted blonde Saran hair, painted side-glancing brown eyes, closed smiling mouth, jointed vinyl body, leopard skin suit and hat, blue club, circa 1964 – 1966, $75.00. *Courtesy Karen McCarthy.*

Ideal Dolls

15" hard plastic "Toni," marked "P-91//Ideal Dolls//Made in U.S.A." on head, "Ideal Doll//P-91" on back, platinum blonde hair, blue sleep eyes, real lashes, eyeshadow, painted lower lashes, closed mouth, five-piece hard plastic body, tagged dress, attached slip, original socks/center-snap shoes, red metal trunk with additional wardrobe, circa 1949, $355.00. *Courtesy McMasters Doll Auctions.*

Left: 14" hard plastic "Toni" marked "P-90//Ideal Doll//Made in U.S.A." on head, "Ideal Doll//P-90" on back, original wig, blue sleep eyes, real lashes, painted lower lashes, single stroke brows, closed mouth, five-piece hard plastic body, original dress with yellow dotted Swiss bodice and sleeves, red skirt, both trimmed with embroidered trim, attached slip, matching panties, replaced rayon socks, center-snap shoes, circa 1949 – 1953, $200.00. *Courtesy McMasters Doll Auctions.*

Right: 15" hard plastic Ideal Toni, marked P-91//Ideal Doll//Made in U.S.A. on head, Ideal Doll//P-91 on back, original wig, sleep eyes, real lashes, painted lower lashes, single stroke brows, closed mouth, five-piece hard plastic body, red and yellow piqué dress with embroidery trim tagged Genuine Toni Doll//with nylon wig//Made by Ideal Novelty & Toy Co., attached half-slip, red center-snap shoes, circa 1949 – 1953, $235.00. *Courtesy McMasters Doll Auctions.*

Kenner Dolls

The "Star Wars" movie was made in 1977, and the sequel, "The Empire Strikes Back," in 1980. Kenner made large Star Wars figures in 1978 in Hong Kong, ranging in heights from 7" to 15" including Princess Leia Organa, Luke Skywalker, R2-D2, Chewbacca, Darth Vader, and C-3P0. In 1979 Boba Fett, Han Solo, Stormtrooper, Ben (Obi-Wan) Kenobi, Jawa, and IG-88 were added. They also made 3" – 4" figures starting in 1979.

What to look for:

Kenner has made a variety of modern character dolls, such as "Bob Scout" with a Boy Scout uniform and accessories, sports figures, and fashion type dolls. Look for a boxed all-original doll, clean with good color. Star War figures are more popular with toy collectors, but always collectible, as are celebrities such as the Six Million Dollar Man figures. Look for them at garage sales, flea markets, and estate sales.

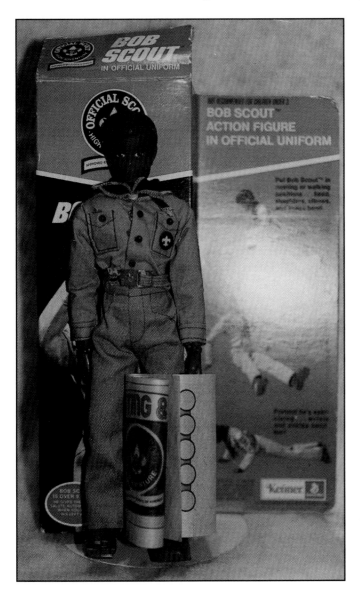

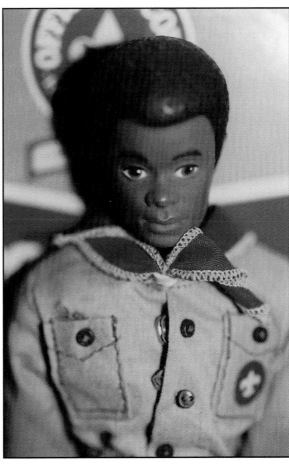

9" vinyl black "Bob Scout," molded painted black hair, painted eyes, molded painted features, fully articulated vinyl body, wearing replica of genuine Boy Scouts of America uniform, in original box with Scout comic book, approved by the Boy Scouts of America, circa 1974, $75.00. *Courtesy Joan Radke.*

Klumpe Dolls

Klumpe is known for caricature figures made of felt-over-wire armature with painted mask faces, produced in Barcelona, Spain, from about 1952 to the mid 1970s. Figures represent professionals, hobbyists, Spanish dancers, historical characters, and contemporary males and females performing a wide variety of tasks. Of the 200 or more different figures, the most common are Spanish dancers, bullfighters, and doctors. Some Klumpes were imported by Effanbee in the early 1950s. Originally the figures had two sewn-on identifying cardboard tags.

What to look for:

These amusing characters may be missing their tags but are still very collectible. Often passed over by more sophisticated collectors, they can still be found for reasonable prices. Look for those with more accessories, tags, or labels. They should be clean, with bright colors. The more intricate the costume and accessories, the more desirable they are to collectors. Must be pristine with all labels to command highest prices. Keep on the lookout at estate sales, antique malls, flea markets, and doll shows for these.

10½" cloth Klumpe girl, felt-over-wire armature with painted mask face, holding umbrella in one hand, yellow basket in other, scarf hat, circa 1952 – 1970s, $175.00. *Courtesy Betty Strong.*

Lenci Dolls

Elena von Konig Scavini was born in Italy in 1886, and after the loss of her firstborn child, she started making cuddly dolls. She called the dolls Lencina or Little Lenci. Her dolls were used as decorative accessories in bedrooms and cars and were carried with designer costumes. Early dolls were characters, tagged with a small Lenci button. Some of the most intricate were made during the 1920s, and this era is noted for rooted hair, hand embroidery, and pieced felt costumes with felt flowers. The American stock market crash threw the company into bankruptcy, and the company was taken over by Pilade Garella who narrowed the product line from clothing, costumes, ceramics, furniture, and handbags to only dolls. The 1930s dolls were simpler with fewer styles. Mascottes (7½") and miniature (9") dolls in regional and nursery rhyme costumes and children's clothes were heavily produced and promoted. Glass flirty eyes were added in 1935. Baby dolls were introduced in the 1930s with two face models but were not popular. Boudoir dolls with elongated arms and legs dressed as celebrities were very popular and were made throughout the company's history. By 1940, Madame Lenci had lost her husband, Enrico, sold her remaining shares, and severed all ties to the Lenci Company. In the 1940s, Lenci quality diminished as production was needed for wartime necessities. In 1942, Beppe Garella, Pilade's son, came into the business, becoming president after his father's death in 1968. In the 1950s, the

Lenci dolls popularity again slowed, and the company made dolls of other materials. In 1978, the company again started making felt dolls, a profitable move. Madame Lenci died in 1974; in 1993, Beppe Garella died; his daughter Bibija now runs the company.

What to look for:

Lenci dolls are made of felt, with double-layer ears and scalloped cotton socks. Early dolls can have rooted mohair wigs, 1930s dolls, may have frizzed played-with looking wigs, and 1940s dolls may have hard cardboard type felt faces. Value depends on condition such as cleanliness, originality, wear, and costumes that are more elaborate.

5½" Lenci "Tea Cozy," advertising "Ye Old Tyme Comfort Shoes" printed on yellow felt apron, painted side-glancing surprise eyes, padded blue felt dress to accommodate a teapot, felt kerchief on her head, no legs, circa 1920s – 1930s, **$400.00.** *Courtesy Nancy Lazenby.*

Lenci Dolls

8½" Lenci Mascotte, marked on bottom of both feet, pressed felt swivel head, red mohair wig in braids, painted brown "surprise" eyes to side, single stroke brows, painted upper lashes, open/closed two-tone mouth, cloth body with felt arms and legs, blue/white polka dot nylon dress with white felt collar and red felt belt, one-piece underwear, red felt sandals, all original, circa 1920s, $150.00. *Courtesy McMasters Doll Auctions.*

10" Lenci boy and 9" girl, marked "Lenci//Torino//Made in Italy" on clothing, "Ungherese" on paper wrist tag of boy, both with pressed felt swivel heads, painted eyes to side, single stroke brows, painted upper lashes, open/closed mouth, applied ears, cloth body, felt arms; boy has felt hair, dressed in felt and cotton regional clothing, girl has mohair wig, dressed in black check silk skirt, red felt cape and bonnet trimmed with fur, circa 1930s, $225.00 pair. *Courtesy McMasters Doll Auctions.*

38" Lenci "Mannequin," marked "Lenci//Turin Italy" on torso, "Kirsh & Reale Inc.//167 Madison Ave.//New York-City" on metal plate, pressed felt swivel head, painted brown side-glancing eyes, closed mouth, applied ears, mohair rooted into felt for hair, felt-covered wooden torso, felt-covered metal or wooden arms/legs, wooden balls from torso and legs pivot for posing, antique shirt, checkered two-piece suit with short pants, circa 1920s, $1,650.00. *Courtesy McMasters Doll Auctions.*

9" Lenci Dutch Boy, blonde hair, surprise eyes, surprise O-shaped mouth, molded/pressed face, black felt jacket, red felt shirt, green and blue felt pants, wooden shoes, circa 1930s, $375.00. *Courtesy Nancy Lazenby.*

14" Lenci-type "Marga Doll," cloth knit body, painted blue side-glancing eyes, closed mouth, auburn wig, elaborate costume, matching hat, knitted socks with flower trim, black shoes, white slip and pantaloons, circa 1930s, $900.00. *Courtesy Nancy Lazenby.*

Monica Dolls

Monica was the creation of Mrs. Hansi Share, owner of the Monica Doll Studios of Hollywood, California, who first advertised her dolls in 1941. Early dolls were 20" and 24" sizes.

In 1947, *Toys and Novelties,* a toy trade publication, advertised 15", 17", and 20" sizes. Individual dolls had names like Veronica, Jean, and Rosalind and later in hard plastic, Elizabeth, Marion, or Linda were offered by high-end stores such as F.A.O. Schwarz and Neiman Marcus. In October 1949 Monica Doll Studios announced the arrival of an all-plastic Marion with rooted hair and sleep eyes.

What was remarkable about this doll from the beginning is the ingenious idea of rooting human hair first in the composition head and then later in the hard plastic one. If any of you endured the 1960s and 1970s era indulging in the tortuous beauty shop treatment of "frosting" your own hair, this is a similar process in reverse. In the beauty shop treatment, a plastic hood was placed over the patron's hair, and the hairdresser pulled the strands of hair through the plastic cap and applied bleach to lighten the hair which gave a "frosted" appearance. Beauty hurt in those days, as the hair was pulled through the tiny holes; fortunately Monica did not have to feel the pain of having hair poked into her composition head.

Mrs. Share managed to come up with a process to place small portions of fragile human hair in the composition and plastic heads during the manufacturing process to give the appearance of "real rooted" hair. Other companies such as American Character fashioned a rooted hair skullcap on Sweet Sue and their 8" Betsy McCall as they tried to adapt this unique patented feature. Hair rooted into the head became an accepted practice with the use of vinyl for making dolls in the 1960s. The Monica Doll Company made dolls until 1952.

The Monica line of dolls is also interesting because it typifies the re-entry of fashion dolls into the world of dolls. A Patsy-type doll of the 1930s such as Patsy and Shirley Temple had an early child-like all-composition body with a pudgy body. In 1935, Effanbee introduced the Patricia line and advertised them as an older sister of about 12 years of age with just the hint of breasts. In 1940, Effanbee showed "Little Lady" dolls still with an older child body, but wearing sophisticated negligees over panties and bras.

Monica dolls in 1941 had all-composition unmarked bodies with flat feet, and the arms and hands seem somewhat heavy and awkward in contrast to the sophistication of the hair, makeup, and facial features. Monica dolls had painted eyes, eyeshadow, a closed mouth, rosy cheeks, and most important, the unique rooted human hair feature. All of this makes the composition dolls dramatic and appealing. In the hard plastic medium, Monica is not as striking because the features become softened. The dramatic look given by the painted eyes diminishes with sleep eyes. These dolls had sophisticated wardrobes and came dressed in fancy short dresses, suits, long evening dresses, or bridal gowns. Additional costumes were available separately. Neiman Marcus's 1945 Christmas catalog featured Monica with a white peasant blouse, red peasant skirt and bolero, fruit-trimmed hat, and black ballerina slippers. Montgomery Ward's 1947 catalog pictures an all-composition Monica in net dress with ruffles, rayon underskirt, rayon panties, and long stockings, and her rooted human hair wig next to an Effanbee doll costumed in transparent black rayon marquisette negligee with matching bra and panties.

Monica, appearing first in composition and making the transition to hard plastic, is an example of a doll that spans the gap from the 1930 child dolls to the more glamorous dolls of the 1950s. She has the same mystique as today's Gene dolls with her sophisticated Hollywood glamour make-up. Her short life, unique features, and Hollywood presence make her an interesting and desirable collectible.

What to look for:

Two identification tips are the rooted hair and painted eyes, although she was later made with sleep eyes. Try to find Monica with great hair and costumes; hard to find is the 11½" size.

11" composition Monica Studios "Monica" is unmarked with rooted human hair, painted eyes, dark eyeliner above eyes, an uncommon rare size, circa 1941 – 1949, $550.00+.
Courtesy Judith Johnson.

20" all composition Monica Studios "Monica" is unmarked and identified by her unusual rooted human hair into composition, painted blue eyes, dark eyeliner above eyes, mauve eyeshadow, soft rosy cheeks, long white charmeuse gown, circa 1941 – 1949, $500.00.
Courtesy Michele Newby.

20" all composition Monica Studios "Monica," rooted human hair wig with center part, painted blue eyes, dark eyeliner above eyes, eyeshadow, soft rosy cheeks, closed mouth, jointed five-piece composition body, pink dress with white organdy sleeves and apron, black shoes, circa 1941 – 1949, $325.00.
Private collection.

Nancy Ann Storybook Dolls

Nancy Ann Storybook Dolls was started in 1936 in San Francisco, California, by Rowena Haskin (Nancy Ann Abbott). The dolls were painted bisque with mohair wigs, painted eyes, head molded to torso, jointed limbs, either with a sticker on the outfit or a hang tag. Later they made an 8" hard plastic Muffie and hard plastic Miss Nancy Ann Style Show, 18", then made 11" Debbie with vinyl head and hard plastic body, and Lori Ann at 7½" with vinyl head and hard plastic body. The company also made vinyl high-heel fashion type dolls in the late 1950s and 1960s, Miss Nancy Ann, 10½", and Little Miss Nancy Ann.

What to look for:

The newer the doll, the more complete and mint it should be. That is what collectors are looking for. In competition, the older, rarer, more mint, original, beautiful doll is the one that catches the judge's eyes. That leaves a lot of dolls, played-with, soiled or with faded clothing or missing accessories dolls that are still collectible, and perhaps you can salvage some great dolls that others have skipped over. You can certainly find enough to collect, but always look for the one with more intricate costume, prettier coloring, and original clothing, tags or labels, or those in boxes.

3½" painted bisque Nancy Ann Storybook baby, marked "Story//Book//Doll//USA," painted hair, painted eyes, closed mouth, fist hands, long white dress, circa 1938+, $200.00. *Courtesy Barbara Hull.*

5½" painted bisque Nancy Ann Storybook, marked "Story//Book//Dolls//USA" on back, painted eyes, closed mouth, red mohair wig, long yellow flower print dress with black lace, straw hat, circa 1941+, $50.00. *Courtesy Barbara Hull.*

4½" painted bisque Nancy Ann Storybook "Bride," marked "Storybook//Dolls//USA// Trademark" on back, painted eyes, closed mouth, blonde mohair wig, one-piece bisque body with head and jointed arms, white dress with lace and net overskirt, net veil with gold crown, circa 1943 – 1947, $50.00. *Courtesy Barbara Hull.*

5½" painted bisque Nancy Ann Storybook "Autumn," #92 from the Season's Series, auburn mohair wig, painted eyes, one-piece head, body and legs, long yellow dress with net skirt overlay, silver label, white box with red polka dots, circa 1943 – 1947, $45.00. *Private collection.*

5½" painted bisque Nancy Ann Storybook "Wednesday's Child, Full of Woe," #182, brunette mohair wig, painted eyes, one-piece head, body, and legs, long white dress with red print and red ribbon trim, silver label, white box with red polka dots, circa 1943 – 1947, $55.00. *Private collection.*

5½" painted bisque Nancy Ann Storybook "One, Two, Button My Shoe," #113, auburn wig, painted eyes, one-piece head, body, and legs, in green plaid dress, painted black boots, in white box with red polka dots, silver label, circa 1943 – 1947, $55.00. *Private collection.*

Nancy Ann Storybook Dolls

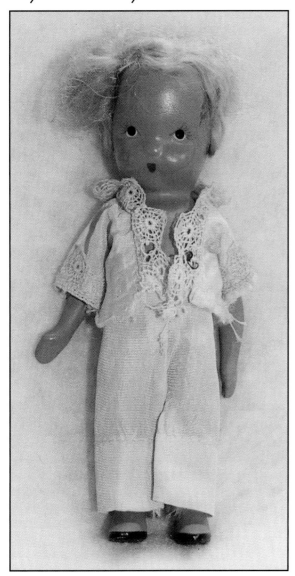

5¼" painted bisque Nancy Ann Storybook "Ring Bearer," marked "Story//Book//Doll// USA" on back, painted eyes, closed mouth, reddish blonde mohair wig, one-piece bisque body with jointed arms, ivory shirt with lace and ivory pants, circa 1939+, $25.00.
Courtesy Barbara Hull.

5½" painted bisque Nancy Ann Storybook "Thursday's Child Has Far to Go," #183, red wig, painted eyes, one-piece head, body, and legs, silver label, gold foil wrist tag, white box with red polka dots, long yellow dress with black lace trim, circa 1943 – 1947, $55.00.
Private collection.

18" hard plastic Nancy Ann Style Show, brown synthetic wig in original set, blue sleep eyes, jointed hard plastic and rigid vinyl body, full lace white formal with white satin shoes, hair bows, mauve sash with pin, circa 1952 – 1955, $795.00. *Courtesy Rita Mauze.*

18" hard plastic Nancy Ann Style Show, brown synthetic wig in original set, blue sleep eyes, hard plastic body, original gold plaid dress with orange trim, matching straw hat with adornment, circa 1952 – 1955, $595.00. *Courtesy Rita Mauze.*

8" hard plastic Nancy Ann Storybook "Muffie," marked "Storybook Dolls//California//MUFFIE," blonde Saran wig, sleep eyes, painted lashes, closed mouth, hard plastic body, with box and boxed outfit, box marked "Muffie//Undressed//#500," circa 1953 – 1956, $395.00. *Courtesy McMasters Doll Auctions.*

Nurse Dolls

Some sources believe that as long ago as 4000 BC, temples were used as hospitals and as training schools for doctors. Primarily, the care of the sick fell to religious groups. Usually there was no formal training; apprentices learned from experienced nurses and in turn, passed on their training to others. There was little or no classroom work. Nurses provided low-cost service to institutions and then worked in private homes or agencies. By 1836, some schools for training nurses were founded in Germany, and in Kaiserswerth one of their pupils was Florence Nightingale. Nightingale was appalled at the lack of sanitation and poorly trained and supervised nurses. When the Crimean War broke out in 1854, she volunteered and organized nurses and provided skilled care during this crisis, significantly dropping the mortality rate among the sick and wounded. At the close of the war in 1860, she founded a nursing school in London, marking the beginning of professional education in nursing.

About this time, a Swiss philanthropist, Jean Henri Dunant, organized world leaders to found societies to care for the wounded in wartime. At a conference in 1864, officials of 12 nations signed the first Geneva Convention specifying rules of treatment for wounded and protection of medical personnel. A symbol of this movement was adopted at this time — a white flag with a red cross. The organization became known as the Red Cross, an international humanitarian agency that alleviates suffering during wars and major disasters and performs other public service. Clara Barton founded the American Red Cross in 1881. Barton was called the "Angel of the Battle" for setting up a supply service during the Civil War, nursing the wounded, and searching for the missing. Congress chartered the Red Cross in 1900.

Little has been documented about nurse dolls as a specific category, but they do rate two pages in *Coleman's Collectors Encyclopedia of Dolls, Vol. II*. Coleman's cites specific nurse dolls as early as 1885. Certainly world events played a role in the popularity of nurse dolls. Before 1900, a nurse was most often portrayed as a nanny who took care of a baby or child. With the advent of World War I, however, dolls with the familiar Red Cross emblem on their costume were seen. In 1934, the birth of the Dionne Quintuplets revived the image of the nurse helping Dr. Dafoe with the quintuplets. Alexander was granted the license to produce the official Dionne Quintuplets. Freundlich and others jumped on the bandwagon with unlicensed quintuplets and nurse sets. World War II again brought dolls dressed in the image of a nurse in a white uniform, blue cape lined with red, and a white cap. They were produced by a variety of manufacturers.

Mattel promoted a television character, Julia, as a nurse, a Barbie-type, circa 1969 – 1971. Still later, Hasbro's military G.I. Joe also had a plastic 10½" GI Action Girl in 1967, authentically outfitted in a white hospital uniform and Red Cross hat with an accessories pack with crutches, bandages, stethoscope, plasma bottle, and more. Nurses as a collectible provide an interesting avenue to pursue and can be a niche category that may be overlooked. The scope and range of this can be as broad or as narrow as you make it.

What to look for:

Both antique and modern dolls can be found. An average day on eBay will find over 100 collectibles listed in the "Nurse" category. The more modern the doll, the more complete it has to be, including all accessories, to be more valuable. Look for costuming that has added details and for dolls that are always clean, bright, tagged, boxed or labeled.

8" hard plastic A&H Doll Co. "Julie," blonde hair, blue sleep eyes, real lashes, closed mouth, jointed hard plastic body, in nurse uniform, box reads "I AM//JULIE//IWALK*I SIT*I SLEEP//DRESS ME//CURL MY HAIR," all original with box, circa 1950s, $100.00. *Courtesy Joan Radke.*

8" hard plastic Elite "Vicki Nurse," synthetic wig, blue sleep eyes, closed mouth, jointed hard plastic body, nurse outfit with hat, socks and shoes, box says "The Walking Doll," mint-in-box, circa 1950s, $95.00. *Courtesy Rita Mauze.*

Old Cottage Toys

This firm was founded around 1948 by Mrs. Margaret E. Fleischmann who fled her native Czechoslovakia to England during the war years. Mrs. Fleischmann first made dolls for her daughter Suzanne and later for sale. The heads are made of a hard composition/hard plastic type material, with bodies of felt-over-padded-wire armature. The features are molded and painted, with mohair wigs. Fleischmann registered her trademark in 1948, and the dolls have an oval paper hang tag with a cottage pictured on one side and marked "Old Cottage Doll Made in England" on the other. They made historical figures, literary figures, English policemen, guards, and pearly figures. In 1968 she made Tweedledee and Tweedledum for a B.B.C. production of Lewis Carroll's "Through the Looking-Glass."

What to look for:

This category of dolls is currently sought-after, very collectible, and rising in value. Most desired are the literary characters, pearly dolls, and dolls with added detail. Lucky you to find Tweedledee or Tweedledum in a box at a sale or shop. Dolls should be clean, tagged, and original to command highest prices.

9" composition "Elizabethan Lady," royalty, dark hair up in curls, painted features, blue eyes, closed smiling mouth, cloth body, molded hands, bell-shaped purple brocade gown, matching hat, white ruffle around neck, necklace, circa 1950+, $175.00. *Courtesy Dorothy Bohlin.*

7½" composition blonde wig, painted features, blue eyes, closed mouth, cloth body, mitt hands, long red velvet dress with gold trim, matching hat, white ruffle at neck, circa 1950+, $125.00+. *Courtesy Dorothy Bohlin.*

8" composition "Elizabethan Boy," brown hair, painted features, blue eyes, closed mouth, cloth body, mitt hands, black felt jacket, matching hat with red feather, red and gold short pants, red stockings, black shoes, circa 1950+, $125.00+. *Courtesy Dorothy Bohlin.*

9¾" composition "Geisha Girl," black mohair wig, painted features, slanted black eyes, closed smiling mouth, cloth body, molded hands, black with yellow flower print kimono, with Old Cottage Doll oval hang tag with house logo, all original with box, circa 1950+, $200.00. *Courtesy Dorothy Bohlin.*

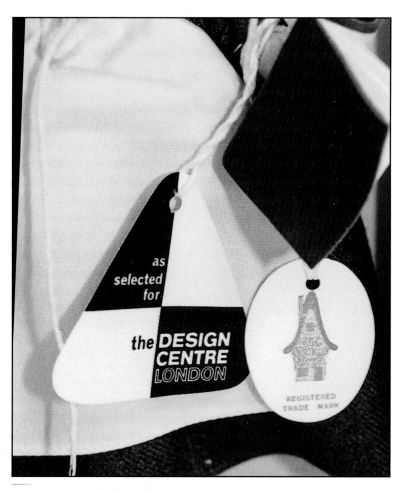

8¾" composition, brown mohair wig, painted features, blue eyes, closed mouth, cloth body, mitt hands, dark gray dress with white collar and apron, matching bonnet, holding book, "Old Cottage Toys" hang tag with house logo, all original with box, circa 1950+, $175.00. *Courtesy Dorothy Bohlin.*

9" composition, dark blonde hair, painted features, blue eyes, closed mouth, mitt hands, cloth body, flower print dress, matching shoes, white apron, white bonnet, holding spoon, hang tag, circa 1960+, $125.00+. *Courtesy Dorothy Bohlin.*

9" composition, brown hair in braids, painted features, blue eyes, closed mouth, mitt hands, cloth body, black felt dress, red felt shawl, red and white checked apron, white cap, black shoes with buckles, circa 1960+, $125.00+. *Courtesy Dorothy Bohlin.*

9" composition, blonde hair in braids, painted features, blue eyes, closed mouth, mitt hands, cloth body, red felt skirt, flower print apron, matching scarf in hair, white shirt, red felt shoes, hang tag with house logo, circa 1960+, $125.00+. *Courtesy Dorothy Bohlin.*

9" composition, blonde hair, painted features, blue eyes, closed mouth, cloth body, mitt hands, in lavender and white striped dress with white pinafore trimmed in lace and matching bonnet, carrying basket of flowers, black shoes, circa 1960+, $125.00+. *Courtesy Dorothy Bohlin.*

9" composition, blonde hair, painted features, blue eyes, closed mouth, mitt hands, cloth body, tan overdress, matching hat, pink/tan/white striped skirt, white shirt, black ribbon on dress and hat, black shoes, hang tag, circa 1960+, $125.00.
Courtesy Dorothy Bohlin.

9" composition, brown hair, painted features, blue eyes, closed mouth, cloth body, mitt hands, white dress trimmed with lace, blue ribbbon and parasol, matching bonnet, with box, circa 1960+, $125.00+.
Courtesy Dorothy Bohlin.

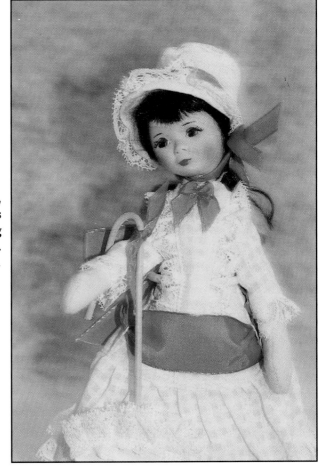

8½" hard plastic, blonde mohair wig in braids, painted features, blue eyes, closed mouth, cloth body, mitt hands, plaid dress, red cape with hood, white apron, red shoes, carrying basket, circa 1960+, $125.00+.
Courtesy Dorothy Bohlin.

8½" composition "Spring Girl," dark blonde mohair wig, painted features, blue eyes, closed mouth, cloth body, mitt hands, green flower print dress with white pinafore, purse, matching shoes, with "Old Cottage Toys" hang tag, all original with box marked "Spring Girl//in Kate Greenaway style//by//Old Cottage Toys//Made in England," circa 1950+, $175.00.
Courtesy Dorothy Bohlin.

8¾" composition, blonde mohair wig, painted features, blue eyes, closed mouth, cloth body, mitt hands, wine colored velvet coat, fur trimmed collar, cuffs, muff, matching fur trimmed hat, wine colored dotted Swiss dress, white pantaloons, leather shoes with buckle, missing hang tag, box, circa 1950+, $175.00. *Courtesy Dorothy Bohlin.*

8½" composition, brown hair in braids, painted features, brown side-glancing eyes, closed mouth, mitt hands, cloth body, white dress with flower print and red trim, red felt hat, red ribbons in hair, red shoes, circa 1960+, $125.00+. *Courtesy Dorothy Bohlin.*

9" composition boy, brown hair, painted features, blue eyes, closed mouth, cloth body, mitt hands, beige coat, brown hat, black pants, red socks, brown shoes with buckle, circa 1960+, $125.00+. *Courtesy Dorothy Bohlin.*

9½" hard plastic, blonde mohair wig in braids, painted features, blue eyes, closed mouth, cloth body, mitt hands, red plaid pants and top, white coat with hood, white shoes, red ribbons in hair, "Old Cottage Toys" hang tag with house logo, circa 1960+, $125.00+. *Courtesy Dorothy Bohlin.*

8½" composition "Girl," dark brown mohair wig, painted features, blue eyes, closed mouth, cloth body, mitt hands, red/white/green plaid dress, red shoes, straw hat, hang tags read "OLD COTTAGE TOYS//HANDMADE IN GREAT BRITAIN," and "as//selected//for//the DESIGN//CEN-TRE//LONDON," all original with box, circa 1950+, $165.00. *Courtesy Dorothy Bohlin.*

Old Cottage Toys

8" composition, blonde mohair wig, painted features, blue eyes, closed mouth, cloth body, mitt hands, yellow pajamas with mouse print, plush house-shoes, "Old Cottage Toys" hang tag, all original with box, circa 1950+, $125.00+. *Courtesy Dorothy Bohlin.*

9½" hard plastic, blonde mohair wig in braids, painted features, blue eyes, closed mouth, cloth body, mitt hands, navy blue jumper, matching hat, white shirt, red tie and belt, red ribbons in hair, white socks, black shoes, "Old Cottage Toys" hang tag with house logo, circa 1960+, $125.00+. *Courtesy Dorothy Bohlin.*

Raggedy Ann & Andy Dolls

Designed by Johnny Gruelle in 1915, the dolls have been made by various companies. Ann wears a dress with apron, and Andy, a shirt and pants with matching hat.

P.J. Volland, 1918 – 1919
Unmarked all cloth, shoe button eyes, skinny brown wool hair, crude hands and feet, no elbow or knee joints, cardboard heart in stuffed body.

P.J. Volland, 1920 – 1934, torso stamped "Patented Sept. 7, 1915"
All cloth, thick brown yarn hair, shoe button eyes, printed features with outlined nose, six eyelashes, crooked thin line smiling mouth, turned-out feet, oversize hands, cardboard heart inside body, striped legs go only to knee.

P.J. Volland, 1920 – 1930
Had only one eyelash, smile had red center, bold triangular eyebrows, no patent stamp. **After 1931**, has arched eyebrows, four eyelashes.

Exposition Doll & Toy Mfg. Co., 1935
Made Raggedy Ann only, produced less than one year, no marks on doll, dress tagged, printed features with pie-cut eyes, red wool hair, no eyebrows or lashes, smile has no red center, toes point forward, stripes to hip, rump designated by darts, oversize hands. This is the rarest of Raggedy Anns.

Molly-'es Doll Outfitters, Mollye Goldman, 1934 – 1937
Marked on chest, "Raggedy Ann and Andy Dolls//Manufactured by Molly'es Doll Outfitters," red yarn wig, printed side-glancing eyes, long outlined nose, red center in smile, three eyelashes, jointed elbows, jointed knees, multicolored striped legs to hips, blue shoes point forward, red printed heart.

Mollye Goldman, 1935 – 1938
Marked on chest: "Raggedy Ann and Andy Dolls Manufactured by Mollye's Doll Outfitters." Nose outlined in black, red heart on chest, reddish orange hair, multicolored legs, blue feet, some have oilcloth faces.

Georgene Novelties, 1938 – 1962
Ann has orange hair and a topknot, six different mouth styles, early dolls had tin eyes, later plastic, six different noses, seams in middle of legs and arms to represent knees and elbows. Feet turn outward, red and white striped legs. All have hearts that read: "I love you" printed on chest. Tag sewn to left side seam, several variations, all say "Georgene Novelties, Inc."

Knickerbocker, 1962 – 1982
Printed features, hair color change from orange to red; there were five mouth and five eyelash variations, tags were located on clothing back or pant seam.

Applause Toy Company, 1981 – 83, Hasbro (Playskool) 1983+
Raggedy Ann storybooks and dolls remain a favorite with doll collectors. They too have a newsletter, *Rags,* devoted to collectors. See Collectors' Network for more information.

What to look for:
Dolls that are clean, no rips or tears, original clothing, tags, or labels. Raggedy Ann was so loved that many are too worn to collect, but they are still available and eagerly sought by collectors.

Raggedy Ann & Andy Dolls

16" cloth Volland Raggedy Ann, black shoebutton eyes, single stroke brows, painted lower lashes, red triangle nose, closed smiling mouth, brown yarn hair, wooden heart in left side of chest, mitten hands, red and white striped legs, brown cloth feet turned outward, original flower print dress and white apron, soil on face, circa 1915 – 1920, $750.00. *Courtesy Joan Sickler.*

22" cloth Georgene Averill "Raggedy Ann and Raggedy Andy," orange yarn hair, black plastic eyes, red triangle painted noses, smiling mouths, red and white striped legs, circa 1947 to early 1950s, $625.00 pair. *Courtesy June Allgeier.*

Scarlett O'Hara Dolls

Scarlett O'Hara is a literary character, the heroine of the 1936 Civil War epic, *Gone With the Wind*, a first novel written by Margaret Mitchell. Mitchell was born November 8, 1900; her father was a lawyer, and she had a five-year-old brother, Stephen. Her family and friends called her Peggy. Her father built a two-story white house with columns on Peachtree Street for the family. Unfortunately, her mother died when she was 20 years old. Peggy went to private schools and she was somewhat spoiled and liked attention. Perhaps from jealousy, she was blackballed from a sorority and the Junior League. She spent her childhood in a large extended family who told stories about the Civil War, and she remembered these tales.

It was the flapper era and Peggy was a petite woman with dark hair and green eyes; she attracted male admirers much like Scarlett. She first met a newspaperman from Kentucky, John Marsh, and dated him, and also met Berrien "Red" Upshaw who gambled and was a bootlegger. She married the wrong man in a home wedding in September of 1922 and alienated her Catholic family. A wedding photo at the Margaret Mitchell Museum in Atlanta shows everyone staring at the photographer except guest John Marsh, who is looking at the bride. Perhaps in her youth, she felt if she pushed John who seems a saint — intelligent, kind, conservative — he would declare himself. The dignified John did the noble thing and let her do the choosing this time. Peggy and Red lived with her father 10 months and then divorced. John helped her to get a job as a reporter, writing about Atlanta and its history. She was good at that.

In 1925 she and John married, and this marriage seems from all accounts a love affair between true soul mates. She was impulsive and outgoing, and John made up for all of her weak points. He was an excellent editor and encouraged her writing. They lived on Peachtree Street in Atlanta in a tiny two-room apartment in an old Tudor-style house that burned to the ground and has been restored with the aid of a $7 million grant from the German automaker, Daimler-Benz. John bought Peggy a small writing table just big enough to hold her typewriter and a stack of paper. She found a niche in the apartment where she worked. She finished the book in 1935, and it was published in 1936. The book was immortalized in a David Selznick movie that premiered December 15, 1939, in Atlanta in time to qualify for the Academy Awards, of which it won several. It starred Vivien Leigh as Scarlett and Clark Gable as Rhett Butler. It remains one of the all-time popular movies just as the book remains a favorite. John and Peggy had no children and their happiness seems short-lived; Peggy was run down by a taxi in Atlanta and died a few days later, August 16, 1949. John died three years later in 1952. Peggy wanted her manuscript burned, and most of her letters were destroyed also.

It was fun to tour the Mitchell apartment in Atlanta and visit the Margaret Mitchell Museum. The apartment was very small, just two rooms and a bath with a closet-sized kitchenette. It had been destroyed by fire and completely rebuilt. Peggy and her brother Stephen had the family house on Peachtree Street torn down because they did not want anyone else to live in it. She was a very interesting woman, and much of her can be found in her heroine Scarlett, I believe. Several biographies have been written about her, including *Margaret Mitchell of Atlanta*, 1965, by Finis Farr, which her brother, Stephen, authorized. In 1983, Anne Edwards wrote *Road to Tara* and Darden Pyron wrote *Southern Daughter* in 1991. In 1993, Marianne Walker wrote *Margaret Mitchell and John Marsh — The Love Story Behind Gone with the Wind*.

With a brief overview of the Mitchell biographies, I could find no mention of any dealings with dolls or the Alexander Doll Company who made the Scarlett doll. Jan Lebow, writing in a *Doll Reader* article in 1995 reports that Madame Alexander created the "Fiction Doll Scarlett" after reading the 1936 *Gone With the Wind* book and dressed the 7" Tiny Betty in a yellow organdy gown with green sash — the first Alexander doll to portray Scarlett before the premier of the movie in 1939.

Scarlett O'Hara Dolls

Madame Alexander began her career dressing dolls, and costuming is one of the trademarks of the Alexander Doll Company. On August 31, 1937, Alexander gained exclusive rights from Selznick and MGM to design, produce, and market Scarlett O'Hara dolls. There is a dizzying array of Scarletts from the beginning of the company up through the present day. The company used dolls in their line and dressed them in Scarlett costumes. The dolls first used were the composition dolls, 7" Tiny Betty (1937 – 1942), 9" Little Betty (1939 – 1941) and then the Wendy Ann face on the 11" Scarlett (1940 – 1943), 14" – 15" (1941 – 1943), 18" (1939 – 1943), and 21" (1942 – 1943). Lebow also reports four styles of Scarlett O'Hara wrist tags, one 2½" x 2¾" with Scarlett holding up her collar in green gown; one 1¾" x 2½" depicting Vivien Leigh in front of Tara; one small card with the name "Madame Alexander" only; and a tiny gold foil-covered medallion with the name "Madame Alexander."

In 1950, Alexander used the Margaret and the Maggie faces in sizes 14" – 16" for a hard plastic Scarlett. They also made a 20" hard plastic Scarlett with a Margaret face. In 1955 they used the vinyl Cissy in the 21" size for Scarlett with a blue taffeta gown with short jacket. In 1958, they produced a Cissy in green velvet jacket and bonnet and in 1961 – 1962, a straight arm Cissy with white organdy with green ribbon inserted in lace tiers wearing a white picture hat.

In 1963 only, Alexander made an 18" hard plastic Scarlett with the Elise face and vinyl arms in a blue organdy dress with rosebuds. Also that year they made a 12" hard plastic Scarlett with Lissy face wearing a green taffeta gown and bonnet.

From 1953 on, Alexander presented a whole host of 8" hard plastic Scarletts with the Wendy Ann face in a wide range of costumes.

In 1965, they made a 21" hard plastic Scarlett with Jacqueline, a hard plastic 21" Coco-faced Scarlett, and also circa 1963 – 1965 with blonde hair a Godey Scarlett. Also in the 1960s, a 10" Scarlett with Cissette face appeared.

Other companies such as Franklin Mint, Mattel, and Robert Tonner have also produced Scarletts. She remains a perennial favorite, triggering again and again the image of Scarlett and the unforgettable *Gone With the Wind*.

**14" composition Alexander "Scarlett,"
blue sleep eyes, eyeshadow, real lashes
above, painted lashes below, closed
mouth, black wig, green velvet dress with
matching feathered hat, with wrist tag
that reads, "Scarlett O'Hara//From//
Gone With//The Wind// by//Madame
Alexander//By Special Permission of//The
Copyright Owners//All Rights Reserved,"
with box, circa 1941 – 1943, $650.00.**
Courtesy Harlene Soucy.

17" composition Madame Alexander "Scarlett," "Scarlett O'Hara//Madame Alexander, N.Y. U.S.A.//All Rights Reserved" on dress tag, black human hair wig, original set, green sleep eyes, real lashes, eyeshadow, painted lashes, feathered brows, closed mouth, five-piece composition body, original flower print with striped skirt dress, green velvet bodice, matching bonnet with plume, hoop slip, matching pantalettes, socks, green leatherette snap shoes, circa 1939 – 1946, $1,050.00.
Courtesy McMasters Doll Auctions.

14" composition Madame Alexander "Scarlett O'Hara," marked "Mme Alexander," green sleep eyes, real lashes, eyeshadow, closed mouth, human hair wig, five-piece composition body, original gold taffeta dress with matching bonnet, dress tagged "Scarlett O'Hara," black velvet jacket, slip with hoop, pantalettes, socks, and shoes, circa 1941 – 1943, $1,100.00. *Courtesy McMasters Doll Auctions.*

11" Madame Alexander composition "Scarlett," with blue sleep eyes, eyeshadow, black wig, and original tagged costume, $525.00. *Courtesy Stephanie Prince.*

14" composition Madame Alexander "Scarlett" in green velveteen long coat and hat worn over plaid dress, circa 1941 – 1943, $1,300.00. *Courtesy Amanda Hash.*

Scarlett O'Hara Dolls

10" hard plastic Alexander "Scarlett" in green taffeta dress trimmed in black braid. In original box, circa 1968, $425.00. *Courtesy McMasters Doll Auctions.*

8" hard plastic Madame Alexander "Scarlett O'Hara," marked "Alex" on body, green sleep eyes, molded lashes, closed mouth, dark brown wig, hard plastic body jointed at shoulders, hips, and knees, walking mechanism so head turns as legs move, white satin dress with green rick-rack trim, tagged "Scarlett O'Hara//by Madame Alexander//New York U.S.A.," straw hat with pale pink roses, all original with wrist tag, circa 1965, $500.00. *Courtesy McMasters Doll Auctions.*

8" hard plastic Alexander "Scarlett" in green velvet, $50.00. *Courtesy Vivian Boucher.*

18" vinyl Robert Tonner Doll Co. "Kitty Collier" dressed as Scarlett O'Hara, in green velvet with gold tassels. Kitty has green plastic eyes, closed red mouth, brown eyebrows, brunette wig, earrings, a 2001 souvenir of the CU Gathering in Atlanta "Return to Tara," **$175.00.** *Courtesy Marilyn Ramsey.*

Shirley Temple Dolls

In 1934, after Shirley Temple stole the show with her performance in "Stand Up and Cheer," Ideal gained the license to produce Shirley Temple dolls, hired Bernard Lipfert to sculpt a prototype, cast her in composition, and soon had a Shirley Temple doll in red and white polka dotted dresses on the market. The costumes were designed by Mollye Goldman during 1934 – 1936 and show the NRA markings on their labels. The costumes were sold separately as well as with the doll.

The composition dolls had sleep eyes or flirty eyes, open mouth with six upper teeth, multi-stroke eyebrows, a 5-piece jointed body, mohair wig, and came in a range of sizes from 11" to 27". The first dolls were packaged with a pin-back button and signed photograph. Dolls were marked on the head and/or torso with "SHIRLEY TEMPLE//IDEAL NOV. & TOY CO." and "SHIRLEY TEMPLE" on the body. In late 1935, a Shirley Temple Baby was introduced followed by baby carriages and accessories. Shirley Temple dolls were popular through the early 1940s, declining when real-life Shirley reached adolescence.

In 1957, Ideal reissued a vinyl 12" Shirley to coincide with the release of her movies to television and Temple's own television series. These dolls have plastic script pins and paper hang tags. In the 1960s, 15", 17", and 19" vinyl dolls were issued. In 1972, to celebrate its 100th anniversary Montgomery Ward issued a 15" vinyl Shirley Temple. In 1982, Ideal made 8" and 12" Shirley Temple dolls costumed as Heidi, Stowaway, Stand Up and Cheer, The Little Colonel, Captain January, and The Littlest Rebel. Danbury Mint has made more recent Shirley Temples, including porcelain 20" dolls costumed from movies, designed by Elke Hutchens. See the Collectors' Network for information on several Shirley Temple publications and groups.

What to look for:

Composition Shirley Temples are difficult to find in excellent condition because the painted finish crazes, and those in very good condition have risen drastically in prices. Collectors may wish to search for the vinyl and newer dolls as they too will eventually become collectible. Check composition dolls for crazing; vinyl should have good color, and clothing should be clean and bright. Shirley collectors like all Shirley Temple related items, such as marked products, paper, and advertising.

Composition

20" composition Ideal "Shirley Temple," marked "Cop. Ideal//N & T Co." on head, NRA tag on dress, wig in original set, hazel sleep eyes, real lashes, painted lower lashes, feathered brows, open mouth, six upper teeth, five-piece composition child body, original blue organdy pleated dress with pink ribbons, underwear combination, socks, center-strap shoes, Shirley Temple button and label on original box, unplayed-with condition, circa 1934+, $1,700.00. *Courtesy McMasters Doll Auctions.*

13" composition Ideal "Shirley Temple" marked "Shirley Temple" on head, "Shirley Temple//13" on back, original mohair wig, hazel sleep eyes, real lashes, painted lashes, feathered brows, open mouth, six upper teeth, felt tongue, five-piece composition body, original Bright Eyes plaid dress, underwear combination, socks and shoes, light crazing, circa 1934+, $500.00. *Courtesy McMasters Doll Auctions.*

25" composition Ideal "Shirley Temple" marked "25//Shirley Temple//Cop Ideal//N & T Co." on head, "Shirley Temple" on back, mohair wig, hazel flirty sleep eyes, real lashes, painted lower lashes, open mouth, six upper teeth, metal tongue, five-piece composition child body, original Shirley Temple button, original blue/white dress, white collar, cuffs and apron, replaced underclothing is copy of original slip and teddy, white socks, center-snap shoes, circa 1934+, $850.00. *Courtesy McMasters Doll Auctions.*

27" composition Ideal "Shirley Temple Ranger," marked "Shirley Temple//Cop Ideal//N & T Co." on head, "Shirley Temple" on back, mohair wig, hazel flirty sleep eyes, real lashes, painted lower lashes, feathered brows, open mouth, six upper teeth, molded tongue, five-piece composition child body, Shirley Temple button, original Ranger outfit with red taffeta shirt and bandana, khaki shorts, leather chaps and vest, replaced holster, gun missing, circa 1934+, $1,325.00. *Courtesy McMasters Doll Auctions.*

13" composition Ideal "Shirley Temple" marked "13//Shirley Temple" on back of head, "Shirley Temple//13" on back, mohair wig in original set, hazel sleep eyes, real lashes, painted lower lashes, feathered brows, open mouth, six upper teeth, five-piece composition body, original plaid "Bright Eyes" dress, underwear combination, replaced socks, original shoes, circa 1934+, $700.00. *Courtesy McMasters Doll Auctions.*

20" composition Ideal Shirley Temple marked "20//Shirley Temple//Cop Ideal//N & T Co." on head, "Shirley Temple//20*" on back, mohair wig, hazel sleep eyes, real lashes, open mouth, six upper teeth, molded tongue, five-piece composition child body, tagged dotted organdy dress with pleats from Curly Top movie, underwear combination, socks and shoes, all original, some crazing, circa 1934+, $500.00. *Courtesy McMasters Doll Auctions.*

27" composition Ideal "Shirley Temple" marked "Shirley Temple//Cop. Ideal N & T Co." on head, "Shirley Temple" on back, mohair wig reset in curls, hazel flirty sleep eyes, real lashes, painted lower lashes, feathered brows, open mouth, six upper teeth, five-piece composition child body, original red/white dress with wrist ties, original underwear combination, replaced socks and shoes, circa 1934+, $550.00. *Courtesy McMasters Doll Auctions.*

Vinyl

12" vinyl Ideal "Shirley Temple" marked "Ideal Doll//ST-12" on head, "ST-12-N" on back, rooted hair in original set, hazel sleep eyes, molded lashes, open/closed mouth, six upper teeth, five-piece vinyl body, original pink nylon slip, panties, socks, black plastic shoes, script pin, original box, sixteen original Shirley Temple outfits, miscellaneous accessories in blue metal trunk by Cass Toys, mint condition, circa 1957, $1,800.00. *Courtesy McMasters Doll Auctions.*

12" vinyl Ideal "Shirley Temple" marked "Ideal Doll//ST-12" on head, "Shirley Temple//made by Ideal Toy Co." on tag on slip, "Shirley Temple" script pin and white purse, rooted hair, hazel sleep eyes, molded lashes, single stroke brows, painted lower lashes, open/closed mouth, teeth, dimples, jointed child body, blue velvet/white dotted Swiss dress, pink nylon slip, matching panties, vinyl shoes, all original w/box, circa 1957, $230.00. *Courtesy McMasters Doll Auctions.*

12" vinyl Ideal "Shirley Temple" marked "Ideal Doll//ST-12" on head, rooted hair in original set with net and plastic clips, hazel sleep eyes, molded lashes, painted lashes, single stroke brows, oen/closed mouth, six upper teeth, five-piece vinyl child body, orange/white tagged dress/lace trim, panties, black vinyl shoes, white vinyl purse, script pin, tagged pink taffeta slip/panties, extra knit panties, unplayed-with condition in original box, circa 1957, $350.00. *Courtesy McMasters Doll Auctions.*

Terri Lee Dolls

Terri Lee dolls were made from 1946 until 1962, in Lincoln, Nebraska, and Apple Valley, California. The first dolls were composition, then hard plastic and vinyl dolls were added. Marked on torso, "TERRI LEE," and early dolls, "PAT. PENDING," Terri Lee dolls have closed pouty mouths, painted eyes, wigs, and jointed bodies.

Recently the Terri Lee molds were acquired to remake Terri Lee dolls, and the new Terri Lees are some of the finest reproductions on the market. See Collectors' Network for more information on collector groups and the bibliography for additional resource material.

What to look for:

Composition dolls are hard to find in good condition, as most have crazing in moderate to severe stages. Hard plastic dolls should be clean with rosy face color and with original clothing when possible. Hair can be restyled and pattern clothes made for nude dolls. Again a stable environment and cleanliness help slow down deterioration of the plastic materials.

16" hard plastic Terri Lee, with brown synthetic wig, brown painted eyes, painted lashes, one stroke brown eyebrows, red dots at nostrils, bright red lips, wearing rose colored velveteen coat and matching hat, fur gloves attached to coat with ribbon, white socks, black shoes, circa 1951 – 1962, $450.00. *Courtesy Diane Vigne.*

16" hard plastic Terri Lee, marked "Terri Lee" on head, back, and dress tag, Saran wig, painted brown eyes, painted upper and lower lashes, single-stroke brows, closed mouth, five-piece hard plastic body, yellow organdy tagged dress, original nylon slip and panties, socks and shoes, circa 1951 – 1962, $425.00. *Courtesy McMasters Doll Auctions.*

16" hard plastic Terri Lee black "Patty Jo," marked "Terri Lee//Pat. Pending" on back, original coarse black wig, large painted brown eyes, painted lashes, heavy arched brows, closed mouth, five-piece brown hard plastic body, black polished cotton dress, tagged Terri Lee slip, cotton panties, rayon socks, white tie leatherette shoes, circa 1950 – 1951, $1,150.00. *Courtesy McMasters Doll Auctions.*

16" hard plastic Terri Lee "Jerri Lee Cowboy" marked "Terri Lee//Pat. Pending" on back, original skin wig, painted brown eyes, painted lashes, single stroke brows, closed mouth, five-piece hard plastic body, "Gene Autry" tagged gold satin shirt, silver piping, "Terri Lee" tagged blue pants, brown oilcloth boots, tagged brown leather vest, cuffs and chaps with beige fringe, holster with silver buckle, gold plastic gun, red felt hat, circa 1950 – 1951, $600.00. *Courtesy McMasters Doll Auctions.*

16" hard plastic Terri Lee look-alike, "Mary Jane" marked "Mary Jane" on dress tag, Saran wig, blue flirty sleep eyes, molded lashes, single stroke brows, painted lower lashes at corners, closed mouth, five-piece hard plastic body with walking mechanism, original tagged yellow polished cotton dress, matching panties, dark green print pinafore, matching hat lined in yellow, rayon socks, white vinly side-fastened shoes marked "Fairyland Toy. Prod.," circa 1950s, $250.00. *Courtesy McMasters Doll Auctions.*

16" hard plastic Terri Lee "Gene Autry," marked "Terri Lee//Pat. Pending" on back, "Gene Autry" on shirt tag, lightly molded and brush stroked hair, feathered brows, painted blue eyes, painted lashes, open/closed mouth with white space for teeth, five-piece hard plastic Terri Lee body, tagged gold satin shirt with silver piping, denim jeans, brown and white cowboy boots, belt, circa 1949 – 1950, $1,700.00. *Courtesy McMasters Doll Auctions.*

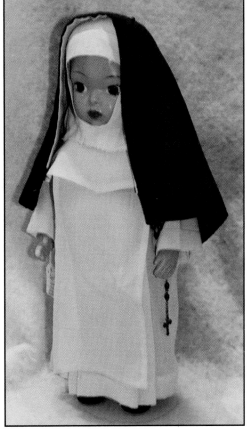

16" hard plastic Terri Lee "Dominican Nun," painted brown eyes, painted lashes, closed mouth, five-piece hard plastic body, authentic outfit with tucked muslin petticoat, jumper with snapped-on sleeves and separate oversleeves, bib covers the jumper, collar goes on last, black shoes, stockings, and correct rosary attached to patent belt, veil is in two parts stitched in the back with headband, circa 1952, $300.00. *Courtesy DeDee Crowe.*

16" hard plastic Terri Lee Bride, marked "Terri Lee" on back and on dress tag, brunette wig, painted brown eyes, single stroke brows, painted lashes, closed mouth, five-piece body, matching veil, panties, satin shoes, comes with nine original outfits in a trunk, including the rare yellow Southern Belle outfit, Girl Scout uniform, Nurse uniform, Cowgirl costume, and more, plus accessories, unplayed-with condition, circa 1951 – 1962, $2,400.00. *Courtesy McMasters Doll Auctions.*

18" hard plastic Terri Lee "Connie Lynn," "Terri Lee Nursery Registration" form, and three "Admission Cards to Terri Lee Hospital;" "Connie Lynn" tag on clothing, caracul wig, blue sleep eyes, real lashes, painted lower lashes at corners of eyes, single stroke brows, closed mouth, hard plastic baby body, original two-piece pink baby outfit, plastic panties, socks, white baby shoes, unplayed-with in original box, circa 1955, $625.00.
Courtesy McMasters Doll Auctions.

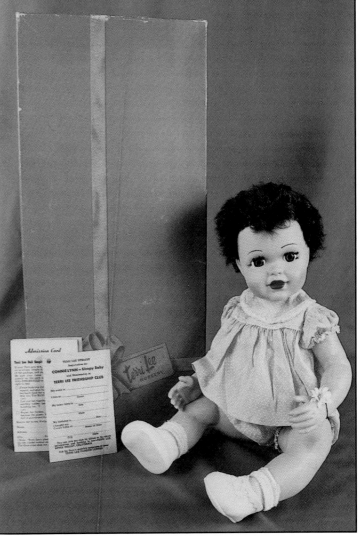

Robert Tonner Doll Company

The Robert Tonner Doll Company began in the early 1990s with multi-jointed porcelain fashion dolls, but hit the jackpot when Tonner first licensed "Betsy McCall" and reproduced her as a 14" vinyl. Betsy is reminiscent of the McCall paper doll from the 1950s and is available dressed or with additional outfits.

In 1999 he also produced a vinyl 10" Ann Estelle from the charming character created by Mary Engelbreit. Ann Estelle has a blonde Dutch bob, blue eyes, and comes dressed in her undies or a special costume. Additional wardrobe is available separately. Tonner also introduced an 8" vinyl Kripplebush Kid with rooted hair and jointed arms and legs that makes a great travel doll.

Eagerly anticipated before its late 1999 introduction, Tonner's new 16" vinyl fashion doll is Tyler Wentworth. Tonner has created a history for Tyler, stating that from an early age she was destined to be a high flyer in the world of high fashion (see pages 160 – 165).

"During the 1950s, Tyler's great-aunt Regina Wentworth established the House of Wentworth in New York City and created innovative collections that set the standard for the 7th Avenue fashion design. Years later, Tyler, who had always loved the glamour and excitement of her great-aunt's business, joined the prestigious house's design staff. She proved to be exceptionally talented, and it was not long until she was promoted to Regina's first assistant.

"With the House of Wentworth's reputation firmly established, Regina began to consider passing the reins to a new talent. Spurring her on was her relationship with Carlos, a young artist who had instantly fallen in love with the chic, elegant, older designer. Soon Regina made her decision to move with Carlos to the south of France, and she turned the company over to Tyler.

"Although young for the job, Tyler quickly showed that she was equal to her new responsibilities. With only a few short seasons of fashion experience, she confidently assumed leadership of the House of Wentworth and received rave reviews over her first collection."

What to look for:

Check eBay, Internet doll shops, doll magazines, and your local doll or gift shop for the latest releases. Special costumed dolls produced in limited editions, like the Roy Rogers version of Betsy McCall from the first Betsy McCall convention and Ann Estelle from the UFDC luncheon in limited edition costume, are available on the secondary market and are increasing in price. Tonner dolls are fun to costume and play with — and fun to collect.

10" vinyl "Ann Estelle," a Mary Engelbreit character, style #ME 8102 "A Good Book," blonde wig, blue eyes, closed mouth, gold-rimmed eyeglasses, rigid vinyl body, black and white striped shirt, red and yellow skirt with suspenders, trimmed red flower embroidery and red rickrack, white socks, black shoes, with book "Life is Just a Chair of Bowlies," outfit only, circa 2001, $89.99. *Courtesy Robert Tonner Doll Company.*

10" vinyl "Ann Estelle," a Mary Engelbreit character, style #ME 0106 "Field Guide," blonde wig, blue eyes, closed mouth, gold rimmed eyeglasses, rigid vinyl body, green and white checked top with buttons, khaki pants, green shoes, straw hat, carrying butterfly net, butterfly container, circa 2001, $89.99. *Courtesy Robert Tonner Doll Company.*

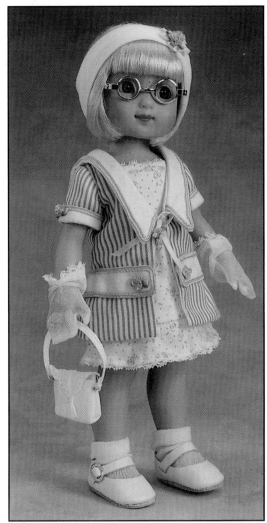

10" vinyl "Ann Estelle," a Mary Engelbreit character, style #ME 0108 "Mother's Day," blonde wig, blue eyes, closed mouth, gold-rimmed eyeglasses, rigid vinyl body, white dress with pink flower print, blue and white striped jacket with white and pink trim, white headband with pink flower, white gloves, white purse, white socks and shoes, circa 2001, $89.99. *Courtesy Robert Tonner Doll Company.*

10" vinyl "Ann Estelle," a Mary Engelbreit character, style #ME 0111 "Prima Ballerina," blonde wig, blue eyes, closed mouth, gold-rimmed eyeglasses, rigid vinyl body, elaborate blue ballerina outfit with attached colored butterflies, lilac shoes with butterflies, shiny stockings, white butterfly tiara, white net cancan slip, circa 2001, $99.99. *Courtesy Robert Tonner Doll Company.*

Robert Tonner Doll Company

10" vinyl "Ann Estelle," a Mary Engel-breit character, style #ME 0114 "Let's Skate," blonde wig, blue eyes, closed mouth, gold-rimmed eyeglasses, rigid vinyl body, green knitted sweater and matching tam with pink pom-pon, pink cuffs, flower print outfit, pink stockings, white skates, cup of hot chocolate, red hand-bag, circa 2001, $99.99. *Courtesy Robert Tonner Doll Company.*

10" vinyl "Ann Estelle," a Mary Engelbreit character, style #ME 0102 "Firecracker Annie," blonde wig, blue eyes, closed mouth, gold-rimmed eyeglasses, rigid vinyl body, denim short overalls with flowers appliquéd on leg, tie-dyed T-shirt, beaded necklace with peace symbol, matching beaded bracelet, white socks with embroi-dery trim around top, brown sandals, flag in pocket, circa 2001, $79.99. *Courtesy Robert Tonner Doll Company.*

10" vinyl "Ann Estelle," a Mary Engelbreit character, style #ME 0113 "Aloha Ann Estelle," blonde wig, blue eyes, closed mouth, gold-rimmed eyeglass-es, rigid vinyl body, orange wrap around skirt with flower print, pink midriff top with puff sleeves, straw hat with fruit decorations, pink sandals, ukulele, circa 2001, $89.99. *Courtesy Robert Tonner Doll Company.*

18" vinyl "Ann Estelle," new larger playmates, a Mary Engelbreit character, style #ME 7101 "Classic Sailor," blonde wig, blue eyes, closed mouth, gold-rimmed eyeglasses, rigid vinyl body, red, white, and blue sailor outfit, orange plaid pleated skirt, straw hat with navy blue band with white polka dots, white socks, black one-strap shoes, circa 2001, $124.99. *Courtesy Robert Tonner Doll Company.*

18" vinyl "Ann Estelle," new larger playmates, a Mary Engelbreit character, style #ME 7103 "Dancing Into My Heart," blonde wig, blue eyes, closed mouth, gold-rimmed eyeglasses, rigid vinyl body, elaborate black and white dress with black pompon trim, white hat with black pompon, white tights, white shoes with black pompon, red flower wrist corsage, circa 2001, $124.99. *Courtesy Robert Tonner Doll Company.*

10" vinyl black "Georgia," a Mary Engelbreit character, friend to Ann Estelle, style #ME 2102, "Georgia The Beachcomber," brown eyes, closed mouth, black wig, rigid vinyl body, two-piece blue with white polka dot swimsuit, trimmed with red, white terrycloth jacket with lining to match swimsuit, red shoes, pail, circa 2001, $79.99. *Courtesy Robert Tonner Doll Company.*

Robert Tonner Doll Company

10" vinyl "Sophie," a Mary Engelbreit character, friend to Ann Estelle, style #ME 1102, "Sophie Boating Party," brown eyes, closed mouth, strawberry blonde wig, rigid vinyl body, blue and white striped dress with puff sleeves, trimmed in dark blue and gold on cuffs, collar, and belt, blue tie, three pleats in front of dress from neck to hem, straw hat with red and white checked ribbon trim, white socks, red shoes, red boat, circa 2001, $89.99. *Courtesy Robert Tonner Doll Company.*

10" vinyl black "Georgia," a Mary Engelbreit character, friend to Ann Estelle, style #ME 2104, "Georgia Overall Comfort," brown eyes, closed mouth, black wig, rigid vinyl body, pink overalls with plaid lining, white turtleneck sweater with pink flower print, blue slippers trimmed with flower print, lime green handbag with pink flower snap, circa 2001, $79.99. *Courtesy Robert Tonner Doll Company.*

10" vinyl "Sophie," a Mary Engelbreit character, friend to Ann Estelle, style #ME 1103, "Sophie Hope," brown eyes, closed mouth, strawberry blonde wig, rigid vinyl body, white knit sweater with red and green flower embroidery, matching tam, red and yellow plaid skirt with scalloped hem, red and white striped stockings, brown lace boots, holding three packages tied with red ribbon, circa 2001, $99.99. *Courtesy Robert Tonner Doll Company.*

10" vinyl "April" from Lynn Johnston's comic strip "For Better or Worse," brown rooted wig, painted eyes to side, closed pouty mouth, jointed body, style #FBFW 0103 "April Flowers," multi-color flower print dress, lilac shoes, shiny stockings, straw hat, circa 2001, $39.95. *Courtesy Robert Tonner Doll Company.*

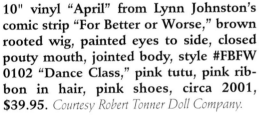

10" vinyl "April" from Lynn Johnston's comic strip "For Better or Worse," brown rooted wig, painted eyes to side, closed pouty mouth, jointed body, style #FBFW 0102 "Dance Class," pink tutu, pink ribbon in hair, pink shoes, circa 2001, $39.95. *Courtesy Robert Tonner Doll Company.*

10" vinyl "April" from Lynn Johnston's comic strip "For Better or Worse," brown rooted wig, painted eyes to side, closed pouty mouth, jointed body, style #FBFW 0104 "Bedtime For Mr. B," white pajamas with pink heart print, pink housecoat, bunny slippers, carrying stuffed bunny, circa 2001, $39.95. *Courtesy Robert Tonner Doll Company.*

Robert Tonner Doll Company

10" vinyl "April" from Lynn Johnston's comic strip "For Better or Worse," brown rooted wig, painted eyes to side, closed pouty mouth, jointed body, style #FBFW 0101, blue denim overalls, orange and yellow striped T-shirt, white tie shoes, circa 2001, $39.95. *Courtesy Robert Tonner Doll Company.*

18" vinyl "Kitty Collier," rooted hair, inset acrylic eyes, closed mouth, painted finger and toenails, jointed vinyl fashion body, high-heel feet, wearing "Hot Spots," style #KC 8101, blue sunsuit with white polka dots, matching long sleeve jacket, white hat, white canvas bag, white high-heeled sandals with flowers, doll, $89.99, outfit only, circa 2001, $39.99. *Courtesy Robert Tonner Doll Company.*

18" vinyl "Kitty Collier," Basic Red, Basic Blonde, and Basic Brown, rooted hair, inset acrylic eyes, closed mouth, painted finger and toenails, jointed vinyl fashion body, high-heel feet, pink lace teddy, nylons, black strap high-heeled shoes, circa 2001, $88.99 each. *Courtesy Robert Tonner Doll Company.*

Robert Tonner Doll Company

18" vinyl "Kitty Collier," rooted hair, inset acrylic eyes, closed mouth, painted finger and toenails, jointed vinyl fashion body, high-heel feet, wearing "My Blue Heaven," style #KC 1105, light blue dress with full skirt, belted waist, yellow flower print, lilac plush coat with lining matching dress, matching hat, lilac high-heeled shoes, bead necklace and matching earrings, circa 2001, $149.99. *Courtesy Robert Tonner Doll Company.*

18" vinyl "Kitty Collier," rooted hair, inset acrylic eyes, closed mouth, painted finger and toenails, jointed vinyl fashion body, high-heel feet, wearing "Patio Party," style #KC 8103, lime dress with green and lilac flower print, full skirt, lilac belt, lilac open-toe high-heeled shoes, outfit only, circa 2001, $44.99. *Courtesy Robert Tonner Doll Company.*

18" vinyl "Kitty Collier," rooted hair, inset acrylic eyes, closed mouth, painted finger and toenails, jointed vinyl fashion body, high-heel feet, wearing "American Beauty," style #KC 1102, white layered full skirt, collar and cuffs, black velvet top, black belt with red rose in front, "pearl" necklace and earrings, black open-toe heels, circa 2001, $99.99. *Courtesy Robert Tonner Doll Company.*

Robert Tonner Doll Company

18" vinyl "Kitty Collier," rooted hair, inset acrylic eyes, closed mouth, painted finger and toenails, jointed vinyl fashion body, high-heel feet, wearing "Picture Perfect," style #KC 1103, pink dress with white tiered lace eyelet ruffles, matching collar ruffle, sheer white gloves with eyelet lace trim, matching large hat, white high-heeled sandals, nylons, "pearl" necklace, matching earrings, circa 2001, $99.99. *Courtesy Robert Tonner Doll Company.*

18" vinyl "Kitty Collier," rooted hair, inset acrylic eyes, closed mouth, painted finger and toe-nails, jointed vinyl fashion body, high-heeled feet, wearing "Scarlet Glamour," style #KC 1104, long red fitted gown with flared skirt at knees, white fur stole around bodice, long white gloves, "diamond" necklace, earrings, and bracelet, circa 2001, $149.99. *Courtesy Robert Tonner Doll Company.*

18" vinyl "Kitty Collier," rooted hair, inset acrylic eyes, closed mouth, painted finger and toenails, jointed vinyl fashion body, high-heel feet, wearing "Enchante," style #KC 1101, "diamond" teardrop earrings, royal blue elegant strapless pantsuit outfit, matching floor-length sheer overcoat with silver buttons, "diamond" belt buckle, high-heeled sandals, dressed doll, circa 2001, $99.99, outfit only, $44.99. *Courtesy Robert Tonner Doll Company.*

18" vinyl "Kitty Collier," rooted hair, inset acrylic eyes, closed mouth, painted finger and toenails, jointed vinyl fashion body, high-heel feet, wearing "Down Mexico Way," style #KC 8102, white peasant top with yarn trim, multicolored skirt with embroidery trim, red shawl with embroidery trim, gold hoop earrings, red shoes, outfit only, circa 2001, $39.99. *Courtesy Robert Tonner Doll Company.*

8" hard plastic Kripplebush Kid "Cowgirl," style #KB 2002, long blonde braided hair, blue plastic sleep eyes, closed mouth, jointed hard plastic body, red and white checked shirt, leather skirt with fringe, leather vest, red cowboy hat, brown boots, circa 2001, $54.99. *Courtesy Robert Tonner Doll Company.*

8" hard plastic Kripplebush Kid "All-American Marni," style #KB 2104, brown hair, blue plastic sleep eyes, closed mouth, jointed hard plastic body, red and white striped T-shirt, blue denim jumper with pockets on front, red ribbon in hair, white socks, white shoes, circa 2001, $49.99. *Courtesy Robert Tonner Doll Company.*

Robert Tonner Doll Company

8" hard plastic Kripplebush Kid "Pinkie," style #KB 1101, auburn hair, blue plastic sleep eyes, closed mouth, jointed hard plastic body, pink organdy dress with net and lace skirt overlay and jacket, trimmed with pink roses, matching stockings, pink boots with three side buttons, matching rose barrettes in hair, circa 2001, $59.99.
Courtesy Robert Tonner Doll Company.

8" hard plastic Kripplebush Kid "Violet Fairy," style #KB 0103, brown hair, blue plastic sleep eyes, closed mouth, jointed hard plastic body, flower print outfit with pink cancan slip, stockings, elaborate flower headdress, bead necklace, circa 2001, $54.99. *Courtesy Robert Tonner Doll Company.*

8" hard plastic Kripplebush Kid "A Scarf from Grandma," style #KB 1102, brown hair, blue plastic sleep eyes, closed mouth, jointed hard plastic body, navy and light blue plaid skirt, matching jacket and tam, red trim, white shirt with flower trim embroidery lace, red crocheted scarf, black button boots, circa 2001, $59.99.
Courtesy Robert Tonner Doll Company.

8" hard plastic Kripple-bush Kid "Swan Lake," style #KB 0104, red hair, blue plastic sleep eyes, closed mouth, jointed hard plastic body, elegant white tutu with netting and lace, headdress, white stock-ings, white shoes, circa 2001, $49.99. *Courtesy Robert Tonner Doll Company.*

8" hard plastic Kripplebush Kid "Trimming The Tree," style #KB 1103, blonde hair, blue plastic sleep eyes, closed mouth, jointed hard plastic body, red satin dress with puff sleeves and heavy white lace trim, holding gold star decora-tion, black boots, circa 2001, $59.99. *Courtesy Robert Tonner Doll Company.*

8" hard plastic Kripplebush Kid "Little Red Riding Hood," style #KB 0102, auburn hair, blue plastic sleep eyes, closed mouth, jointed hard plastic body, red hooded cape with black trim, white petticoat, white shirt with black and red trim, red skirt with flowered trim and black and white checked trim, black shoes, carrying basket, circa 2001, $59.99. *Courtesy Robert Tonner Doll Company.*

Robert Tonner Doll Company

8" hard plastic Kripplebush Kid "Stars and Stripes Marni," style #KB 3106, brown hair, blue plastic sleep eyes, closed mouth, jointed hard plastic body, red, white, and blue satin dress with lace-trimmed short sleeves, white stockings, red one-strap shoes, circa 2001, $59.99. *Courtesy Robert Tonner Doll Company.*

8" hard plastic Kripplebush Kid "Practically Magic Eliza," style #KB 3105, auburn hair, blue plastic sleep eyes, closed mouth, jointed hard plastic body, orange dress trimmed in black, Halloween print pinafore, orange and black and orange shoes, black pointed hat, circa 2001, $59.99. *Courtesy Robert Tonner Doll Company.*

8" hard plastic Kripplebush Kid "Noelle," style #KB 3107, brown hair, blue plastic sleep eyes, closed mouth, jointed hard plastic body, red plaid dress trimmed in white lace, red velvet overdress, matching hooded jacket with white fur cuffs and hood trim, circa 2001, $59.99. *Courtesy Robert Tonner Doll Company.*

Vogue Dolls

Jennie Graves started her Vogue Doll Shop business in Somerville, Massachusetts, in 1922, dressing German dolls for department stores. She used cottage industry home sewers as her business expanded. Just before the war, she established a storefront, but depended on home workers again during the war years, as all able-bodied workers were needed in the defense plants. In 1945, she incorporated Vogue Dolls, Inc. and opened a factory in Medford, Massachusetts. By 1949, she contracted Commonwealth Plastics Company to make an 8" hard plastic doll. At no time did she manufacture dolls, but she did open a 15,000 square-foot factory where the dolls were dressed and packed for shipment.

Graves designed the costumes for over 20 years. She dressed German Armand Marseille bisque Just Me dolls in Vogue's early years, and these are highly prized today for the costumes. She also used imported German Kammer & Reinhardt (K&R) doll as well as composition dolls made by Arranbee and Ideal. In 1937, Graves had doll designer Bernard Lipfert design an 8" composition doll Toddles which she produced until 1948 when she had the doll made in hard plastic and named her Ginny. In the 1950s, Graves promoted a doll with wardrobe to increase year-around sales. Vogue advertising promoted Ginny as a leader in the doll fashion society and noted she had 50 outfits available. This brought such a spurt of growth that Graves had to borrow money to open another factory in 1953. Her success gave rise to competition such as Ginger by the Cosmopolitan Doll Company.

In 1957, Vogue became the largest doll manufacturer in the U.S. In 1958, Vogue purchased Arranbee Doll Company and reported gross sales of over $6 million. Graves retired in 1960 and turned the control of the company over to her daughter Virginia Graves Carlson, and son-in-law, Ted Carlson, in 1966 when Virginia retired. In 1972, Vogue was sold to Tonka Corp. who began manufacturing the dolls in Asia, and in 1977, the company was purchased by Lesney Products. During the Lesney era, Ginny was redesigned with a much slimmer body. After several changes of ownership, Meritus in 1984 and R. Dakin in 1986, the rights to all Vogue dolls and molds, including Ginny, were purchased by Vogue Doll Company, Inc., founded in 1995 by Linda and Jim Smith. Today, Vogue, under the guidance of President Linda Smith, is a family company that is making Ginny, once again, a great collectible doll.

What to look for:

Early composition dolls should have minimal crazing and good color. Hard plastic dolls should have good color and original clothing. Clean dolls that have no mold or odor are important considerations. Hair can be restyled with patience. Vogue's Ginny dolls were a big favorite of the Baby Boomers during the 1950s and remain an appealing collectible with the new dolls of today, attracting first-time as well as older collectors.

8" hard plastic Ginny "Coronation Queen," marked "Vogue Doll" on back, original wig, sleep eyes, painted lashes, closed mouth, five-piece strung hard plastic body, dressed in rare 1953 outfit to commemorate coronation of Queen Elizabeth, brocade dress trimmed with beads, sequins, and pearls, blue ribbon sash with star decoration, taffeta slip, panties, purple velvet long cape with fur trim, replica of St. Edward's crown, gold scepter, circa 1953, $725.00. *Courtesy McMasters Doll Auctions.*

8" hard platic "Ginny," painted lashes, blonde synthetic wig, rosy cheeks, sleep eyes, straight leg, wearing red floral pattern dress, with yellow, red, and green felt trim, yellow bias tape, red roller skates, hat, circa 1950 – 1954, **$500.00.** *Courtesy Marilyn Ramsey.*

8" hard platic "Ginny," painted lashes, blonde synthetic wig, rosy cheeks, sleep eyes, straight leg, red and blue fur-trimmed ski outfit with skis with extra shoes attached and poles, hat, circa 1950 – 1954, **$600.00.** *Courtesy Marilyn Ramsey.*

8" hard plastic "Ginny," painted lashes, blonde synthetic wig, rosy cheeks, sleep eyes, straight leg, wearing pink and purple skating costume, with lime and pink felt trim, skates, hat, circa 1950 – 1954, **$500.00.** *Courtesy Marilyn Ramsey.*

8" hard plastic "Bunny Hop" Ginny, from That's Just Ginny Collection, marked "Ginny's Signature TM//1988//The Vogue Doll Company//Made in China," red rooted hair, green plastic sleep eyes, jointed hard plastic body, painted bunny face with white buckteeth, white plush bunny costume, holding large orange carrot, circa 2001, $39.95. *Courtesy Vogue Doll Company.*

8" hard plastic "Dandelion" Ginny, from the Botanical Babies Collection, marked "Ginny's Signature TM//1988//The Vogue Doll Company//Made in China," blonde rooted hair, blue plastic sleep eyes, jointed hard plastic body, gray and brown dandelion costume with white feathery hat, circa 2001, $39.95. *Courtesy Vogue Doll Company.*

8" hard plastic "Forget-Me-Not" Ginny, from the Botanical Babies Collection, marked "Ginny's Signature TM//1988// The Vogue Doll Company// Made in China," blonde rooted hair in sausage curls, blue plastic sleep eyes, jointed hard plastic body, blue and green embroidered felt costume, circa 2001, $39.95. *Courtesy Vogue Doll Company.*

Vogue Dolls

8" hard plastic "Pansy" Ginny, from the Botanical Babies Collection, marked "Ginny's Signature TM// 1988//The Vogue Doll Company// Made in China," red rooted hair, brown plastic sleep eyes, jointed hard plastic body, shaded violet and lavender embroidered felt outfit, green tights, circa 2001, $39.95. *Courtesy Vogue Doll Company.*

8" hard plastic black "Sunflower" Ginny, from the Botanical Babies Collection, marked "Ginny's Signature TM//1988//The Vogue Doll Company//Made in China," brown rooted hair, brown plastic sleep eyes, jointed hard plastic body, green felt costume, green tights, yellow and brown sunflower headdress, circa 2001, $39.95. *Courtesy Vogue Doll Company.*

8" hard plastic "First Communion Brunette" Ginny, from Ginny Celebrates Collection, marked "Ginny's Signature TM//1988//The Vogue Doll Company// Made in China," brunette rooted hair, brown plastic sleep eyes, jointed hard plastic body, pristine white dress of cotton lace and silky taffeta is set off by a headpiece of pearls and tulle; she carries a white Bible and wears a tiny gold cross, white tights, white patent leather shoes, circa 2001, $45.00. *Courtesy Vogue Doll Company.*

8" hard plastic "Goldilocks" Ginny, from The Fairy Tales Collection, marked "Ginny's Signature TM// 1988//The Vogue Doll Company// Made in China," blonde rooted hair in curls, blue plastic sleep eyes, jointed hard plastic body, blue jacket trimmed in gold, matching band in hair, blue and white dress trimmed in gold, gold shoes, circa 2001, $45.00. *Courtesy Vogue Doll Company.*

8" hard plastic "Gretel" Ginny, from The Fairy Tales Collection, marked "Ginny's Signature TM//1988//The Vogue Doll Company// Made in China," blonde rooted hair in braids, blue plastic sleep eyes, jointed hard plastic body, red, white, and gold outfit, matching hat, black shoes, circa 2001, $45.00. *Courtesy Vogue Doll Company.*

8" hard plastic "Little Red Riding Hood" Ginny, from The Fairy Tales Collection, marked "Ginny's Signature TM//1988//The Vogue Doll Company//Made in China," brown rooted hair in braids, green plastic sleep eyes, jointed hard plastic body, red felt cape, a crewel embroidered cotton apron tops her peasant dirndl, carries a basket of goodies, circa 2001, $45.00. *Courtesy Vogue Doll Company.*

8" hard plastic "Forever '50s" Ginny, from Rock 'N' Roll Collection, marked "Ginny's Signature TM//1988//The Vogue Doll Company//Made in China," blonde rooted hair, blue plastic sleep eyes, jointed hard plastic body, dressed in a quintessentially fifties circle-skirted dress of hot pink edged with black piping and decorated with a Sputnik motif, black leatherette halter bodice, hot pink scarf holds her ponytail, black socks, saddle shoes, circa 2001, $39.95. *Courtesy Vogue Doll Company.*

8" hard plastic "Wake Up Little Ginny," from Rock 'N' Roll Collection, marked "Ginny's Signature TM//1988//The Vogue Doll Company//Made in China," blonde rooted hair, blue plastic sleep eyes, jointed hard plastic body, turquoise halter dress with black Z's embroidered around skirt, black trim, black bouffant slip, black shoes, and black scarf tied around ponytail, circa 2001, $39.95. *Courtesy Vogue Doll Company.*

8" hard plastic "She's So Fine" Ginny, from Rock 'N' Roll Collection, marked "Ginny's Signature TM//1988//The Vogue Doll Company//Made in China," brown rooted hair, brown plastic sleep eyes, jointed hard plastic body, white wool cheerleading outfit with red block G sweater, red socks, saddle shoes, red megaphone, circa 2001, $39.95. *Courtesy Vogue Doll Company.*

8" hard plastic "Going to the Chapel" Ginny, from Rock 'N' Roll Collection, marked "Ginny's Signature TM//1988//The Vogue Doll Company//Made in China," dark brown rooted hair, brown plastic sleep eyes, jointed hard plastic body, pearl encrusted white satin skirt and fuzzy white bolero, tulle hair bow, saddle shoes, white socks, circa 2001, $39.95. *Courtesy Vogue Doll Company.*

8" hard plastic "Teen Idol" Ginny, from Rock 'N' Roll Collection, marked "Ginny's Signature TM//1988//The Vogue Doll Company//Made in China," dark brown rooted hair, green plastic sleep eyes, jointed hard plastic body, white satin pantsuit slashed with silver and studded with sparkles, red neck scarf, circa 2001, $39.95. *Courtesy Vogue Doll Company.*

8" hard plastic "Spring Chick" Ginny, from That's Just Ginny Collection, marked "Ginny's Signature TM//1988// The Vogue Doll Company//Made in China," blonde rooted hair, blue plastic sleep eyes, jointed hard plastic body, yellow newly-hatched chick outfit, circa 2001, $39.95. *Courtesy Vogue Doll Company.*

8" hard plastic "Beary Cute" Ginny, from That's Just Ginny Collection, marked "Ginny's Signature TM//1988//The Vogue Doll Company//Made in China," brown rooted hair, brown plastic sleep eyes, jointed hard plastic body, brown painted nose, caramel colored fur bear suit, carrying a felt beehive, circa 2001, $39.95. *Courtesy Vogue Doll Company.*

8" hard plastic "Pretty Kitty" Ginny, from That's Just Ginny Collection, marked "Ginny's Signature TM//1988// The Vogue Doll Company//Made in China," blonde rooted hair, blue plastic sleep eyes, jointed hard plastic body, painted nose, gray fur kitten suit with white tipped feet and tail, carrying a red ball of yarn, circa 2001, $39.95. *Courtesy Vogue Doll Company.*

8" hard plastic "Puppy Love" Ginny, from That's Just Ginny Collection, marked "Ginny's Signature TM//1988//The Vogue Doll Company//Made in China," brunette rooted hair, brown plastic sleep eyes, jointed hard plastic body, black painted nose, Dalmatian costume of plush white with black spots, red collar and brass dog tag, circa 2001, $39.95. *Courtesy Vogue Doll Company.*

8" hard plastic "Ginny the Wavette Hair Doll" reissue, from The Ginny Doll Club, marked "Ginny's Signature TM//1988//The Vogue Doll Company// Made in China," blonde rooted hair, brown plastic sleep eyes, jointed hard plastic body. Vogue dolls introduced the first Ginny in 1951. The Ginny Doll Club celebrates 50 years of Ginny by recreating "Ginny the Wavette Hair Doll." Dressed as in 1951 in her red checked gingham dress and straw hat, circa 2001, $45.00. *Courtesy Vogue Doll Company.*

8" hard plastic "Gift of Life Ginny" from Ginny Lends a Hand, marked "Ginny's Signature TM//1988//The Vogue Doll Company//Made in China," auburn rooted hair, brown plastic sleep eyes, jointed hard plastic body, dressed as a nurse in blue and white striped dress, white apron, and matching cap. Vogue will donate $5.00 per doll sold to The Gift of Life, a non-profit organization that brings children to the U.S. for life-saving heart surgery. Circa 2001, $39.95. *Courtesy Vogue Doll Company.*

8" hard plastic "Dinner at Eight" Ginny, from The Hat Shoppe Collection, marked "Ginny's Signature TM//1988//The Vogue Doll Company//Made in China," blonde rooted hair, blue plastic sleep eyes, jointed hard plastic body, silky pink dress is adorned with sequins at the collar, matching pink hat with veil and purse, matching pink shoes, nylons, faux fur stole, long white gloves, pearl necklace, circa 2001, $49.90. *Courtesy Vogue Doll Company.*

8" hard plastic "Pretty as a Picture" Ginny, from The Hat Shoppe Collection, marked "Ginny's Signature TM//1988//The Vogue Doll Company//Made in China," blonde rooted hair, brown plastic sleep eyes, jointed hard plastic body, golden yellow picture hat and jacket atop a black and white polka dotted dress, black netting on hat, nylons, black lace gloves, black shoes, carrying a yellow Vogue Hat Shoppe hatbox, circa 2001, $49.90. *Courtesy Vogue Doll Company.*

8" hard plastic "Cloche to You" Ginny, from The Hat Shoppe Collection, marked "Ginny's Signature TM//1988// The Vogue Doll Company//Made in China," brown rooted hair, brown plastic sleep eyes, jointed hard plastic body, navy and white polka dot dress with lace trim, red felt cloche hat, matching purse with her name, white socks, red one-strap shoes, circa 2001, $39.95. *Courtesy Vogue Doll Company.*

8" hard plastic Vogue "Picture Perfect" Ginny, from The Hat Shoppe Collection, marked "Ginny's Signature TM//1988//The Vogue Doll Company//Made in China," blonde rooted hair, blue plastic sleep eyes, jointed hard plastic body, wearing a light, airy floral dress trimmed in lace and pink ribbon and matching picture hat, lace gloves, nylons, pink one-strap shoes, carrying a pink Vogue Hat Shoppe hatbox, circa 2001, $49.90. *Courtesy Vogue Doll Company.*

8" hard plastic "Pretty in Pink" Ginny, from The Hat Shoppe Collection, marked "Ginny's Signature TM//1988//The Vogue Doll Company//Made in China," blonde rooted hair, blue plastic sleep eyes, jointed hard plastic body, pink brushed cotton dress and bloomers, white cardigan lace trimmed sweater, pink sequined hat and matching purse, white lace topped socks, pink one-strap shoes, circa 2001, $45.00. *Courtesy Vogue Doll Company.*

8" hard plastic "Puddle Jumping" Ginny, from The Hat Shoppe Collection, marked "Ginny's Signature TM//1988//The Vogue Doll Company//Made in China," brown rooted hair, brown plastic sleep eyes, jointed hard plastic body, red and white checked dress and bloomers, clear plastic raincoat trimmed in red, big floppy red rain hat, matching red umbrella, red one-strap shoes, circa 2001, $45.00. *Courtesy Vogue Doll Company.*

8" hard plastic "Crystal Blue Ballet" Ginny, from Ginny Celebrates Collection, marked "Ginny's Signature TM//1988//The Vogue Doll Company//Made in China," brown rooted hair, blue plastic sleep eyes, jointed hard plastic body, prima ballerina costume in a sparkling tutu of icy blue topped with ivory re-embroidered lace and sprinkled with crystal sequins and tiny pearls, matching headpiece of beaded lace, white tights, blue ballet slippers, circa 2001, $39.95. *Courtesy Vogue Doll Company.*

Vogue Dolls

8" hard plastic "Old Fashion Christmas" Ginny, from Ginny Celebrates Collection, Limited to 2000, marked "Ginny's Signature TM//1988// The Vogue Doll Company//Made in China," brown rooted hair, brown plastic sleep eyes, jointed hard plastic body, attired in a stunning Christmas ensemble of cranberry velveteen trimmed with faux fur and an intricate braid, matching fur-trimmed cape, bonnet and a fur muff, circa 2001, $49.90. *Courtesy Vogue Doll Company.*

8" hard plastic "Easter Bonnet" Ginny, from Ginny Celebrates Collection, marked "Ginny's Signature TM//1988//The Vogue Doll Company//Made in China," brown rooted hair, blue plastic sleep eyes, jointed hard plastic body, dress and matching bonnet are embroidered dotted Swiss batiste, white socks, blue center-snap shoes, carrying an Easter basket with a tiny chick, release date 2002. *Courtesy Vogue Doll Company.*

8" hard plastic "Ginny's Rockin' Christmas," from Ginny Celebrates Collection, Limited to 2000, marked "Ginny's Signature TM//1988//The Vogue Doll Company//Made in China," blonde rooted hair, green plastic sleep eyes, jointed hard plastic body, a 1950s Christmas outfit with evergreen velveteen circle skirt edged with a peppermint twist and trimmed with ribbon and a dimensional satin ornament to match her satin jacket, red one-strap shoes, circa 2001, $39.95. *Courtesy Vogue Doll Company.*

8" hard plastic "First Communion Blonde" Ginny, from Ginny Celebrates Collection, marked "Ginny's Signature TM//1988//The Vogue Doll Company// Made in China," blonde rooted hair, blue plastic sleep eyes, jointed hard plastic body, pristine white dress of cotton lace and silky taffeta is set off by a headpiece of pearls and tulle, she carries a white Bible and wears a tiny gold cross, white tights, and white patent leather shoes, circa 2001, $45.00. *Courtesy Vogue Doll Company.*

8" hard plastic "Easter Basket" Ginny, from Ginny Celebrates Collection, marked "Ginny's Signature TM//1988//The Vogue Doll Company//Made in China," auburn rooted hair, brown plastic sleep eyes, jointed hard plastic body, lavender organdy over satin party dress with a yellow sash, matching bonnet, yellow center-snap shoes, white socks, carrying an Easter basket with a plush white bunny, circa 2001, $45.00. *Courtesy Vogue Doll Company.*

Collectors' Network

It is strongly recommended when contacting these references and requesting information that you enclose an SASE (self-addressed stamped envelope) if you wish to receive a reply. Do not ask those who have volunteered to network to assume the postage burden; not only you but 100 other collectors may be wanting an answer. These networking collectors may already have many obligations on their time and resources, but they are more likely to answer if they receive an envelope ready for return.

ACCESSORIES
Best Dressed Doll
PO Box 12689
Salem, OR 97309
Phone: 1-800-255-2313
Catalog, $3.00
E-mail: Tonilady@aol.com

AMERICAN CHARACTER — TRESSY
Debby Davis, Collector/Dealer
3905 N. 15th St.
Milwaukee, WI 53206

ANTIQUE
Can research your wants

Matrix
PO Box 1410
New York, NY 10002

ANTIQUE & MODERN
Rosalie Whyel Museum of Doll Art
1116 108th Avenue N.E.
Bellevue, WA 98004
Phone: 206-455-1116
Fax: 206-455-4793

AUCTION HOUSES
Call or write for a list of upcoming auctions or if you need information about selling a collection.

McMasters Doll Auctions
James and Shari McMasters
PO Box 1755
Cambridge, OH 43725
Phone: 1-800-842-3526
Phone: 614-432-4419
Fax: 614-432-3191

Dream Dolls Gallery & More
5700 Okeechobee Blvd. #20
West Palm Beach, FL 33417
Phone: 1-888-839-3655
E-mail: dollnmore@aol.com

Jaci Jueden, Collector/Dealer
575 Galice Rd.
Merlin, OR, 97532
E-mail: fudd@cdsnet.net

Steven Pim, Collector/Dealer
3535 17th St.
San Francisco, CA 94110

BETSY MCCALL
Betsy's Fan Club
PO Box 946
Quincy, CA 95971
Marci Van Ausdall, Editor
Quarterly, $15.50 per year

CELEBRITY
Celebrity Doll Journal
Loraine Burdick, Editor
413 10th Ave. Ct. NE
Puyallup, WA 98372
Quarterly, $10.00 per year

CHATTY CATHY, MATTEL
Chatty Cathy Collector's Club
Lisa Eisenstein, Editor
PO Box 140
Readington, NJ 08870-0140
Quarterly newsletter, $28.00
E-mail: Chatty@eclipse.net

COMPOSITION
Effanbee's Patsy Family
Patsy & Friends Newsletter
12415 W. Monte Vista Road
Avondale, AZ 85323
Quarterly, $20.00 per year
Send address for sample copy
E-mail: moddoll@yahoo.com

COSTUMING
Doll Costumer's Guild of America, Inc.
341 S. McCadden Pl.
Los Angeles, CA 90020
Bimonthly, $18.00 per year

French Fashion Gazette
Adele Leurquin, Editor
1862 Sequoia SE
Port Orchard, WA 98366

DELUXE READING
Penny Brite
Dealer/Collector
Carole Fisher
RD 2, Box 301
Palmyra, PA 17078-9738
E-mail: Rcfisher@voicenet.com

DIONNE QUINTUPLETS
Quint News
Jimmy and Fay Rodolfos, Editors
PO Box 2527
Woburn, MA 01888

Connie Lee Martin, Collector/Dealer
4018 East 17th St.
Tucson, AZ 85711

DOLL ARTISTS
Jamie G. Anderson, Doll Artist
10990 Greenlefe, P.O. Box 806
Rolla, MO 65402
Phone: 573-364-7347
E-mail: Jastudio@rollanet.org

Martha Armstrong-Hand, Doll Artist
575 Worcester Drive
Cambria, CA 93428
Phone: 805-927-3997

Betsy Baker, Doll Artist
81 Hy-Vue Terrace
Cold Spring, NY 10516

Cynthia Baron, Doll Artist
7796 W. Port Madison
Bainbridge Is., WA 98110
Phone: 206-780-9003

Charles Batte, Doll Artist
272 Divisadero St. #4
San Francisco, CA 94117
Phone: 415-252-7440

Atelier Bets van Boxel, Doll Artist
De Poppenstee
't Vaartje 14
5165 NB Waspik – Holland
Web: www.poppenstee.nl
E-mail: bets@poppenstee.nl

Cheryl Bollenbach, Doll Artist
PO Box 740922
Arvada, CO 80006-0922
Phone: 303-424-8578
E-mail: cdboll@aol.com

Kathleen Campbell
5802 Oak
Omaha, NE 68106
Phone: 402-346-7689
E-mail: katc39@hotmail.com

Stephanie Cauley
10523 Shadow Lake Drive
Geismar, LA 70734
Phone: 225-647-0620
E-mail: caulynn@eatel.net

Laura Clark
PO Box 596
Mesilla, NM 88046

Ankie Daanen Doll-Art
Anton Mauvestraat 1
2102 BA HEEMSTEDE NL
Phone: 023-5477980
Fax: 023-5477981

Jane Darin, Doll Artist
5648 Camber Drive
San Diego, CA 92117
Phone: 619-514-8145
E-mail: Jdarin@san.rr.com
Web: http://www.janedarin.com

Jacques Dorier
2567 E. Madison St.
Seattle, WA 98112
Phone: 206-325-3650
E-mail: washij@aol.com

Marleen Engeler, Doll Artist
m'laine dolls
Noordeinde 67 1141 AH Monnickendam
The Netherlands
Phone: 31-299656814
E-mail: Mlwent4.2@globalxs.nl

Yvonne Flipse
Roelshoekweg 14,
4413 NG
Krabbendijke Nederland
E-mail: maskerade@zeelandnet.NC

Judith & Lucia Friedericy, Doll Artists
Friedericy Dolls
1260 Wesley Avenue
Pasadena, CA 91104
Phone: 626-296-0065
E-mail: Friedericy@aol.com

Originals by Goldie, Doll Artist
8517 Edgeworth Drive
Capitol Heights, MD 20743
Phone: 301-350-4119

Marilyn Henke
5422 SW 43 Ave.
Owatonna, MN 55060
Phone: 507-451-8979
E-mail: mhenke99@mnic.net

Lillian Hopkins, Doll Artist
2315 29th Street
Santa Monica, CA 90405
Phone: 310-396-3266
E-mail: LilyArt@Compuserve.com

Marylynn Huston, Doll Artist
101 Mountain View Drive
Pflugerville, TX 78660
Phone: 512-252-1192

Kathryn Williams Klushman, Doll Artist
Nellie Lamers, Doll Artist
The Enchantment Peddlers
HC 6 Box 0
Reeds Spring, MO 65737
Phone: 417-272-3768
E-mail:
Theenchantmentpeddlers@yahoo.com
Web: www.inter-linc.net/TheEnchant-mentPeddlers/

Lebba Kropp
Rt. 2, Box 778
Hearne, TX 77859
Phone: 409-279-6030

Denise Lemmon
6713 296th St. E.
Graham, WA 98338
Phone: 253-847-6479
E-mail: patnde@earthlink.net

Diane Little
42 Juniper Rd.
Placitas, NM 87043
Phone: 505-867-1306

Pat Moulton
4320 Barbara's Court
Camino, CA 95709
E-mail: patmoulton@directcon.net

Joyce Patterson, Doll Artist
FabricImages
PO Box 1599
Brazoria, TX 77422
Phone: 409-798-9890
E-mail: Clothdol@tgn.net

W. Harry Perzyk
2860 Chiplay St.
Sacramento, CA 95826

Daryl Poole, Doll Artist
450 Pioneer Trail
Dripping Springs, TX 78620
Phone: 512-858-7181
E-mail: Eltummo@aol.com

Peggy Ann Ridley, Doll Artist
17 Ridlon Road
Lisbon, ME 04250
Phone: 207-353-8827

Anne Sanregret, Doll Artist
22910 Estorial Drive, #6
Diamond Bar, CA 91765
Phone: 909-860-8007

Sandy Simonds, Doll Artist
334 Woodhurst Dr.
Coppell, TX 75019
Web: www.lindaleesutton.com
E-mail: linda@lindaleesutton.com

Linda Lee Sutton, Doll Artist
PO Box 3725
Central Point, OR 97502

Goldie Wilson, Doll Artist
8517 Edgeworth Drive
Capitol Heights, MD 20743

DOLL REPAIRS
Doc. Doc. Assoc.
1406 Sycamore Rd.
Montoursville, PA 17754
Phone: 717-323-9604

Fresno Doll Hospital
1512 N. College
Fresno, CA 93728
Phone: 209-266-1108

Kandyland Dolls
PO Box 146
Grande Ronde, OR 97347
Phone: 503-879-5153

Life's Little Treasures
PO Box 585
Winston, OR 97496
Phone: 541-679-3472

Oleta's Doll Hospital
1413 Seville Way
Modesto, CA 95355
Phone: 209-523-6669

GIRL SCOUTS
Girl Scout Doll Collectors Patch
Pidd Miller
PO Box 631092
Houston, TX 77263

Diane Miller/Collector
13151 Roberta Place
Garden Grove, CA 92643

Ann Sutton, Collector/Dealer
2555 Prine Rd.
Lakeland, FL 33810-5703
E-mail: Sydneys@aol.com

Collectors' Network

HASBRO — JEM
Linda E. Holton, Collector/Dealer
P.O. Box 6753
San Rafael, CA 94903

HITTY
Artists
Judy Brown
506 N. Brighton Ct.
Sterling, VA 20164

Ruth Brown
1606 SW Heather Dr.
Grants Pass, OR 97526

DeAnn R. Cote
5555 – 22nd Avenue South
Seattle, WA 98108-2912
E-mail: DRCDesign@aol.com
Web:
http://members@aol.com/DRCDesign

Janci
Jill Sanders/ Nancy Elliot
2442 Hathaway Court
Muskegon, MI 49441-4435

Lotz Studio
Jean Lotz
PO Box 1308
Lacombe, LA 70445-1308
Phone: 504-882-3482

Friends of Hitty Newsletter
Virginia Ann Heyerdahl, Editor
2704 Bellview Ave
Cheverly, MD 20785
Quarterly, $12.00 per year

IDEAL
Ideal Collectors Newsletter
Judith Izen, Editor
PO Box 623
Lexington, MA 02173
Quarterly, $20.00 per year
E-mail: Jizen@aol.com

INTERNET
eBay Auction site
http://www.ebay.com

About.com Doll Collecting
Denise Van Patten
Web: http://collectdolls.about.com
E-mail: denise@dollymaker.com

AG Collector List
For American Girl, Heidi Ott and other 18"
play dolls, no selling, just talk, e-mail: ag_collector_request@lists.best.com

Barbie chat
E-mail: Fashion-l@ga.unc.edu

Dolls n' Stuff
E-mail: Dollsnstuff@home.ease.lsoft.com

Doll Chat List
Friendly collectors talk dolls, no flaming permitted, a great group.
E-mail is forwarded to your email address from host, no fees. To subscribe, e-mail: DollChat-Request@nbi.com, type subscribe in body of message.

Not Just Dollmakers
http://www.notjustdollmakers.com
Information: e-mail, carls@isrv.com

Sasha
E-mail: sasha-1-subscribe@makelist.com

Shirley Temple
E-mail:
shirleycollect-subscribe@makelist.com

KLUMPE
Sondra Gast, Collector/Dealer
PO Box 252
Spring Valley, CA 91976
Fax: 619-444-4215

LAWTON, WENDY
Lawton Collectors Guild
PO Box 969
Turlock, CA 95381

Toni Winder, Collector/Dealer
1484 N. Vagedes
Fresno, CA 93728
E-mail: TTUK77B@prodigy.com

LIDDLE KIDDLES
For a signed copy of her book, *Liddle Kiddles*, $22.95 postpd., write:
Paris Langford
415 Dodge Ave
Jefferson, LA 70127
Phone: 504-733-0676

MANUFACTURERS
Alexander Doll Company, Inc.
Herbert Brown
Chairman & CEO
615 West 131st Street
New York, NY 10027
Phone: 212-283-5900
Fax: 212-283-6042

American Girl
8400 Fairway Place
PO Box 620190
Middleton, WI 53562-0190

Collectible Concepts
Ivonne Heather
President
945 Hickory Run Lane
Great Falls, VA 22066
Phone: 703-821-0607
Fax: 703-759-0408
E-mail: ivonnehccc@aol.com

Effanbee Doll Company
19 Lexington Ave.
East Brunswick, NJ 08816
Phone: 732-613-3852
Fax: 732-613-8366

Gene — Ashton-Drake Galleries
1-888-For Gene
9200 N. Maryland Ave.
Niles, Il 60714-9853

Susan Wakeen Doll Company, Inc.
PO Box 1321
Litchfield, CT 06759
Phone: 860-567-0007
Fax: 908-788-1955
E-mail: Pkaverud@blast.net

Robert Tonner Doll Company
Robert Tonner Doll Club
PO Box 1187
Kingston, NY 12402
Dues: $19.95
Credit Card: 914-339-9537
Fax: 914-339-1259

Vogue Doll Company
PO Box 756
Oakdale, CA 95361-0756
Phone: 209-848-0300
Fax: 209-848-4423
Web: http://www.voguedolls.com

MODERN DOLL COLLECTORS, INC.
Judy Whorton
17017 Hwy. 61 N
Wilsonville, AL 35186
Phone: 205-669-6219

MUSEUMS
Arizona Doll & Toy Museum
602 E. Adams St.
Phoenix, AZ 85004
(Stevens House in Heritage Square)
Phone: 602-253-9337
Tues. – Sun., adm. $2.50, closed Aug.

Enchanted World Doll Museum
"The castle across from the Corn Palace"
615 North Main
Mitchell, SD, 57301
Phone: 606-996-9896
Fax: 605-996-0210

Land of Enchantment Doll Museum
5201 Constitution Ave.
Albuquerque, NM 87110-5813
Phone: 505-255-8555
Fax: 505-255-1259

Margaret Woodbury Strong Museum
1 Manhattan Square
Rochester, NY 14607
Phone: 716-263-2700

Rosalie Whyel Museum of Doll Art
1116 108th Avenue N.E.
Bellevue, WA 98004
Phone: 206-455-1116
Fax: 206-455-4793
Web: www.dollart.com

NANCY ANN STORYBOOK
Elaine Pardee, Collector/Dealer
PO Box 6108
Santa Rosa, CA 95406
Phone: 707-585-3655

PRESERVATION
Twin Pines
Web: www.twinpines.com

PUBLICATIONS — MAGAZINES
Contemporary Doll Collector
Scott Publications
30595 Eight Mile
Livonia, MI 48152-1798
Subscriptions: 800-458-8237

Doll Reader
Cumberland Publishing, Inc.
6405 Flank Dr.
Harrisburg, PA 17112
Subcriptions: 1-800-829-3340
E-mail: dollreader@palmcoastd.com

Dolls
170 Fifth Ave, 12th Fl.
New York, NY 10010
Phone: 212-989-8700
Fax: 212-645-8976
E-mail: snowyw@lsol.net

PUBLICATIONS — NEWSLETTERS
Alexander Doll Company
The Review
Official publication of the Madame
Alexander Doll Club,
Quarterly, plus 2 "Shoppers"
$20.00 per year.
PO Box 330
Mundelein, IL 60060-0330
Phone: 847-949-9200
Fax: 847-949-9201
Web: http://www.madc.org

Chere Amies de Bleuette
Barbara Hilliker
4515 Walking Stick Lane
Gainesville, GA 30506
Quarterly, $20.00 per year

Collectors United
711 S. 3rd Ave.
Chatsworth, GA 30705
Phone: 706-695-8242
Fax: 706-895-0770
E-mail: Collun@Alltel.net

Ninsyo Journal — JADE
Japanese American Dolls Enthusiasts
406 Koser Ave
Iowa City, Iowa 52246
E-mail: vickyd@jadejapandolls.com

Patsy & Friends Newsletter
12415 W. Monte Vista Road
Avondale, AZ 85323
Quarterly, $20.00 per year, 36 pages
E-mail: moddoll@yahoo.com

RAGGEDY ANN
Rags newsletter
Quarterly $16.00
Barbara Barth, Editor
PO Box 823
Atlanta, GA 30301

ROLDAN
Sondra Gast, Collector/Dealer
PO Box 252
Spring Valley, CA 91976
Fax: 619-444-4215

SANDRA SUE
Peggy Millhouse, Collector/Dealer
510 Green Hill Road
Conestoga, PA 17516
E-mail: peggyin717@aol.com

SASHA
Friends of Sasha
Quarterly newsletter
Dorisanne Osborn, Editor
Box 187
Keuka Park, NY 14478

SHIRLEY TEMPLE
**Australian Shirley Temple
Collectors News**
Quarterly newsletter
Victoria Horne, Editor
39 How Ave.
North Dandenong
Victoria 3175, Australia
$25.00 U.S.

Lollipop News
Shirley Temple Collectors By the Sea
PO Box 6203
Oxnard, CA 93031
Membership dues: $14.00 year

Shirley Temple Collectors News
Rita Dubas, Editor
881 Colonial Rd
Brooklyn, NY 11209
Quarterly, $20.00 year
Web:
http://www.ritadubasdesign.com/shirley/

TERRI LEE
Daisy Chain Newsletter
$20.00 per year
Editor, Terry Bukowski
3010 Sundland Dr
Alamogordo, NM 88310
E-mail: bukowski@wazoo.com

Ann Sutton, Collector/Dealer
2555 Prine Rd.
Lakeland, FL 33810-5703
E-mail: Sydneys@aol.com

Betty J. Woten, Collector/Dealer
12 Big Bend Cut Off
Cloudcroft, NM 88317-9411

UNITED FEDERATION
OF DOLL CLUBS
10920 N. Ambassador Dr., Suite 130
Kansas City, MO 64153
Phone: 816-891-7040
Fax: 816-891-8360
Web: http://www.ufdc.org/

VOGUE
Ginny Doll Club
PO Box 338
Oakdale, CA 95361-0338
Phone: 1-800-554-1447

WOODS, ROBIN
Toni Winder, Collector/Dealer
1484 N. Vagedes
Fresno, CA 93728

Bibliography

Anderson, Johana Gast
_____. *Twentieth Century Dolls,* Wallace Homestead, 1971.
_____. *More Twentieth Century Dolls,* Wallace Homestead, 1974.
_____. *Cloth Dolls,* Wallace Homestead, 1984.
Axe, John
_____. *Effanbee, A Collector's Encyclopedia 1949 – 1983,* Hobby House Press, 1983.
_____. *The Encyclopedia of Celebrity Dolls,* Hobby House Press, 1983.
_____. *Tammy and Her Family of Dolls,* Hobby House Press, 1995.
Blitman, Joe
_____. *Francie & Her Mod, Mod, Mod, Mod World of Fashion,* Hobby House Press, 1996.
Casper, Peggy Wiedman,
_____. *Fashionable Terri Lee Dolls,* Hobby House Press, 1988.
Crowsey, Linda
_____. *Madame Alexander Collector's Dolls Price Guide #25,* Collector Books, 2000.
Clark, Debra,
_____. *Troll Identification & Price Guide,* Collector Books, 1993.
Coleman, Dorothy S., Elizabeth Ann and Evelyn Jane
_____. *The Collector's Book of Dolls Clothes,* Crown Publishers, 1975.
_____. *The Collectors Encyclopedia of Dolls, Vol. I & II,* Crown Publishers, 1968, 1986.
Cook, Carolyn
_____. *Gene,* Hobby House Press, 1998.
DeWein, Sibyl and Ashabraner, Joan
_____. *The Collectors Encyclopedia of Barbie Dolls and Collectibles,* Collector Books, 1977.
Garrison, Susan Ann
_____. *The Raggedy Ann & Andy Family Album,* Schiffer Publishing, 1989.
Hedrick, Susan & Matchette, Vilma
_____. *World Colors, Dolls & Dress,* Hobby House Press, 1997.
Hoyer, Mary
_____. *Mary Hoyer and Her Dolls,* Hobby House Press, 1982.
Izen, Judith
_____. *A Collector's Guide to Ideal Dolls,* Collector Books, 1994.
_____. *Collector's Encyclopedia of Vogue Dolls,* Collector Books, 1998.
Jensen, Don
_____. *Collector's Encyclopedia of Horsman Dolls, 1865 – 1950,* Collector Books, 2002.
Judd, Polly and Pam
_____. *African and Asian Costumed Dolls,* Hobby House Press, 1995.
_____. *Cloth Dolls,* Hobby House Press, 1990.
_____. *Compo Dolls, Vol. I & II,* Hobby House Press, 1991, 1994.
_____. *European Costumed Dolls,* Hobby House Press, 1994.
_____. *Hard Plastic Dolls, Vol. I & II,* Hobby House Press, 1987, 1989.
_____. *Glamour Dolls of the 1950s & 1960s,* Hobby House Press, 1988.
_____. *Santa Dolls & Figurines,* Hobby House Press, 1992.
Langford, Paris
_____. *Liddle Kiddles,* Collector Books, 1996.
Lewis, Kathy and Don
_____. *Chatty Cathy Dolls,* Collector Books, 1994.
Mandeville, A. Glen
_____. *Ginny, An American Toddler Doll,* Hobby House Press, 1994.
Mansell, Colette
_____. *The Collector's Guide to British Dolls Since 1920,* Robert Hale, 1983.
Mertz, Ursula
_____. *Collector's Encyclopedia of American Composition Dolls, 1900 – 1950,* Collector Books, 1999.
Morris, Thomas G.
_____. *The Carnival Chalk Prize, Vol. I & II,* Prize Publishers, 1985, 1994.

Moyer, Patsy
_____. *Doll Values*, Collector Books, 1997, 1998, 1999.
_____. *Modern Collectible Dolls, Vol. I, II & III*, Collector Books, 1997, 1998, 1999.
Niswonger, Jeanne D.
_____. *That Doll Ginny*, Cody Publishing, 1978.
_____. *The Ginny Doll Family*, 1996.
Olds, Patrick C.
_____. *The Barbie Years*, Collector Books, 1996.
Outwater, Myra Yellin
_____. *Advertising Dolls*, Schiffer, 1998.
Pardella, Edward R.
_____. *Shirley Temple Dolls and Fashions*, Schiffer Publishing, 1992, 1999.
Perkins, Myla
_____. *Black Dolls*, Collector Books, 1993.
_____. *Black Dolls Book II*, Collector Books, 1995.
Robison, Joleen Ashman and Sellers, Kay
_____. *Advertising Dolls*, Collector Books, 1992.
Schoonmaker, Patricia N.
_____. *Effanbee Dolls: The Formative Years, 1910 – 1929*, Hobby House Press, 1984.
_____. *Patsy Doll Family Encyclopedia, Vol. I*, Hobby House Press, 1992.
_____. *Patsy Doll Family Encyclopedia, Vol. II*, Hobby House Press, 1998.
Smith, Patricia R.
_____. *Madame Alexander Collector Dolls*, Collector Books, 1978.
_____. *Modern Collector's Dolls, Series 1 – 8*, Collector Books.
Tabbat, Andrew
_____. *Raggedy Ann and Andy*, Gold Horse Publishing, 1998.
_____. *The Collector's World of Raggedy Ann and Andy*, Gold Horse Publishing, Vol. I, 1996; Vol. II, 1997.

Index

Acme Toy Company 107
Adam 108
Adorable Silk Victorian 24
advertising dolls ....8 – 10
Alex (see Alexandra Fairchild Ford)
Alexander Doll Company ......11 – 29
Alexander-kins 14
Alexandra Fairchild Ford....141 – 147
Alice in Wonderland 12, 14
American Character Doll
    Company ......30 – 35, 73 – 76, 190
American Children Collection 120
American Indian dolls........129 – 131
Ann Estelle ....222 – 225
Anne-Shirley 119, 120
Annie Oakley 30
Applause Toy Company 207
Arranbee Doll
    Company ....36 – 41, 235
Artist Dolls ....42 – 56
Ashton-Drake Galleries......148 – 160
Austria 132
Averill, Georgene 100, 106, 208
Avon 168
Baby Snooks 182
Baby Sue 30
Baitz...................................132
Bamm-Bamm 183
Barbie dolls ....57 – 71
    Number One Barbie..57, 58, 61, 71
    Number Two Barbie 57, 71
    Number Three Barbie 57
    Number Four Barbie 57
    Number Five Barbie 57, 58
    Number Six Barbie 58
Basketbabies 42
Bavaria.................................134
Beatles, The............................94
Best Friend 24
Bets van Boxel, Atelier 42, 43
Betsy McCall ....72 – 81, 222
Betty 12
Binnie Walker 14
black dolls ....82 – 87
Black Sambo 83
Blue Mist Angel........................20
Bo Peep 37
Bob Scout 185
Bow Tie Company 166, 169
bride 15
Brown, Judy 175
Brownie 168
Bubblecut Barbie 59, 60
Buddy Lee 10
Cameo dolls 88

Campbell, Kathleen 43, 44
Campbell Kids.........................176
Cauley, Stephanie 44, 45
Century Doll Company 108
celebrity dolls ....89 – 96
Chad Valley 101
chalkware dolls ....97 – 99
Champagne Lady 122
Chase, Martha.........................101
Children of the World................43
Christie 64
Cinderella 80
cloth dolls ....100 – 105
Cissy ....26 – 28
"A Day in the Life of Cissy" trunk
    set 27
Cochran, Dewees 120
comic dolls 106
composition dolls....107 – 114, 119 –
    121, 123 – 128, 131, 133, 135 –
    138, 140, 177, 180, 182, 191,
    198 – 206, 210, 211, 214 – 216
Crown Toy Company 118
Czechoslovakia 12
Darin, Jane 45
Debu'Teen..........................37, 41
Deluxe Reading...................115, 116
Disney dolls 117, 118
Dollywood Studios 101
Dorier, Jacques 46
Dream World 108
Durbin, Deanna 94
Eegee 109
Effanbee dolls...........119 – 128, 167,
                                    170, 190
Eloise 29
Engelbreit, Mary ....222 – 225
Engeler, Marleen 46
Eskimo.................................130
Esme 160, 162, 164, 165
ethnic dolls ....129 – 140
Eugenia Doll Company..............171
Fall Angel 21
Fanny Brice 182
fashion dolls ....141 – 165
Fashion Queen Barbie 61
Flipse, Yvonne 47
France 133
Francie 65, 66
Frazier, Madeline 109
Gene dolls ....148 – 160
Gene Marshall..................148 – 154
George, Ruth Elena 167
Germany 134
Ginny ....173, 235 – 247

Girl Scout dolls ....166 – 170
Goldman, Mollye 207, 214
Golliwogs 82, 83
Gorham 102
Greece 135
Grizzly Adams 95
Gund 106, 118
groom 16
Happiness Candy Stores, Inc. 112
hard plastic.........122, 130, 132, 134,
                    139, 140, 171 – 173, 177,
                    180, 181, 184, 195, 197,
                    203, 205, 206, 212,
                    218 – 221, 231 – 247
Heavenly Pink Angel..................20
Henie, Sonja ....89 – 93
Henke, Marilyn 48
Hitty dolls 174, 175
Holland 133
Hollywood 110
Horsman 81, 176, 177
Hoyer, Mary dolls ....178 – 181
Ideal 9, 72, 94, 96, 122,
                                182 – 184, 214
Imperial Doll Company 110
India 135
Indian 130, 131
Innocent Silk Victorian 25
Italy 136
Jacqueline 18
Janci ....174 – 175
Jeannie Walker 12
Jiminy Cricket 118
Julia 95
Kamkins 102
Kammer & Reinhardt 235
Kenner dolls 185
Kestner 117
Kitty Collier..............213, 228 – 231
Klumpe dolls 186
Knickerbocker 117, 207
Knorr dolls
    Dutch 8
    French...................................8
    Norwegian 9
    Swiss 9
Kripplebush Kid ....222, 231 – 234
Kropp, Lebba..........................48, 49
Kruse, Kathe 102
Lady Churchill.........................16
Lapland 137
Lee, H.D. Company 10
Lemmon, Denise 49, 50
Lenci dolls ....187 – 189
Lipfert, Bernard......72, 123, 214, 235

Little Audrey 106
Little Bo Peep 12
Little, Diane 50
Little Lady 121
Little Love Angel
    pink 20
    lavender 21
Little Red Riding Hood 233, 239
Little Women, Amy 14
Live Action Barbie 63
Lloyderson 102
L.W. Company 112
Madame Alexander 92, 93, 95,
        143 – 147, 209 – 212
Madra Lord ....148, 149, 155 – 159
Maggie Walker 16
Mama Doll 111
Marseille, Armand 235
Martin, Lori 96
Mary Lee 128
Mattel 95, 96, 210
McAboy, Mary 131
McGuffey Ana 12, 13
Mego 96
Menjou, Adolph 94
Mexico 138
Meyer, Mary 170
Mickey Mouse 117
Midge 59, 66
Mimi 16
Miss Curity 9
Molly'es 103
Monica dolls 190, 191
Mortimer Snerd 182
Moulton, Pat 51
Mountain Babies 49, 50
Muffie 195
My Dream Baby 36
Nancy 38
Nancy Ann Storybook
    dolls ....192 – 195
Nancy Ann Style Show 195
Nancy (comic character) 106
Nancy Lee 39
Nanette ....39 – 41
Novelties, Georgene 207
nurse dolls 196, 197
Old Cottage Toys ....198 – 206
Paris Doll Company 171
Patricia-Kin 127
Patsy ..110, 111, 113, 123 – 128, 190

Patsy Ann 125
Patsyette 124
Patsy Joan 125, 126
Patsy Lou 126, 127
Patsy Ruth 127
Pebbles 183
Penny Brite 116
Peru 138
Perzyk, W. Harry 52, 53
Pinocchio 118
P.J. 67
Ponytail Barbie 60, 61
Prince Charles 17, 18
Queen Elizabeth 17
Queen Elizabeth II 15
Raggedy Ann & Andy 207, 208
Raggedy Doodle 103
Raleigh, Jesse McCutcheon 113
Roberta Doll Company 172
Saalfield Publishing Company 104
Santa Claus, Mr. and Mrs. 48
Scarlett O'Hara ....209 – 213
Scootles 85
Scotland 139
Sheppard, J.B. & Company 104
Sherrod, Myra 53
Shindana 82, 83, 87
Shipstead & Johnson 104
Skipper 68
Skippy 128
Skookums 131
Skooter 68
Sleeping Beauty 13
Sluggo 106
Snow White 17, 88, 182
Sophisticated Silk Victorian 25
Sound of Music
    Brigitta 19
    Friedrich 19
    Gretl 19
    Liesl 19
    Louisa 19
    Maria 19
    Marta 19
Spain 140
Spring Angel 22
Star Wars 185
Steffie 67
Storybook doll 38
Summer Angel 22
Sutton, Linda Lee 53, 54

Suzette 121
Suzy Cute 115
Sweet Silk Victorian 26
Sweet Sue ....31 – 33
Switzerland 140
Sydney Chase 160, 165
Talking Barbie 64
Temple, Shirley 97, 99, 190, 214
Terri Lee ....86, 218 – 221
Three in One Doll Corp. 114
Tintair 122
Tiny Betsy ....75, 77 – 79
Tiny Tears 34
Tiny Town Doll 105
Toni 34, 122, 184
Tonner, Robert Doll
    Company ....75 – 81, 160 – 165,
        210, 222 – 234
treetoppers
    Caroler 23
    Golden Dream 23
    Holiday Trimmings 23
    Shining Bright Angel 21
    Starburst Angel 21
Trent Osborn 149
Tutti 68, 69
Twiggy 96
Twist 'n Turn Barbie 62
Tyler Wentworth ....160 – 164, 222
Uneeda 72, 96
Victorian Marigold 25
vinyl ....122, 130, 143 – 147,
        150 – 159, 161 – 165,
        183, 213, 217, 222 – 231
Violet Waters 149
Vogue dolls ....235 – 247
Volland, P.J. 207, 208
Waltons 96
Wee Patsy 123
Wellings, Norah 105
Well Made Toy Manufacturing
    Corp. 166, 170
Welsh Morris Doll Company 172
Wendy Bride 18
Whimsie 35
Wick, Faith 55
Wilson, Goldie 55, 56
Winter Angel 22
Withers, Jane 95

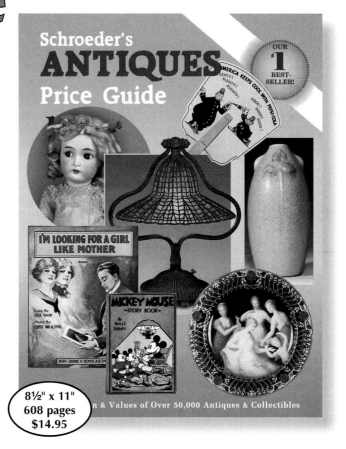